City-State and World State

CITY-STATE AND WORLD STATE IN GREEK

AND ROMAN POLITICAL THEORY UNTIL AUGUSTUS

MASON HAMMOND

BIBLO and TANNEN
NEW YORK
1966

320.937
H227

CUI DONO LEPIDUM NOVUM LIBELLUM

E PRELO MODO CANDIDUM EXEUNTEM?

F.P.H., TIBI; NAMQUE TU SOLEBAS

MEAS ESSE ALIQUID PUTARE CURAS.

PREFACE

THE SUBSTANCE OF THIS BOOK WAS DELIVERED AS SIX LECTURES under the auspices of the Lowell Institute of Boston, Mass., in the spring of 1948. The author is grateful to the Trustee of the Lowell Institute, Ralph Lowell, Esq., and to the Curator, Professor William H. Lawrence, for the invitation to lecture on this distinguished foundation and for the impetus and encouragement thereby given towards the preparation of this book, in which the original lectures have been entirely rewritten and enlarged. The author is indebted to Miss Janice M. Didsbury for preparing the typescript, to his wife for constructive criticism of the style and presentation, and to an anonymous reader of the Harvard University Press for helpful criticism. Thanks are also due to the Cambridge University Press for permission to quote a passage by Ernest Barker from *The Cambridge Ancient History* and to the Harvard University Press for permission to quote a passage from the translation of Polybius by W. R. Paton in the Loeb Classical Library.

The book is intended for the student of the general history of political theory and not for the specialist in the political theory of the Greeks and Romans. It is therefore neither detailed nor argumentative. Greek words have been transliterated, and often pluralized in English. The bibliography aims to guide the reader to the more readily accessible literature upon which the treatment chiefly depends and in which may be found fuller reference to and discussion of the ancient sources and modern research. The notes either give references for the principal quotations from the ancient sources or elaborate on statements which might otherwise seem unjustifiably categorical.

MASON HAMMOND

Cambridge, Massachusetts, 1951

CONTENTS

INTRODUCTION

THE FOLLOWING CHAPTERS DO NOT ATTEMPT TO TRACE THE HIS-
torical development of the world state, whether that of Alexander or that of the Romans. They are concerned primarily with
the conflict in political thought between the dominant political
concept of the city-state, as established by Aristotle and Plato and
developed in the Hellenistic period in the theory of the mixed
constitution, and the pressing need to find some theoretical basis
for the larger political organizations which arose in fact in the
Hellenistic and Roman periods.[1] Historical material is presented,
therefore, only in so far as it either illuminates political thought or
has provided the material for political thinkers. The chapters are
not concerned with the political experience of the Hellenistic
world and the degree to which this was taken over by Augustus
and his successors.[2] In particular, many aspects of the development
of the Roman empire and of the contributions thereto of individual Romans like Flamininus, Cato the Elder, Sulla, Lucullus, or
Pompey have been slighted because they apparently had no great
effect on the political thought of Polybius and of Cicero. Cicero's
own practical concern with the problems of provincial government, as evidenced, for instance, in the speeches against Verres
or the correspondence from Cilicia with Caelius, similarly had
little influence on his political doctrine as expressed in the *de Republica*, the *de Legibus*, and to some extent in the *de Officiis*. Thus

the central chapters of this book, which are concerned with Cicero, may seem to some to neglect important historical aspects of the development of the Roman world state.

This neglect may find a partial excuse in the attempt to keep the treatment to a modest scale. It may also be justified by the aim of interpreting political thought, not political history, and by the conviction of the author that the significant value of the ancient experience for modern students lies not in its factual achievements and failures, interesting and instructive as these may be, but in its intellectual inability to escape from a dominant concept and to find a theoretical basis for the world state which had in practice become the necessary form of political organization. The factual achievements and failures may be attributed to the particular conditions which existed in the ancient world, and any attempt to generalize upon them in terms of modern conditions is open to dispute. The lessons of the past for the present are valid only in very broad terms of human reactions to existing conditions. It is the author's persuasion that one of the principal lessons taught by the experience of the Greeks and Romans is that too great respect for tradition is fatal to any society.

Mankind today feels the urgency of achieving "One World." The prejudices inherent in national political institutions and, more important, in national political thought must be overcome in favor of some sort of world-wide political coöperation. Professor Toynbee may or may not be right when he argues that the emergence of world states in previous societies has been a symptom of their decay.[3] Perhaps this time, as he hopes despite the logic of his study of previous societies, things will turn out differently and a revitalized Christianity will permit Western society to forge ahead. Or his examples may be too few to justify his generalization. Whether his conclusion be accepted or rejected, it underlines the necessity of choosing between a world state and the possibility of a war destructive on a scale as yet unimaginable. The success of a world state will depend on the ability of nations — that is, of the individuals composing them — to put aside political traditions and prejudices and to give rational consideration to the political situation which confronts them.

Only one of the societies in which Professor Toynbee traces the emergence of world states affords a glimpse behind the historical facts to the political thought that conditioned them. This society, which he calls the "Hellenic," was that of Greece and Rome. During three centuries it wrestled with the problem of achieving "one world." Alexander first posed the problem to Greek thought in the late fourth century B.C., when he brought the Persian empire under Greek rule. Towards the end of the first century B.C., Augustus finally established an enduring unified government for what was then considered the area inhabited by civilized men, the "oecumene." The Augustan solution resulted, to be sure, from a long historical process. But its form was determined by the pressure of political theory and it is with the development and nature of this theory rather than with the historical process that the present discussion is concerned. The theory culminated in the political doctrine and ideals of a Roman statesman who best exemplified both the strength and the weakness of Greco-Roman political thinkers in meeting the problem of "one world." That statesman was Cicero.

Cicero needs no introduction even in a day when the study of Greece and Rome has an ever smaller place in education. Cicero and Virgil constitute the core of Rome's contribution to the culture of Western Europe. Cicero is in fact perhaps the best known of all the personages of classical antiquity because of his revelation of himself in his writings. This intimacy has in modern times militated to some extent against his fame both as a statesman and as a thinker. He has revealed to later ages the inner doubts and uncertainties behind the façade of his political leadership. His letters admit the reader behind the scenes of his career; they reveal how the compromises and changes in his practical politics fell below his ideals of statesmanship and his higher motives.[4]

Moreover, the shift in intellectual interest from Rome to Greece that has taken place since the eighteenth century has demoted Cicero from the position which he occupied during the Middle Ages and the Renaissance as an outstanding teacher and philosopher. He has been shown to have drawn heavily if not entirely upon his Greek predecessors so that his intellectual stature has been reduced almost to that of a compiler of popular textbooks. In consequence, while there has been a great deal of learned research into the sources of Cicero's philosophical, rhetorical, and political writings, the general lives of Cicero, particularly those in English, tend to concentrate on Cicero the man and the politician and to give but little attention to Cicero the thinker.

Yet Cicero is one of the very few who consciously theorized about the Roman state. Roman literature is pervaded by implications, assumptions, and even statements about the political achievement of Rome, but compared to the literature of Greece, or of later Western Europe, it is singularly lacking in reasoned political theory. This difference between mere political thought and political theory has been well expressed by Ernest Barker in a chapter in *The Cambridge Ancient History* on the political thought of Greece in the fourth century:[5]

"A distinction may perhaps be drawn, which is based on a real difference, between political theory and political thought. Political theory is the speculation of individual minds (though it may well become, and in the process of time often does become, the dogma of a school); and, as such, it is an activity of conscious thought, which is aware both of itself as it thinks and of the facts about which it thinks. Political thought is the thought of a whole society; and it is not necessarily, or often, self-conscious. It is an activity of the mind; but one naturally thinks of it as a substance or content rather than as an activity. It is the complex of ideas which is entertained — but not, as a rule, apprehended — by all who are concerned in affairs of state at a given period of time. It is such thought which makes history; and history is the mirrored reflection, or the reverse side, of such thought. Political thought and history are two aspects of one process — the process of the human spirit: they are two sides of a single coin. There is thus a political thought which is immanent in each historical process; and there is a political theory which is distinct from the process, and yet — because it cannot but be influenced by the process, either in the way of attraction, or in the way of repulsion — is part and parcel of it. It is easy to think of political thought as the active and determining maker of history, and to regard political theory as a speculation of the detached mind, remote from the motive force of events. Such a distinction is perhaps nowhere true. Thinking which is directed to human conduct becomes a factor in human action; speculation that seems airy may bring down an abundant rain of events; the theory of Rousseau, for example, was a stuff which made and unmade states. The distinction is certainly untrue if it is applied to ancient Greece. Here political theory was conceived as a 'practical science' — a theory, indeed, or speculation, but not a mere theory or speculation, which left things as they were because they could not be otherwise. It was regarded as dealing with those human things which 'might be otherwise than they were,' and charged with the duty of showing how they might become otherwise in the sense of becoming better. Because it was practical, it was idealistic; because it was concerned with making men and states better, it issued in the construction of ideal states, which were meant to be realized — immediately and directly realized. Political theory in the modern world only becomes active and practical when it becomes political thought, and the many are converted to the teaching of the few. We submit, as it were, to a mediation between theory and action. The note of Greek political theory is immediacy. It moves directly to action . . ."

In the history of Roman literature only three men can seriously be regarded as political theorists, and not merely as political thinkers: the Greek Polybius, who stands practically at the opening of conscious Latin literature and who will figure largely in the present discussion; Cicero, who stands, as was said, at the center of Rome's intellectual development; and Saint Augustine, who comes at the end of the long tradition of Latin letters but who, despite his outward continuance of this tradition and in particular his admiration for Cicero, was separated from the classical world by the great intellectual gulf imposed by the spiritual collapse of paganism and the triumph of Christianity in the third and fourth centuries.[6]

The following eleven chapters have, therefore, the limited objective of presenting the development during the Greco-Roman period of the theory of the city-state. They will deal only secondarily with the historical evolution of the world state. The first six will consider the evolution of the orthodox view of the Greek city-state, the failure of this theory to adapt itself to the experience of the Hellenistic monarchies, and the application of the orthodox theory by Polybius to Roman history. The last five will discuss the degree to which contemporary conditions influenced Cicero's thought, his own political ideals and doctrine, and the way in which his expression of the orthodox theory of the city-state conditioned, whether explicitly or implicitly, the compromise solution which Augustus devised for governing a world state in the framework of a city-state constitution.

I

GREEK POLITICAL THOUGHT BEFORE PLATO: MONARCHY, ARISTOCRACY, AND DEMOCRACY

THE LINE OF THOUGHT WHICH CULMINATED IN THE ORTHODOX theory of the Greek city-state developed consistently from the earliest surviving Greek literature, Homer and Hesiod. Whatever the actual date at which the two epics that come down under the name of Homer were composed, they reveal Greek society as still governed by monarchs, or tribal chieftains. The monarchs were limited by a council of elders or, where the monarch was, like Agamemnon, commander-in-chief of a federation of chiefs, by a council of other chiefs. Final appeal was to an assembly of the people or of the soldiers. This form of government survived in the historic period in Sparta, whose political development was immobilized by the reform attributed to Lycurgus and dated by modern scholars at the end of the seventh century B.C. An earlier spirit of progress, attested by Doric lyric poetry and by archaeological discoveries at Sparta, was deliberately stifled, apparently because of the need of disciplining the state to keep in check its recently subjected neighbors in Messene. The reform of Lycurgus perpetuated in Sparta a titular monarchy, in the persons of two kings selected from two royal families. In fact, however, the kings had real power only when they exercised military command in the field. At home, the power rested with a council, the *Gerousia*, composed of the two kings and twenty-eight elders selected for life from the noble families. There was a board of five annual magistrates in charge of domestic affairs, called *Ephors*, but they were subject to the *Gerousia*. Finally, there was an assembly of all Spartans capable of carrying arms, the *Apella*, which elected the *Ephors* and passed on major decisions but which had little real initiative as against the *Gerousia*. The Spartans, men, women, and children, led a semicommunal life subject to rules and training of a rigid and military sort. They, a minority of the total population, were supported by estates worked by serfs called *Helots* and by the contribution of free but noncitizen peasants dwelling on the frontiers and called *Perioeci*. The Spartan constitution merits this brief description because it impressed the political thinkers of Greece by its stability, which they attributed to its mixed form in which the aristocratic element predominated, and by its discipline, so contrary to the fickleness of the ordinary Greek democracy.

By the time of Hesiod, monarchy had generally been displaced by an aristocracy of prominent landowners which already displayed the vices of selfishness and of oppression of the lesser landowners. Yet the aristocratic society of the seventh and sixth centuries B.C. afforded the background and patronage which fostered Greek lyric poetry, culminating in Pindar of Thebes, early Greek philosophy, and archaic Greek art. A conservative, aristocratic government based on the ownership of land survived in those Greek communities, such as Thebes, which, being relatively cut off from the sea, remained untouched by the commercial expansion of the sixth and fifth centuries B.C. Order and adherence to tradition, as against the excesses and innovations of tyranny and democracy, recommended aristocratic government to Greek political thinkers. But its tendency to be a government for the benefit of the few and to deprive the average citizen of any real participation in public affairs, even when it did not result in actual oppression of the poor, counted against it.

Those Greek cities which were accessible by sea to contact with the outside world, notably those along the Aegean coast of Asia Minor, those in Sicily and southern Italy, and Corinth and Athens in Greece itself, witnessed a popular movement during the sixth century B.C. against control by the rich landowners. This movement expressed itself in the emergence of a leader who, generally without actual alteration of the constitution, became dominant in the state. In most instances, this "tyrant," as he was called, directed the state according to his own arbitrary will. In Athens, the first figure so to emerge, Solon, was a man of great public spirit and idealism. He refused to retain the control of the state which popular support gave him and, after successfully reforming the constitution and strengthening the position of Athens in her external relations, withdrew from public office. Later tradition was to regard him as the founder of democracy at Athens. Though it is likely that this term, with its connotations, only appeared in the Periclean age and that Solon's reforms were primarily favorable to the well-to-do, he did give recognition to forms of wealth other than land and he did protect the poor from the arbitrariness of the rich.

Yet his reforms did not save Athens from the normal cycle of Greek political change. In the middle of the sixth century B.C., Peisistratus made himself tyrant by winning the support of the poor against the rich. He may be taken as an example of the Greek tyrant at his best. For the tyrants were by no means as evil as later tradition made them out to be. Most of them came to power through the support of the mass of the population who were tired of the oppression of the rich. Once they achieved power, they continued to cultivate popular support. The ill repute under which tyranny labored in later Greek political thought was due to several causes. The second generation of early tyrants became arbitrary and oppressive, as did the sons of Peisistratus at Athens. The term "tyrant" was applied to later rulers who, in the fifth and fourth centuries B.C., gained power under different circumstances, often as military *condottieri*, and sometimes maintained themselves by ruthless police methods. The tyrants of all periods were hostile to the aristocracy. And finally the concept of the arbitrary rule of an individual, not empowered by regular process, not restricted by tradition or law, and not responsible to a popular assembly, was alien to Greek political sentiment. Yet the unpopularity of tyranny did not prevent later Greek thinkers from praising the rule of a single individual who was wise, disinterested, and accepted by his state, whether he was hereditary monarch or newly created tyrant.

The expulsion of the sons of Peisistratus from Athens at the end of the sixth century B.C. made possible a restoration and further liberalizing of the Solonian constitution. This reform was again the work of an individual, Cleisthenes. Cleisthenes was later regarded as the second founder of Athenian democracy, but he appears to have been concerned primarily with limiting the power of the magistrates, making them responsible to law, and rendering them accountable to the assembly — in short, for what the Greeks called "isonomia," equal obedience to law by all, including magistrates. The Cleisthenic constitution remained fundamentally that of Athens during the fifth century. It was further liberalized as a result of the Persian Wars, in which Athens' final victory was not the work of the conservative, propertied hoplites who had defeated the first Persian attack at Marathon, but that of the sailors and poorer city dwellers who manned the fleet that won at Salamis.

It is unnecessary to recount the familiar story of the achievement by Athens of an imperial position in the Aegean or of the effect which this position had in increasing the power of the Athenian assembly, the *Ecclesia*, as against the magistrates, the *Archons*, the traditional council of elders, the *Areopagus*, and the Cleisthenic elective council, the *Boule*. The power of the Assembly during the second half of the fifth century B.C. permitted the man who could command its support to rule the state as effectively as might a tyrant, though more indirectly and in accordance with law

and custom. The personality and achievements of Pericles so dazzled his contemporaries and later generations that the individual,
or monarchical, character of his control has been obscured. He
was possibly the prototype for Plato's philosopher-king. It was
under Pericles that there appeared the concept of "democracy,"
the rule of the "people" as against that of any single individual or
clique of the well born or well-to-do. Later writers, such as Aristotle, disillusioned by the excesses of Athenian democracy, looked
on the government under Pericles as a degeneration from the sim-
pler, more conservative ideals of Cleisthenes and even of Solon,
whom they came to regard as the first promoters of democratic
ideals. In fact, however, Pericles appears to have the best claim to
this title. Periclean Athens in its literature and its art showed the
heights to which a people proud of its freedom and its achievement
could carry its artistic self-expression.[1]

When Pericles died in 429 B.C., in the opening years of the
Peloponnesian War, the control of the Assembly passed to men of
lesser stature and greater selfishness, such as the demagogue Cleon
and the brilliant aristocrat Alcibiades. These men, according to
Thucydides, frankly justified the Athenian empire and the prosecution of the war in terms of power politics. Their denial of any
fundamental concept of political right and wrong originated from
the Sophistic examination into all accepted conventions. Plato puts
in the mouth of the Sophist Thrasymachus, at a dramatic date of
about 420 B.C., the classic expression of this political philosophy:
justice is the advantage of the stronger.[2] A similar utilitarian argument for the Athenian empire is presented in an anonymous treatise on the Athenian constitution, preserved among the works of
Xenophon, but probably written by a person of oligarchic sympathies either before the outbreak of the Peloponnesian War in
432 B.C., or at the conclusion of its first phase, the Archidamian
War, in the late 420's.[3] Thucydides, who probably wrote toward
the close of the war, at the end of the century, was even more conscious of the problem of justice as against self-interest, the conflict

between *to dikaion* and *to xumpheron*. He places the arguments for self-interest in the mouths of the demagogic imperialists. He has given classic expression to the opposition between the two political motives in such dramatic scenes as the Mytilenean and Melian debates. The problem continued basic for political theorists and is rehandled by Cicero in the third book of his *de Republica*.[4]

The excesses, both in practical affairs and in attitude, into which the demagogues led the Assembly resulted finally in the devastating defeat of Athens by Sparta. The experience of Athens during these years and the general reaction toward conservatism that swept over Greece during the fourth century B.C. put democracy out of favor with political theorists. It must be remembered that for the Greeks democracy did not mean, as for modern thinkers, a system of government in which every person and every point of view was permitted to express itself freely; it meant a system of government by the masses and for the masses. The few, the rich aristocrats, were not disenfranchised, but political power rested with the masses, who used it for their own advantage.

A further result of the experience of Athenian democracy, coupled with the second emergence of tyranny at Syracuse in Sicily during the early fourth century B.C., was to persuade Plato that the tyrant was a creature of the democratic mob and not, as the early tyrannies had been, a transitional phase between aristocracy and democracy. In general, however, the political experience of Greece down to the time of Plato, which has been briefly reviewed, supported historically his scheme for the succession of constitutions, which he tried to explain on rational grounds. This fact is often forgotten by those who regard Plato's *Republic* as purely an expression of political theory, based on a logical line of reasoning but not related to Greek political experience.

A final remark should be made concerning the Greek political experience. Change in a form of government was almost always either actually the work of, or at least attributed to, a specific individual. The development of the government of the Greek city-

states is marked by a succession of outstanding "lawgivers": Lycurgus, Solon, Cleisthenes, to mention only a few. This was to constitute a notable point of difference from the Roman political
experience, a difference to which Cicero calls attention in his
de Republica. For it must be remembered that the Greek background of Roman political thought comprised not only philosophy
but also history.

By the middle of the fifth century B.C., Greek political experience had witnessed the emergence of three major forms of government: monarchy, or the rule of an individual; aristocracy, or the
rule of the few whose superior quality depended generally on
landed property; and democracy, or the rule of the mass of the
people. As has been remarked, for the Greeks the essential difference between these three forms consisted in the group in which
political control was vested and, to some extent, for whose advantage the government was conducted. However, it came to be realized that the government might also be conducted in any one of
these three ways for the benefit of the community as a whole. The
latter attitude came to be thought of as "justice," the former as
"utility."

Apart from the implications with respect to various types of
government in such writers as Homer, representing monarchy,
Pindar and Theognis, representing aristocracy, and the Athenian
tragedians, representing the development of democracy, the first
explicit confrontation of the three forms is in the third book of
Herodotus' *History*, which was probably composed sometime between 450 and 430 B.C. Herodotus stages a discussion on the best
form of government between the Persian nobles who, in 521 B.C.,
assassinated the pretender who had seized the throne on the death
of Cambyses. He asserts that this discussion actually took place, but
the terms in which the respective merits of monarchy, aristocracy,
and democracy are expounded are purely Greek. Whether the discussion reflects debates among the sophists or whether Herodotus'
Persian or Ionian informants related a historical event to him in

Greek terms is uncertain. But the passage may justly be called the earliest surviving piece of explicit political theory. Herodotus gives the palm to democracy, although he admits that practical considerations led the Persian conspirators to continue the monarchy in the person of Darius. Whether or not Herodotus reflects Athenian thought of the Periclean Age and whether or not there is a change in his point of view between the earlier and later books, he established for later Greek thought the dark picture of tyranny. Yet he recognizes the achievements of such men as Polycrates of Samos and Peisistratus of Athens. With Aeschylus, he draws the classic contrast between political freedom and slavery in his exaltation of the Athens of Miltiades and Themistocles as opposed to the Persia of Darius and Xerxes. Yet here again he glorifies the virtues of the Persians of an earlier date during their rise to power under Cyrus. In general, Herodotus sees in history two chief conflicting political principles — the rule of one against the rule of the whole community, monarchy or tyranny against democracy, slavery against freedom. The struggle between the few and the many, *hoi oligoi* against *hoi polloi*, which had been adumbrated in Theognis and which became the dominant theme in Athens during the fifth century, does not appear in Herodotus.[5]

Allusion has already been made to the attack of the so-called Sophists on accepted belief during the later fifth century. It should be remembered that the Sophists were not a school but simply a group of men, each of whom held his own views, but all of whom were similar in their critical attitude toward accepted opinion and institutions in the various fields of human activity, in their pretensions to knowledge superior to that of the ordinary run of men, and in their claim to be able to teach this knowledge, so as to enable a man to succeed, particularly in politics.[6] Aristophanes, the conservative writer of comedies during the Peloponnesian War, had considerable justification when he took Socrates as the type of this new group of thinkers, even though Plato, in his *Apology*, makes Socrates distinguish himself sharply from the Sophists on the ground that he did not teach, and certainly not for money, and that he did not pretend to any knowledge but only attempted to find the flaws in other people's pretensions.[7] The great contribution of the Sophists to Greek political thought was to inspire men to consider critically opinions and institutions which had simply been taken for granted as proved and honored by tradition. Their chief harm was that such criticism easily became a skeptical cynicism which argued that, since no principle could withstand criticism, political and ethical principles could be regarded as purely matters of convention, to be perverted by the clever politician for his own ends. It was against such abuses of knowledge that Socrates directed his searching attack. However, the degree to which the teaching of Socrates had a positive content has been the subject of so much debate that for the purpose of the present discussion it is better to pass directly to Plato, who attributed his fundamental ideas to his master.

II

PLATO AND ARISTOTLE: THE ORTHODOX THEORY OF THE MIXED CONSTITUTION

PLATO WAS BORN OF A RICH, ARISTOCRATIC, AND CONSERVATIVE Athenian family in 428/7 B.C., soon after the opening of the Peloponnesian War. He grew up under the extreme democratic regime which finally brought down in ruin the great artistic, intellectual, and political achievement which Athens had represented under Pericles. During these years at the end of the fifth century B.C., Plato fell under the spell of Socrates. Socrates, though a man of the people, preached that virtue and knowledge could be achieved only by those few aristocrats of mind and character who had the ability and courage thoroughly to analyze their traditional prejudices and to attain a rational understanding of intellectual and moral truth, which for him were identical. From the Socratic teaching Plato derived increased distrust of the prejudices of ordinary people, a distrust which was only confirmed when an Athenian jury yielded to the persuasions of certain narrow conservatives. These conservatives disapproved of the questioning of tradition which Socrates, like the Sophists, encouraged. In 399 B.C., they secured his conviction and execution as a corrupter of young men and as irreligious.

Plato is generally presented as a political theorist who constructed his theories according to a logical scheme rather than as a result of an analysis of historical development. At heart he was a mathematician, which in Greece meant primarily a geometrician. Either in consequence of his disgust at the execution of Socrates or because he was temperamentally unsuited to public life, he remained aloof from politics. His one attempt to put his theories into practice, as counsellor of the younger Dionysius in Syracuse, resulted in failure and disappointment. It is therefore argued that his political theory was constructed with the consistency of a geometrical proof and with no room for the pragmatic irregularities of human nature. But in fact Greek history afforded plenty of evidence which, had he wished, he could have adduced to support his political theories.

Plato held that behind the shift and change of the particular objects and actions of the actual world lay permanent patterns whose interrelations were fixed and whose validity was eternal. For him, the truths of science and of morality were ultimately part of one and the same eternal scheme, in which goodness is truth and truth goodness. In the ideal state, as described in his *Republic*, the rulers should by rigorous study have attained to knowledge of the eternal patterns of science and morality and of their interrelation in terms of ends, since to be good is to be good for something.

Plato conceived that the perfect society should be organized according to a rigid division of function. This division paralleled the tripartite division of states which, as has been shown, had become orthodox for the Greeks of the fifth century B.C. But he made this division functional by assigning the task of ruling to the one or few wise men, the philosopher kings; the task of defense to men of spirit, the aristocrats; and the task of labor to the vast mass of people. Though the masses have a sort of knowledge and skill suited to their particular pursuits, they lack political wisdom and courage. Hence their primary civic virtue must be that of temperance, of sticking to their task and not trying to interfere in

spheres for which they lack qualifications. The harmonious coöperation of the three political classes, representing respectively the
three virtues of wisdom, courage, and temperance, produces in the
state the fourth of the traditional virtues, justice, whereby each person does and receives what is in the highest sense his due. A state
thus pervaded by justice will not need the restraints of positive law
since the rule of the wise will be accepted without demur by the
temperate masses. Plato's concept of a state in which the three forms
of government traditional in Greece were represented by elements
exercising certain virtues and performing certain functions became
orthodox for later Greek political thought.

In addition to his theory of the perfect state, Plato developed
a cycle for the political evolution and degeneration of society, based
on what he conceived to have been the growth and decay of Greek
city-states. In primitive times, the most elementary form of society,
the family, lived simply off natural products. As families grew and
the different branches continued to cohere, the need for mutual
support and protection necessitated more organization. The greater
needs of the more complex society induced trade; trade created
wealth; wealth encouraged greed; and greed led to war. Hence a
fully developed state required not only laborers but also defenders
and rulers. A stable balance between these groups could be maintained only if justice pervaded their mutual relations. But Plato did
not think that the just state would evolve naturally out of the need
for organized defense and government. The tradition of Greek constitutions always went back to some specific lawgiver who had invented and imposed them. Thus Plato felt that a conscious, specific,
and drastic reform would be necessary to institute the ideal constitution. Indeed, in his later life he lost hope in the possibility of
realizing the perfect society and referred to it simply as a pattern
laid up in the eternal realm of the ideas. The best that could be
achieved in this faulty world of material things was a second-best
constitution equipped with an elaborate code of laws. This he described in his last work, the *Laws*.

Moreover, according to the scheme set forth in the *Republic*, a degeneration from the ideal state would inevitably occur because of an inescapable tendency of human nature to fall away from perfection. This degeneration would follow a cycle for which Plato could also have adduced parallels from Greek history. The perfect state, whether a monarchy or ruled by several wise men, would give way, in pursuance of the natural law that all human institutions change, to what he called a timocracy, in which the aristocratic element would vie for honors. This in turn would become an oligarchy, in which those few who had power would use it to accumulate wealth. The mass of the population would then revolt against the oppression of the oligarchy and establish a democracy in which there would be a free-for-all of competing interests. Finally one forceful individual would play upon the passions of the mob until it accepted his leadership. Once in control, he would consolidate his position as a tyrant. Such a government, the dominance of the state by one evil individual, was for Plato the last form of degeneration, which he had witnessed in the domination of the Athenian democracy by Cleon or in the corruption by power of the younger Dionysius at Syracuse. His view reflects on a high plane of political morality the prejudice that tyranny had created against itself during the sixth and fifth centuries B.C. and from which it was to suffer throughout the remainder of Greek and Roman history.

In later life, when Plato had come to feel that the most practicable constitution would be one which fell short of the ideal, he concluded that each of the degenerate types of state might nevertheless have a better or worse manifestation according to its aims. Therefore, in a dialogue on the statesman, the *Politicus*, he set his ideal constitution to one side as unattainable in practice and divided possible forms of government into the traditional three types, depending on the number of those who exercise the political power, namely, one, a few, or the mass of the citizens. Each of these three types may have a good and a bad manifestation. If the single ruler rules by consent, he is a monarch; if by force, a tyrant. If the few who rule are wealthy in their own right, they rule well and constitute an aristocracy; if they are poor and therefore greedy for self-enrichment, they become an oligarchy. If the mass of citizens govern the state according to law, they are a good democracy; if according to the lawless whims and passions of the moment, they are a bad democracy. In this scheme, monarchy is the best and tyranny the worst, but a good democracy comes next after the ideal monarchy, since in a good democracy law takes the place of the wisdom of the ideal monarch.

The concept of law as the guiding principle of the state and as the expression in a particular state of the "idea" of justice did not originate with Plato; it may be found in the speculations of the earlier, "physical" philosophers who were concerned with the problem of whether the universe ran according to principles or not. Even the Hippocratic writers on medicine conceived of health as a sort of just balance between the elements of the body, whose maintenance could be expressed in "laws" of diet and treatment. Plato's elevation of law to the ruling position in his second-best state was to be fruitful both for Aristotle and for the Stoics and, through them, for Cicero. Yet, despite the contribution of Plato and his successors to the development of a philosophy of jurisprudence, their speculations fell short of achieving the concept of a generalized system of legal principles, a *ius naturale*, which existed as a part of the universal order in the universal mind. This, as will appear later, was a major contribution of Cicero to later political theory.[1]

Aristotle, long a student under Plato, derived his political theories from those expressed in the *Politicus* and the *Laws*. During Aristotle's lifetime, Alexander outmoded the self-sufficient city-state and introduced into Greek political thought the concept of the world empire, the superstate in which would be absorbed both the particularist Greek cities and the tribal kingdoms of the Near East. But Aristotle was blind to the significance of Alexander's achievements; he continued to think along the traditional lines of Greek politics. Like Plato and Greek thinkers in general, he emphasized the close connection between ethics and politics. Whereas Plato had sought to define the good life by considering the state as the individual writ large, Aristotle began by analyzing the moral life of the individual in his *Ethics*. In consequence his *Politics* is more strictly political than either Plato's *Republic* or his *Laws*. Moreover, Aristotle had a biological attitude whereas Plato was a geometrician. Hence Aristotle based his generalizations not on logical concepts but on the analysis of extant forms. He is said to have had prepared studies of 158 actual constitutions as a basis for the *Politics*.[2] Aristotle came, moreover, from a middle-class, not an aristocratic, background, and was born not in Athens but in Stageira, on the borders of Macedonia. While he was not an active politician, he came to be closely and successfully associated with the rulers of Macedonia, Philip and Alexander. Hence his theory of the Greek city-state is more practical, historical, and balanced than that of Plato.[3]

Aristotle regarded politics as an art with an end, not as a theoretical science. Whereas ethics show how the individual may lead the good life, politics show how this good life is possible only in a well-ordered society. Though historically the individual comes first, logically man is a political animal and the existence of the state is a prerequisite for his fullest self-realization. Basically, therefore, Aristotle agreed with Plato that the good man and the good society are inseparable. But Aristotle substituted the concept of the "end," or perfect function which the individual or institution should perform in relation to the universe, for Plato's "idea," or pattern which they should approximate within the all embracing meaning given to the other ideas by the idea of the "good." For Aristotle, the state develops naturally from the union of male and female through the family to the village and city. The basis of political life is, as for Plato, justice, or the principle which determines the relations, rights, and duties of each person on the basis

of his individual qualifications. Like Plato, also, Aristotle defined
the optimum size for a city-state as that which would permit all
citizens to participate according to their abilities, namely, about
five thousand. This figure does not, of course, include women,
children, foreigners, and slaves. Aristotle, unlike Plato, regarded
women as by nature inferior to men, and also held that some men
were by nature fitted to be slaves. In both cases the inferiority con-
sists in the lack of the guiding principle of reason.

Theoretically, Aristotle would have preferred the rule of the
best, or an aristocratic form of government. In practice, however,
he was fully cognizant of the oligarchic abuses into which Greek
aristocracies had usually lapsed. He felt that the most stable and
enduring form of government was that which gave political power
to all those who had enough wealth to equip themselves as heavy-
armed soldiers or hoplites. Such men were capable of meeting his
definition of citizenship, the capacity to rule and be ruled in turn.[4]
Aristotle's practical goal was, therefore, a middle-class democracy
in which the poorer citizens were excluded from any effective share
in the government. Aristotle also discussed the three functions of
government, namely, the deliberative, the magisterial, and the judicial. But this division of function, so important in the eighteenth-
century theories of a balanced constitution, did not in antiquity
supersede the division into three types according to the element in
which political control was vested. In Greek practice, the various
organs of government, such as magistrates, senates, assemblies, and
courts, were never so strictly delimited with respect to function as
they are, for instance, in the Constitution of the United States.

Aristotle employed the same scheme of good and bad manifestations of the three traditional types of government which Plato had
expounded in his later works. On the one side stand monarchy,
aristocracy, and what Aristotle called a "polity," or constitution
par excellence. On the other are ranged tyranny, oligarchy, and
democracy. A polity, which is equivalent to Plato's "good democracy," should combine the best elements of the three traditional

types. From democracy, it should take equality, but in a proportional, not an absolute, form; from aristocracy, virtue; and from monarchy, firm government. The desirable mingling will be achieved if obedience to law prevails, if each element in the community is treated according to their particular ambitions, if the rulers are kept from becoming too powerful, and if the aim of government is the interest of the whole, not that of any class or individual. Moreover, Aristotle conceived of law not as something generally valid but as a means to the end of the formation of character under a given constitution. Each system of law must therefore be suited to its particular constitution.[5] In general, the polity of Aristotle, while very similar to Plato's "second-best" constitution, is less aristocratic and represents, as was said, a middle-class and democratic compromise between the three pure types. As such, it was destined to become the orthodox theory of the Hellenistic period.

The political experience of the fourth century seemed to support the theories of Plato and Aristotle. And this experience continued in Greece during the Hellenistic period. Alexander attempted to propagate throughout the lands which he conquered the Greek city-state as the typical form of civilized life; to this extent he put into practice the teachings of Aristotle. In fact, however, an empire such as he envisaged left no room for the political independence of the city-state. A city might manage its local affairs and provide the framework for civilized living, but it could not be an active participant in world politics. The consequences of Alexander's imperialism will be traced in a later chapter; for the moment it must suffice to note that the Ptolemies in Egypt established only one or two Greek city-states with any measure of self-government. The most important, Alexandria, always remained apart from the rest of Egypt as the Hellenic center from which the country was governed.[6] Although the Seleucids in Syria adhered to Alexander's policy of prolific municipalization, their foundations never attained more than a semblance of municipal life.

Hence the tradition of the city-state remained vital only in the Greek homeland and to some extent along the Aegean shore of Asia Minor, in the ancient Greek cities of Ionia, and in those of Sicily and Southern Italy. This vitality was in part due to the enlightened treatment of Greece and Ionia which characterized respectively the rulers of Macedonia, the family of Antigonus, and the rulers of Pergamum in northwest Asia Minor, the family of Attalus. Moreover, the rivalries between the great monarchies prevented any single one from becoming completely dominant in the Aegean area, so that many cities enjoyed a fair measure of independence. In consequence, during the nearly two centuries which elapsed between the death of Alexander in 323 B.C. and the sack of Corinth by the Romans in 146 B.C., the cities of Greece experienced many forms of government; the Macedonian kings imposed garrisons, local tyrants seized power, communistic revolutions occurred in Sparta, and a number of experiments in federation were tried, notably among certain cities of the Peloponnesus, which formed the Achaean League, and among the more primitive tribal communities of western Greece, which formed the Aetolian League. The most successful and stable of these various forms of government seemed to contemporaries to be those which vested power in the hands of the conservatives and which guaranteed the rights of property without reducing the mass of citizens either to penury or to disenfranchisement.

On the theoretical side, the successors of Plato in the Academy turned to abstract science, particularly to geometry, or to epistemological speculations that resulted in increasing skepticism as to the possibility of certain knowledge. The new philosophical schools of the Stoics and Epicureans emphasized the moral aspects of the Socratic tradition. They sought to develop within the individual intellectual and moral attitudes which would withstand the ups and downs of fortune so common in the new ecumenical world — a world where personal rectitude had far less relation to outward well-being than it had had in the closely knit life of the city-state.

The study of the social and physical sciences, those requiring observation and comparison of fact rather than abstract speculation,
were particularly the province of the successors of Aristotle, the
so-called Peripatetics. It was among this group that there were to
be found the great historians of the early Hellenistic period, Ephorus
and Theopompus; the student of individual characters, Theophrastus; and finally a political theorist named Dicaearchus. To the last
has been attributed, though on uncertain evidence, the final per-
fecting of Aristotle's polity in what came to be called the theory
of the "mixed constitution." [7]

The mixed constitution aimed to combine the best features of
the three pure types of monarchy, aristocracy, and democarcy. It
must be remembered that these terms had acquired connotations
beyond the simple meaning of the rule respectively of one, a few,
and the masses. They now implied political domination by social
groups. Monarchy, to be sure, still meant the rule of a single individual, normally a king, whether hereditary or self-made, since the
name of tyrant had fallen into such disrepute. But the "best" or
the "few" of an aristocracy meant the conservative propertied
class, whose wealth continued to be invested chiefly in land despite
the great fortunes that might be made initially in trade, banking,
or even mercenary warfare. And the "people" who governed in a
democracy were not the whole citizenry but the masses, both urban
and rural, who had slight propertied stake in the community and
were eager chiefly for what political control would mean in more
food, entertainment, and jobs, no matter how the bills might be
paid. Plato had underlined how readily any of these three types
could be corrupted unless either wisdom or law prevailed. Aristotle
had doubted the possibility of maintaining any one of the pure
types in a good status even where wisdom or law were present,
since man is naturally imperfect and incapable of long maintaining
that peak of tension which represents the perfect balance, or mean,
between one and another excess. Hence the most stable constitution, in the light both of Aristotle's teaching and of the experience

of contemporary events, would be one in which the three elements whose domination characterized the three simple types should be played off against each other to counteract their respective defects. Moreover, as Plato and Aristotle had tended to suggest, the functions of the three elements were increasingly identified with administration, deliberation, and legislation. It may be noted parenthetically that the judicial function was not specifically assigned, since in practice it might be exercised by any one of the elements. The monarchical element was supposed to find its expression and function in the administrative officials or magistrates, drawn from the propertied classes; the aristocratic, in the deliberative councils or senates, which were generally composed of ex-magistrates; and the democratic element, in the popular assemblies, which remained the final source of law and justice. In theory, the mixed constitution seemed a happy and just solution of the problem of stable government in a city-state; in practice, it vested the real power in the propertied classes. Only they could afford to hold the public offices and in consequence they composed the councils. Moreover, the poorer masses were to a large extent dependent economically for a livelihood on the purchasing power of the rich.

In short, the political experience of the Greeks from the fifth through the second century B.C. and the political theory of Plato, Aristotle, and the Peripatetics established four beliefs which constituted the orthodox theory of the city-state. First, man is a political animal and can attain his highest self-realization only in a rationally organized society. Second, this rationally organized society should be an economically self-sufficient and politically sovereign community small enough for all full citizens to participate directly, according to their qualifications, in its political life. Third, the best form of government for such a society is one which gives scope to the functions of three traditional elements, the administrative function of the officials, representing monarchy, the deliberative function of the council, representing aristocracy, and the legislative function of the popular assembly, representing democracy. Fourth, the most stable of these three elements is the aristocratic, the proper-tied class, which has the means and leisure to devote itself to public affairs and in which, therefore, should rest the ultimate direction of these affairs.

It must be remembered that in the Greek city-state only full citizens participated in political activity and that they formed a minority of the total inhabitants. Not only were women and chil-dren disenfranchised; slavery was frankly recognized as a social necessity if not a natural phenomenon. Resident foreigners and noncitizen workers or peasants also had no political share in the government. Thus even the mass of less well-to-do citizens repre-sented an aristocracy in relation to the large bulk of noncitizen residents, and the state was operated for the benefit of the citizens rather than of all the inhabitants. The view that the resources of the state, raised principally by taxation or contributions levied on the rich, should be expended for the benefit of the masses was perhaps an inheritance from Pericles, who had thus used the resources of the Athenian empire. This doctrine enjoyed increasing vogue in the Hellenistic period and produced social experiments which recall on a small scale modern socialism or the "New Deal."

This aristocratically controlled but democratically organized type of city-state government, with its conservative tone, its sense of the responsibility of the rich to hold public office, and its nascent concept of social welfare, was that which the Romans found preva-lent in Greek political theory and practice when, during the third and second centuries B.C., their own political and intellectual ex-pansion brought them in contact with the Hellenistic world. As will be shown in later chapters, the practical situation in which they found themselves in relation to their conquests demanded a wholly different approach to government. But the orthodox theory of the mixed constitution so admirably fitted the institutions and way of life which they had themselves developed historically that they fell naturally under its intellectual dominance.

III

HELLENISTIC LEAGUES AND MONARCHIES

THE ORTHODOX THEORY OF THE MIXED CONSTITUTION REACHED ITS final form in a period when in fact the Greek city-state had become outmoded. This was unfortunate because the authority of Plato and Aristotle over later thought established their concept of the ideal human society so firmly that other theories had little chance to secure recognition. The domination of authority and tradition was characteristic of Greek and Roman civilization in all its aspects. It constitutes at least one of the reasons why in the long run classical thought, for all its great achievements, failed to keep pace with the changing conditions of life, and eventually became sterile and purely imitative. With regard to the present discussion, the inability to look beyond the city-state prevented the Greeks from developing an adequate theoretical basis for the organization of society on the scale necessitated pragmatically by the conquests of Alexander. Two forms of social organization did in fact appear on a scale larger than the city-state. Federalism developed in the fourth century, and monarchies arose in consequence of the expansion of Macedonia. The present chapter will discuss the failure of federalism and the adaptation to the Hellenistic world of the absolutist monarchies of the Near East by Alexander and his successors.

Federalism had a long tradition in Greek political experience. Thebes had from early times dominated Boeotia because it controlled a league of neighboring communities. Sparta organized the city-states of the Peloponnesus during the sixth and fifth centuries B.C. into a Peloponnesian League. The Athenian empire in the fifth century B.C. began as the Delian League. In all these and other similar cases, there existed some sort of common council, attended by representatives of the member states. But such leagues fell short of being true federations in two respects. First, representation was of states, not of people, and therefore the size of the individual states did not affect their representation. Second, the league fell under the leadership, hegemony, or domination, of a single powerful member.

In a true federation, communities equally sovereign send representatives to a council and surrender to it some of their sovereignty so that either it conducts certain common affairs, such as war or diplomatic negotiations, or it makes decisions to be followed without question by the members in the conduct of their own affairs. Such true federation played little or no part in Greek politics before the Hellenistic period. After the Battle of Chaeronea had placed all Greece under his control in 338 B.C., Philip II of Macedon, perhaps inspired by his study of Boeotian federalism during his youthful sojourn in Thebes, sought to unite all the Greek city-states in a true federation of Panhellenic scope. The resultant League of Corinth, or, more correctly, League of the Hellenes, had as its organ of government an assembly of representatives of the individual larger states and of groups of smaller communities. It lacked any common citizenship and it fell too much under the domination of its leader, the king of Macedon. Moreover, for reasons which remain uncertain, Alexander preferred to construct his new empire independently of the League. Thus, though the League lingered on even after Alexander's death, it never became an effective instrument for Panhellenic unity.[1]

During the Hellenistic period, only the strongest city-states, like Athens, Sparta, or Rhodes, could maintain their independence single-handedly against the various rulers who competed for the control of Greece and the Aegean. In consequence, the smaller Greek states continued to form federations. Two of these federations, the Achaean League in the Peloponnesus and the Aetolian League in western Greece, were the most successful and enduring.[2] They went beyond the League of Corinth in that citizens of member cities enjoyed in addition a common citizenship in the league. This departure from the traditionally exclusive nature of citizenship perhaps pointed the way toward the development under the Roman empire of the view that one could be a citizen both of one's own community and of Rome. But in the leagues, the general assembly continued to represent communities rather than, directly, all the individual citizens. Hence, while the Hellenistic leagues represent the achievement of representative federalism, they did not develop representative government directly responsible to the electorate. More important for the present discussion, they stimulated no intellectual attempt to devise a political theory of federalism which might compete with the orthodox theory of the city-state. In consequence the various federations left no lasting mark on the history of political theory, as against political practice. Apparently the Greeks looked upon them as diplomatic arrangements between the member communities rather than as a new form of political organization capable of theoretical analysis.

The failure of the federal idea meant that the organization of areas larger than the city-state was conceivable only in the form of the domination of one state over another, as in the Athenian empire or later in the growth of Rome, or in the form of a congeries of different political entities united in subservience to a single will, as in the empires of Persia and of Alexander.[3] Moreover, this failure meant that citizenship continued to be thought of as something which must be exercised directly and not through elected representatives. Fundamentally, the failure affords an instance of the inability of Greek and Roman thought to break the bonds of tradition and to develop from practical experience fresh and fruitful solutions for new political problems.

The concept of common race which had been present among the Greeks from the earliest days might have afforded grounds for forming a Panhellenic state. Panhellenism had, indeed, been approximated in the union of most of the Greek states against the common Persian foe in the early fifth century B.C. under the hegemony first of Sparta and then of Athens. But the particularism of the mainland states and the jealousy between Athens and Sparta prevented the continuation of this union on any wider scale than the Delian League or the Peloponnesian League. Nevertheless, at the end of the Peloponnesian War, Gorgias pleaded for Panhellenic unity at the Olympic Games in 408 B.C. Twenty years later, Lysias did the same. And the idea of Panhellenism found its warmest advocate in the outstanding political pamphleteer of the fourth century B.C., Isocrates.

Isocrates continued throughout his long life to urge the Greek states to put aside their particularistic rivalries and to unite on the basis of their common blood in a common cause. The common cause which he advanced was a crusade against Persia, a second "expedition against Troy," which would finally complete the repulse of the Persians by freeing those Greek cities in Asia Minor which had been surrendered to Persian rule under the Peace of Antalcides in 387 B.C. The union which Isocrates advocated was not a true federation but rather a league under the hegemony of an outstanding state or ruler. He sought in the contemporary world for some state or individual to occupy the position which Athens had held in the Persian War but which she had lost by converting the Delian League into an empire. When Athens tried to revive her league in the early fourth century B.C. with the express promise to avoid her previous abuses, Isocrates hoped that she might resume the leadership of all Greece. To this hope he returned intermittently throughout his life. But the hegemony of Greece passed first to Sparta, then to Thebes. Isocrates turned, therefore, to various contemporary rulers who, monarchs in their own states, might become, like Agamemnon, leaders of a Panhellenic alliance.

Philip of Macedon finally achieved in the League of Corinth the hegemony which Isocrates desired. It may be doubted, however, whether Philip was initially inspired by any such high ideals as those preached by the pamphleteer. He was clever enough to add to his armory of diplomacy, bribery, and force, the appeal to Panhellenic sentiment which Isocrates put in his hands. Philip set the seal on his hegemony by his victory over Athens at Chaeronea in 338 B.C. Athens, roused by the fiery oratory of Demosthenes, had organized against the Macedonian invader a last-ditch defense of Greek liberty and particularism. Her defeat spelled the end for all practical purposes of the traditional political pattern in Greece, the coexistence of sovereign, self-sufficient city-states. Thereafter, individual city-states might from time to time regain a measure of independence, but in fact they would always exist under the shadow, and by the tolerance, of some larger power. Shortly after the battle of Chaeronea, Isocrates died, while two years later Philip was assassinated. But the message of the one and the achievement of the other found a worthy heir in the youthful Alexander. Alexander, pupil of Aristotle and devotee of Homer, almost certainly had in mind Isocrates' program of a summoning of the Greek hosts for a Panhellenic crusade when he united the Greek states by oaths of direct loyalty to himself and levied forces from each for his Asiatic venture. His pattern may well have been Agamemnon summoning the Greek chiefs to honor their sworn promise and to lead their contingents under his command against Troy.

Alexander's Asiatic venture, however, resulted far differently than Isocrates might have hoped or than Alexander probably first planned. True, the shadow of a Panhellenic League was maintained for a time in Greece. But Alexander's conquest of the Persian Empire brought him face to face with a system of government and a justification of rule which was alien to previous Greek experience and theory. For all practical purposes he was forced to supersede the league by a new form of government. In this he was no longer a leader, a "hegemon," on the model of his father Philip or Homer's Agamemnon; he became as absolute as had been the Pharaohs in Egypt or the "Great Kings" of Persia.

The Persian Empire in the fourth century B.C. extended from the Hellespont to the Sudan, from the Mediterranean to Turkestan. Within this vast area there was no well-organized state with a uniform culture, but rather a loose union of many peoples, each of whom enjoyed a considerable degree of racial and cultural integrity under the absolute sway of a king who ruled by divine right. The Greeks had long been fascinated by the extent of the Persian Empire and by the magnificence of its "Great King." But the Persian power had in fact steadily declined from its high tide of expansion at the time of the invasion of Greece in the early fifth century B.C. When Alexander challenged it in 334 B.C., the central government no longer exercised effective control over the outlying areas. The Persian army consisted of national levies without a common tongue or a uniform organization. Hence both government and army disintegrated before the shock of Alexander's compact, heavily armed Macedonian phalanx. In the brief space of ten years and after a series of brilliant military campaigns, Alexander found himself master of all and more than the Persians had ruled. He faced the problem of himself establishing a system of government for these vast territories and diverse peoples. To solve this problem he could find no answer in Greek political experience and theory, limited as this had been to the self-sufficient and closely-knit city-state. He naturally turned to the centuries-old experience of the areas which he must rule. Within the Persian Empire had been absorbed two long traditions of government on a large scale, the Egyptian and the Mesopotamian.

Egypt is a country almost wholly protected from foreign attack and at the same time dependent for its existence on the proper con-

trol of the floods of the Nile. Hence it early developed a high degree
of internal organization whose continuity was seldom disturbed
by foreign invasion. The ruler, or Pharaoh, was sole owner of the
land and sole arbiter of the destinies of the people. He stood so far
above them that he basked in the effulgence of divine favor and
was regarded, to all intents and purposes, as a god on earth. Sig-
nificantly, tradition asserts, whether rightly or not is disputed, that
Alexander chose the shrine of the Egyptian god Ammon-Ra at
Siwa for the announcement of his divine birth from a union between
Zeus, whom the Greeks equated with Ammon, and his own mortal
mother, Olympia.

Since Alexander did not remain long in Egypt, his final concept
of empire derived mainly from his more intimate knowledge of
the Persian system of government. This, in turn, was the consummation of thousands of years of political development in the Mesopotamian valley. Mesopotamia, unlike Egypt, had from time im-
memorial been exposed to conquest, chiefly by the hill tribes along
its north and east edges. Its wealth had also lured the more western
powers eastward so that the northern section, the "fertile crescent,"
became a historic battle ground between East and West. Hence the
function of government in the Mesopotamian valley had not been
primarily economic, as it was in Egypt, but defensive and military.
The governments which established themselves successively never
developed a highly centralized administrative machine like that of
the Pharaohs. They were rather loosely knit and, if the term may
be used, feudal. Unity and control depended largely on the personal loyalty of local officials to the "Great King." Once this loyalty weakened or the vigor of the kings themselves failed, the empires became easy preys to fresh invaders. Moreover, the empires
had no such racial and cultural homogeneity as characterized Egypt.
They were congeries of peoples. Sovereignty over such a state
could not proceed from the people; it must derive either from
heredity or from a belief in a divine right to rule. Membership in
such a state could not be citizenship in the Aristotelian sense of an

opportunity for each to rule and be ruled in turn; it must be simply complete subjection to the despotic will of the ruler.[4]

The last of the conquerors of Mesopotamia before Alexander, the Persians, based their claim and the claim of their king to govern on the teachings of Zoroaster. Zoroastrianism, like the previous religions of Mesopotamia, taught that the supreme deity was a Lord of Good, Ahura-Mazda, engaged throughout the universe in a truceless war against the Lord of Evil, Ahriman. The favor shown by Ahura-Mazda to the king and his rule were justified because the latter headed this conflict as representative of the Lord of Good among men. He therefore embodied the justice which characterized the Lord of Good. As such, his utterances were divinely inspired rules, and he himself was, as it has been expressed, "animate law."

Alexander sought to conform his position to the Persian concept of empire. He gave equal recognition to Persians with his Greeks. He required all alike to perform before himself the deep bow which was customary before oriental gods and rulers. He may even have begun issuing orders to the Greek cities whose validity was to be supraconstitutional, like instructions from the oracles of the gods. Naturally, the free spirit of his Macedonians, whose king was traditionally elected by the assembled people and was only a chief among equals, and of the Greek cities, with their concept of constitutional sovereignty, were equally alienated by these innovations.

After Alexander's untimely death in 323 B.C., no one of his generals proved strong enough to hold together his conquests. Out of some twenty years of conflict emerged three major monarchies. Antigonus Gonatas and his descendants ruled in Macedonia. Seleucus, in whose family this name alternated with Antiochus, kept Syria and a tenuous hold on Mesopotamia. Ptolemy, whose successors used only this name as the Egyptian kings had used Pharaoh, secured Egypt. No one of them, apparently, carried out completely the political program of Alexander; each perpetuated certain aspects but was forced to adapt his form of government on the one side to the local tradition and on the other to the need of retaining the support of his Greek troops and officials.

In Egypt, the Ptolemies ruled the Egyptians as successors to the Pharaohs, absolute and quasi-divine masters. But they administered the country with Macedonian soldiers and Greek officials, and kept the native Egyptians, particularly the previously powerful priests, out of public office and out of the army. For the Macedonians and Greeks, the Ptolemies continued to be simply national kings. However, there was a gradual tendency for the regime to become Egyptianized. Whereas the first two Ptolemies gave divine honors only to deceased predecessors, the third made himself and his sister-queen gods during their lifetime. Under their successors, the Egyptians were admitted to a somewhat greater share in the administration and the army. Inscriptions and the remains of Alexandrian literature show that the Greeks themselves, notorious flatterers, adopted the exaggerated oriental concepts of the divine ruler.

In Syria, the Seleucids employed chiefly Greeks as administrative officers. They also actively fostered the Hellenization of the natives, particularly by the foundation of cities. But they depended largely on native levies for their military forces. They themselves, as against the Ptolemies, seem to have treated their Greek subjects on the same level as non-Greeks. On the other hand, the Seleucids did not attempt to deify themselves to the same degree as did the Ptolemies. In fact, they inherited the general position and concept of the Persian monarch. Though they did not go as far as had Alexander in equalizing their oriental subjects with their Greeks, they came closest of the Hellenistic monarchs to the ecumenical concept of a kingdom embracing on the same terms a wide diversity of peoples and cultures.

The Antigonids remained true to the traditions of the Macedonian kingship. This was undoubtedly in origin a tribal chieftainship, and even in historic times seems to have retained an almost Homeric character. The office had been hereditary in the family of the Argeadae, but the new king apparently had to be accepted, or even "elected," by the army, representing an original assembly of males capable of bearing arms. A direct heir might be passed over in favor of a more competent relative. Though the army had no official share in the government, it does seem to have acted as an ultimate court of justice. Obviously, under such conditions, the ruler had so to conduct himself as not to alienate the sympathies of the army, which, being a general levy, really represented public opinion. Naturally, the more influential Macedonians, the "nobility," like the more prominent Homeric warriors, played a considerable part both directly and indirectly in the government, and the king had particularly to consider their opinions.[5] Moreover, in the fourth century Philip achieved a dominant position in Greece, and the Greeks, to salve their pride, recognized their new rulers as fellow Hellenes rather than as alien barbarians. The Macedonians prided themselves on thus being accepted into the circle of "civilized" peoples.[6] Even though they did not maintain at all times their domination over the Greek cities, they were constantly trying to do so and for that reason wished their monarchy to appear in the form most acceptable to the cities. Finally, Antigonus Gonatas, founder of the dynasty, fell strongly under the influence of Stoic political theory, which will be discussed in the next chapter. For all these reasons, the Antigonids were the least absolute, the least divine, and, if the phrase may be permitted, the most "constitutional" of the three great dynasties.

The Hellenistic period witnessed two practical attempts to organize society on a scale larger than the city-state. The first of these, the League of city-states, might have been fruitful in anticipating the modern concept of the federal state. But contemporary thinkers failed to provide for it a theoretical justification, and also the slight beginnings of representation withered. It was the monarchical form of state which succeeded. While this had some background in early Greek society, its real models were in the ancient divine or semidivine monarchies of the Near East. In these ancient monarchies, the divinity of the king as well as the practical need for effective executive control set such a gulf between ruler and subject that responsible government became impossible.[7] Absolutism was, however, tempered by a sense of the obligation of the ruler toward the ruled in those two monarchies which were most Hellenic in character, the lesser kingdom of Pergamum and particularly Macedonia. The theoretical justifications for monarchy which were advanced during the Hellenistic period followed, therefore, two lines — absolutist for the Seleucid and Ptolemaic monarchies, and "constitutional" for the Antigonid.

IV

PHILOSOPHIC JUSTIFICATIONS FOR THE HELLENISTIC MONARCHIES

THE ORTHODOX VIEW OF THE CITY-STATE SO DOMINATED THE FIELD of political theory during the Hellenistic and Roman periods that little if anything has survived to show if and how contemporary thinkers tried to justify philosophically the Hellenistic monarchies. It does appear that two lines of thought were adopted, the first in connection with the Seleucid and Ptolemaic states and the second in connection with the Antigonid. The first line had its roots in oriental ideas of divine kingship, and it may have been pursued among thinkers who belonged to the Pythagorean school and wrote in a literary Dorian language. How far the views which they expressed in fact derived from early Pythagoreanism and had any real connection with the survival of monarchy in Sparta is questionable. Moreover, the fragments of the works in which this absolutist theory of the divine monarch as living law finds expression have recently been placed, on the grounds both of language and of thought, not in the Hellenistic period but in the late second or third century A.D., and connected with the new concept of the Roman emperor which then developed. Despite this uncertainty, it seems not unlikely that the views expressed in these neo-Pythagorean treatises on royalty, the fragments of which are quoted by Stobaeus in the fifth century A.D., were first worked out in the Hellenistic period to adapt to the Hellenistic monarchies the traditions of divine kingship which derived from the Egyptians and the Persians.[1]

The absolutist view recognized two sources of law — inanimate, or written, and animate, expressed in the person of a ruler. Plato shows traces of such a theory in his contrast between the ideal state of the philosopher-king in the *Republic* and the second-best state ruled by law in the *Laws*. In the former, the philosopher-king rules because of his knowledge of the ultimate principles of the universe, the "ideas." Rule is therefore an "art" or *techne* practiced by the ruler and accepted by the rest of the inhabitants, whether citizens or not, because they have the virtue of temperance. In such a state, the restraints of written law are unnecessary. But in the second-best state, described in the *Laws*, an elaborate code replaces the adaptable wisdom of the ruler and regulates according to a fixed pattern the detailed functioning of government. Parallels for the absolutist theory can also be found both in the Egyptian concept that the Pharaoh was inspired by a special ray from the sun-god and even more in the Persian concept that royal glory was especially bestowed by the Lord of Good and was symbolized by the eagle who can behold the sun face to face. According to the absolutist theory, therefore, the Hellenistic monarch was animate law, whose rule was personal and unrestricted by any formal code or constitution. He was also the superhuman Savior who afforded to his subjects a dynamic and personal manifestation of divinity. He possessed preëminent virtue and preëminent reason, or what the Greeks called *logos*.

The concept of the ruler as a divine and animate source of law may have made it easier for the Greek city-states to accept the enactments of the monarchs as law even though their constitution provided for no sovereignty above that of the assemblies. But there is so little evidence for this view that it may be questioned whether the Greeks themselves ever attempted to make any such philosophic adjustment between the orthodox theory of the self-sufficient, sovereign city-state and the existence of an overriding monarch. The absolutist theory may therefore be assumed to have been developed primarily against the oriental background and traditions of the Seleucid and Ptolemaic monarchies. Though it was to play its part in the development of the Roman imperial government, it did not contribute directly to the political theory of Cicero.

If oriental absolutism did not satisfy the Greeks as a theoretical justification for the Hellenistic monarchies, it was still possible that their own philosophers might have provided a solution to the problem. However, of the four major schools of philosophy in the Hellenistic period, neither the Academy of Plato nor the Peripatetic successors of Aristotle took cognizance of the new political problem presented by the conquests of Alexander. They remained loyal to the traditional and orthodox city-state. Their failure in this respect arose from their general lack of response to the underlying philosophic challenge presented by the Hellenistic world, the need to redefine man's relation to morality and metaphysics in terms suited to his altered position in society. Their failure therefore merits consideration before the responses of the other two schools, the Epicurean and the Stoic, to the challenge are discussed.

The Academy of Plato devoted itself to problems of mathematics and to the possibility of certainty. In the third and second centuries B.C., the so-called Middle Academy reached a position of complete skepticism with respect to the possibility of certain knowledge. In consequence, its thinkers maintained that all positions were equally tenable and apparently applied this view to politics. The result was a return on the part of Carneades, who headed the Academy in the middle of the second century B.C., to the pragmatic view of the Sophists in the fifth century, that might makes right and that arguments on behalf of justice are only specious excuses for the fact of rule. The skepticism of the Academy when the Romans first came in contact with it undoubtedly accounts in part for the fact that Stoicism rather than Platonism became the accepted philosophy at Rome.

The successors of Aristotle, the Peripatetics or Lyceum, devoted themselves to many fields of learning and attempted to base their conclusions on careful observation of fact. At the instigation of the second Ptolemy, they were the founders of a great school for research in the so-called "Shrine of the Muses" or Museum at Alexandria. But, as the previous chapter showed, in politics they perpetuated the orthodoxy of Plato and Aristotle with regard to the city-state and perfected their doctrine that the only satisfactory form for society was a mixed constitution in a self-contained, sovereign community small enough for all citizens to rule and be ruled in turn. The mixed type of constitution was in fact spread throughout the conquests of Alexander by his successors, who regarded Hellenism as the highest form of civilization and the city-state as the political expression of Hellenism. But their policy provided no means for integrating either the individual or the city-state as an active participant in the new monarchical states.

The influence of Socrates had not, however, been perpetuated during the fourth century only by Plato and, through him, by Aristotle. Other philosophers had concentrated on the ethical aspect of his teaching, namely, that goodness depended more on inner character than on the externals of wealth, success, good health, and the like. This train of thought, which Plato and Aristotle accepted in moderation, could be pursued to two extreme conclusions: first, that the good life does not depend on the external environment of society but must be attained within the individual; and, concomitantly, that the external demands of society distract the individual from his own self-perfection. Such conclusions, so alien to Aristotle, nevertheless received considerable support from the conditions of life during the fourth century B.C. As the complex of political and economic conditions transcended the limits of the particularistic city-states and attained a Panhellenic, not to say a Mediterranean, scope, the inner merit of the individual bore less and less relation to his position in the community or to the accidents which might overtake him. Clever but unprincipled men went far in the confused politics of the time, nor did their sins catch up with them. Wars and economic crises over which the ordinary man had no control and in whose issues he had no concern might sweep away his possessions and reduce his person to slavery. People felt the need for an ethic which would justify morality against the obvious fact that success or failure visited good and bad with no apparent relevance to their character and which would assure the individual of an inner calm and self-confidence in the face of the unpredictable chances of life. One simple answer, of course, was to regard the dominant force in the universe as chance, and, in fact, Chance personified, *Tyche*, became one of the important refuges of thought during the Hellenistic period. But if chance ruled the externals of life, how much more necessary for the individual to have within himself the moral force to cope with her inequities. Herein consisted the moral challenge which the new age presented to philosophy.

According to later tradition, two pupils of Socrates, Aristippus of Cyrene and Antisthenes, whose followers came to be called Cynics, were said to have attempted to answer this problem, the one negatively and the other positively.[2] During the fourth century, these two lines of ethical speculation had been overshadowed by the dominant thought of Isocrates, Plato, and Aristotle. Moreover, there still remained sufficient vigor in the city-state to justify the traditional relation of ethics and politics. But the conquests of Alexander initiated an era of world politics. Not merely the individual city-states but even Greece herself was reduced to a minor role. Chance, or *Tyche*, had ever more spectacular opportunities to make sport of the individual. The ethical points of view later attributed to Aristippus and Antisthenes came to the fore at the opening of the third century in the teaching of two more prominent philosophers, Epicurus and Zeno. Their schools, not Plato's Academy or Aristotle's Lyceum, were destined to reign supreme, at least for the general public, as the accepted ethical guides for the Hellenistic and Roman eras.

Of these two schools, the Epicureans offered an answer to the political and moral problem which was negative, not to say anarchistic. Epicurus urged the individual to live as pleasantly as he could. Though this doctrine came to be used as an excuse for self-indulgence and excess, especially among the Romans, Epicurus himself had an almost ascetic concept of pleasure. Bodily self-indulgence, which might bring on illness or which might lead to regret if one were ever deprived of the enjoyment, was as much a mistake as excessive self-denial. Simplicity, moderation, and getting along with the minimum dependence on external goods, were the only certain ways to preserve oneself from the suffering that reverses of fortune might bring. From the point of view of the present discussion, however, this aspect of Epicureanism is not so important as the doctrine that the intelligent man should withdraw as far as possible from the world of affairs. He should not take part in politics because there, if anywhere, the blows of fortune would be most keenly felt; he should not even become involved in family affections because death, ingratitude, and similar accidents might bring pain. Finally, he should be skeptical toward religion because from religion arises superstition, the fear of the unknown, the incalculable will of the gods. Epicurus admitted that the gods might exist, in their own happy Epicurean world above. But he held that they could not be concerned with the affairs of men.

This doctrine of withdrawal from a world which one could not reform has precedents in Plato. Plato theoretically insisted that the philosopher, once his education is complete, should return from the contemplation of the abstract "ideas" and become a king to rule men in accordance with the eternal truths which he had learned. In fact, however, he was discouraged from active participation in politics, probably by his failure to induce the younger Dionysius to establish the ideal state in Syracuse. In the words of his own simile, he retired into the shelter of a wall from the dust and hail raised by the whirlwind of contemporary politics.[3] He withdrew with his pupils to the grove of the hero Academus, in the Attic countryside. And thereafter his Academy became cut off from real life and devoted to the pursuit of "pure" mathematics and other intellectual pursuits. Similarly, Epicurus established his school in a garden outside of Athens. The "Garden" became a symbol of retirement from the world into a pleasant and tranquil but entirely self-centered existence, such as the gods led in their remote heaven. Epicurus took as the ideal of life the Greek word *apraxia* or "inactivity," almost *dolce far niente.*

Epicureanism, despite the personal attractiveness of its founder, could never become a popular philosophy. Self-denial and the severance of the normal human ties required a high degree of inner self-sufficiency and skepticism toward accepted values. It also demanded sufficient means to permit of the self-contained life. It was therefore definitely a philosophy of the well-to-do. Moreover, the disciples of Epicurus adhered almost religiously to the very words of their master. Hence the school displayed no philosophical growth and stimulated no continuing intellectual effort. In view of this limited appeal and negative character, it is astonishing that Epicurean doctrines aroused such hostility among both Romans and later Christians. Christian hostility is easier to explain on the ground of the atheistic and purely mechanistic metaphysics of Epicurus. The Roman antipathy represented a reaction which arose from their deep-seated conviction of the individual's duty towards the state. Traditionally, no Roman could live for himself alone; his individual existence and desires were subordinated to those of the family or the community. Cicero, consistently with his devotion to the Roman commonwealth, found nothing good in Epicureanism.[4] From the point of view of the present discussion, therefore, Epicureanism made no positive contribution to Hellenistic or Roman political theory. It attempted to tear down the beliefs on which the orthodox theory of the city-state depended. But it offered no alternative solution for the relation of the individual to the monarchic state except acceptance combined with personal withdrawal and inactivity.

Zeno, contemporary with Epicurus and founder of Stoicism, is ιid to have come from Cyprus and to have had Phoenician, that is, Semitic, blood in his veins. How far the Stoic doctrine was his and how far it was elaborated by his immediate successors, Chrysippus and Cleanthes, cannot be determined. Scholars have attributed to Zeno's Semitic blood that moral fervor and monotheistic belief which, in Stoicism, recalls the Hebrew prophets. But the same moral fervor was also characteristic of the purely Greek Cynics, cognates and perhaps predecessors of the Stoics. Even in the second century of the Roman empire, Cynic preachers, on street corners of the cities, after the tradition of Socrates, Diogenes, and Bion of Borysthenes, still made an ostentatious display of poverty and called on men to turn into the paths of virtue. Monotheism also can be traced in Greek thought as early as Xenophanes, a writer of the sixth century B.C. It attained an elevated, impersonal purity in Plato's identification of the idea of the good as the all-embracing and eternal spirit. Hence it is not necessary to look beyond the Socratic tradition for the sources of Zeno's thought, and in particular of his ethical, social, and political theories.

The early Stoics agreed in several respects with the Epicureans. The aim of philosophy should be to free men from the disturbances of the soul created by the external accidents of fortune. The first step in achieving this ideal was to form a true judgment of the unessential nature of externals, popularly regarded as goods. To this extent Zeno was as ascetic as a Cynic and more so than Epicurus. Where, however, the Cynics preached a homely, practical wisdom of making the best of life, whether good or bad, with the consciousness that happiness and virtue are within oneself, not outside of one, Zeno preached an impossible ideal of absolute perfection and wisdom, the Wise Man, the *sophos* or *sapiens*, who alone was free because he alone lived the life of complete inner self-sufficiency, unaffected by externals. Where Epicurus advocated lack of activity, *apraxia*, the Stoics urged that one be not upset, *ataraxia*.

In another respect, the Stoics resembled the Epicureans; they realized that the active integration of the individual and the state had become impossible, now that the sphere of politics was no longer the city but the inhabited world, the *oecumene*. Instead, however, of using this as an argument for withdrawal from affairs, the Stoics recognized that the concept of citizenship must be enlarged to include the whole world. Moreover, if knowledge in the Platonic sense could no longer serve as the guide for life, conduct could; and that conduct should find expression in performance of duty. As a practical illustration of this doctrine, Zeno did his teaching in no retired Academy, Lyceum, or Garden, to select and qualified disciples. Like Socrates, he held forth to any who cared to listen, rich or poor, in a public colonnade in the center of Athens, the "painted Stoa" from which his school took its name. The early Stoics also made explicit the implications of their theory of world citizenship; namely, that all men had a common brotherhood; that no man was by nature, as Aristotle had argued, a slave, except in so far as he was a slave to passion and fear; and that Greeks were as men in no wise different from barbarians. Ethically, therefore, Stoicism offered a solution at once practical and noble to the problem of the relation of the individual to the state in the new monarchies. Yet this solution was not wholly satisfactory because it was one-sided. It placed on the individual a duty toward his fellow men but it offered him no corresponding privilege, such as citizenship had constituted in the city-state. Few men are idealistic, or disciplined, enough to live by duty alone; though if any ancient people were so, it was the Romans. The discipline and sense of duty to the state inbred in the Romans explain the appeal which Stoicism had for them.

With respect to political theory, the Stoics did offer a philosophic justification for the Hellenistic monarchies. They conceived that the affairs of the world were guided not by the interplay of mechanistic movements, as Epicurus held, but by reason. This universal reason was not a thing apart, as had been the ancient gods or Aristotle's "prime mover," which was itself immobile and outside of the moving universe. Reason, like Plato's idea of the good, pervaded the whole universe, held it together, motivated and controlled it. Plato had maintained that only those who had been trained by a rigorous course of education until they beheld the correlation of all lesser concepts in the all-embracing, all-enlightening idea of the good were fit to manage the affairs of the state. Similarly, the Stoics taught that monarchy is the best form of government but that the monarch must be enlightened enough to rule in accordance with the universal reason. If he has not the time himself to become a philosopher, he should at least guide his government in accordance with the teachings of philosophers.[5]

Zeno was more fortunate than Plato; he found in Antigonus Gonatas a monarch who could play this role. Antigonus, as governor of Greece on behalf of his father Demetrius in the 290's B.C., became a disciple and friend of Zeno and their mutual admiration continued throughout their lives. Antigonus as king of Macedonia gathered about himself a circle of poets, philosophers, and historians which was largely Stoic in color. There seems to be no reason to doubt that Antigonus consciously conformed to the Stoic concept of the ruler. The ancient sources describe his character as *atuphos*, lacking in self-deception, free from the illusion of false pride. They refer to his gentleness and his love for mankind, *philanthropia*. This quality the Romans were to elevate into the concept of *humanitas*, the quality that characterizes man at his best. And one ancient writer, Aelian, reports that when Antigonus' son had used his subjects severely and roughly, the king said, "Knowest thou not, my son, that our kingship is a noble servitude?"[6]

The Stoic view of kingship was not, indeed, very remote from the Oriental. It was accident that kingship in Macedonia preserved a flavor of the ancient tribal chieftainship which, though it had ordinarily passed by inheritance, was probably confirmed by the assem-

bly of people under arms. As Tarn points out, Antigonus Gonatas
did not achieve his monarchy by inheritance or by popular acclaim.
In the terms which the Byzantine scholar Suidas applies to the successors, the *Diadochi*, of Alexander, neither birth, that is, inheritance, nor justice, that is, lawful succession, gave him the rule,
but his own ability to raise an army and to handle affairs intelli-
gently.[7] In so far as he was acceptable to the people, this acceptance
was after the event; in so far as he ruled for their benefit, he did
so of his own will and not in response to theirs; his sovereignty derived not from the will of the people but from his own achievements; he passed his rule on to his children so that the succession
did not revert to the people. It was an accident of temperament that
Antigonus accepted Stoic teachings and refused the deification by
which the Seleucids and Ptolemies came to conceal the arbitrary
sources of their power.

Yet, despite the part which accident played in making the Stoic
justification of monarchy the official view of the kingdom of Macedonia, the Stoics alone among the important schools of the Hellenistic period advanced a political theory which coped seriously with
the problem. Certainly if monarchy was the only possible form of
government for areas larger than the city-state, no nobler justification could be propounded than that of the Stoics. The doctrine that
all men are common citizens of the world supported the establishment of a world or ecumenical state. The doctrine that the individual has a duty toward his fellow men meant that all men had a
duty to work together for the common good. The doctrine that
reason pervaded the universe gave rise to the concept that law was
the expression for human relations of this universal reason and that
behind the particular codes of individual states lay a universal,
natural law based on the character of man as man, not on the
particular character of a specific state. The doctrine that the king
was the exponent on earth of the universal reason assumed that
he would rule in accordance with law for the benefit of the whole
community. Nevertheless, despite the nobility of the Stoic politi-

cal theory, it fell short, as has been indicated, of bridging the gap between governed and governor. The ruler was not responsible to the will of the people, since he was wiser than they and ruled in virtue of his wisdom, not of election. The people, therefore, had only such share in rule as the king, in recognition of the wisdom of individuals, might choose to give them.

Thus, in political theory, the Hellenistic period achieved no satisfactory substitute for the orthodox theory of the city-state which might afford a philosophic justification for government on a larger scale than the city. Federation was tried and had a certain practical success. The Achaean League, for instance, survived for nearly a century and a half. It started about 280 B.C. and was dissolved by the Romans after the sack of Corinth in 146 B.C. It produced a series of able and, for the most part, disinterested leaders, notably Aratus and Philopoemen. Yet even its last outstanding figure, the historian Polybius, made no attempt to justify federation on a philosophic basis. He discussed it always in terms of practical politics and diplomacy.

Alexander and his successors in Egypt and Syria, the Ptolemies and Seleucids, inherited from the Pharaohs and the Persian kings monarchies which were absolute, which surrounded the ruler with an aura of divine favor, which based sovereignty on heredity in a quasi-divine family, and which accepted the word of the ruler as divinely inspired law. From Persia the Seleucids also inherited through Alexander the concept of an empire embracing many different people on terms of equality, even if only of equal subjection to the will of a single ruler, not of equal participation in the government. As against the Ptolemies, moreover, the Seleucids, while maintaining the superiority of Greek culture, were far more ready to admit excellence wherever found and to distinguish Greeks and barbarians on the basis not of blood but of civilization. Thus the Seleucids most nearly maintained the ecumenical concept of rule which Alexander had introduced to the Greeks.

Such an ecumenical concept of an all-embracing, multiracial

empire was, however, alien to the character of Greek political life and thought. Hence, though traces survive of attempts to develop a philosophic justification and basis for absolute, divine monarchy in the Hellenistic period, these made no headway against the orthodox theory of the city-state and contributed little to Roman political thought. It is noteworthy that although the Roman emperors borrowed many of the external trappings of the eastern monarchies, including the aura of divinity, Augustus and his successors for two centuries did not adopt the philosophic implications thereof, that sovereignty came from above and that rule should be hereditary. Heredity and the support of the troops in fact determined the succession at Rome; in theory the outward forms of the grant of power by the senate and the acceptance of the emperor by the people alone made his rule legally valid. Even at the end of the second century A.D., when the Severi were laying the foundations of what became the absolute, divine, monarchy of the Later Empire, the Roman lawyers could still trace the power of the emperor to a popular enactment, a *lex*, and could still say that although the emperor was above the law, yet it should be his duty preëminently to abide by the law.[8]

Though the significant contribution of the Near East was to the political practice of Hellenistic monarchy rather than to its theoretical justification, it might be expected that the Greek genius, which had so successfully founded the institutions of the city-state on the theory of citizenship, might also have discovered some theoretical justification for the monarchical state. But of the four chief philosophic schools which flourished during the Hellenistic period, only one, the Stoics, grappled positively with this problem. Their solution, moreover, was secondary to their major concern with the ethical orientation of the individual in an expanding and complex society. The Stoics abandoned the traditional view that Greeks were distinct from and superior to other peoples, to "barbarians." They taught that the individual is a brother to all men, even to slaves and aliens. In consequence his traditional duty toward the community became for them a duty toward the all-embracing commonwealth of mankind. The Stoics likewise established for the ruler a standard of behavior in accord with universal reason and natural law, based on the realization that rule should be not merely an opportunity for self-aggrandizement but rather for the service of the commonwealth. Moreover, the later Stoics, abandoning to some extent the extreme position of the founders, admitted that while the perfect wise man might be only an unrealizable ideal, still the ordinary individual could lead the good life by trying always to do what was proper rather than what was simply useful. They also accepted the fact that, within the framework of universal brotherhood, smaller political entities must exist. They therefore advocated as the practicable form of society the orthodox city-state with a mixed constitution. This was their position in the second century B.C. when the Romans came in contact with them and found that both their ethics and their politics most nearly suited the native Roman character and constitution. Even the Stoics, however, failed to find an adequate solution by which Aristotle's fundamental criterion of political life, that citizens rule and are ruled in turn, could be extended beyond the limits of the city-state. The Stoics could only offer as a solution for the relation of the individual to the new monarchical states the doctrine that while subjects should work for the state and rulers rule for the state, both were placed in their station of life in accordance with their capacities and, in particular, the ruler governed not in response to the will of the people but as the exponent of universal reason.

The Hellenistic monarchies succeeded practically in governing large areas, particularly those in which absolute monarchies were traditional. They offered an attractive pattern on which Romans like Caesar and Antony attempted to organize Rome's domination over the Mediterranean basin. But the noble Stoic justification for monarchy did not satisfy the traditional feeling of both Greeks and Romans that the citizen should participate actively in politics and that sovereignty should originate from the people rather than from above. The orthodox theory of the city-state remained dominant in the field of theory. The Romans, particularly Cicero, were familiar with the Hellenistic monarchies. But they refused to abandon their traditional city-state form of government in favor of monarchy even when faced with the problem of organizing their empire. Their refusal finally caused the downfall of the Roman Republic. Equally, failure to recognize the loyalty of men like Cicero to the orthodox theory of the city-state led Caesar to the Ides of March. The success of Augustus in founding the Roman empire lay in his ability to resolve by compromise this conflict between theory and practice.

V

THE DEVELOPMENT OF THE ROMAN CONSTITUTION

THE ADAPTATION OF THE GREEK THEORY OF THE MIXED CONSTITUTION
to the Roman government was, so far as surviving literature goes,
first consciously made by a Greek historian of Rome, Polybius, in
the latter half of the second century B.C. This adaptation was conditioned by what Polybius thought that the historical development
of the Roman government had been and, undoubtedly, by what
had been said by previous writers, both in Greek and in Latin, on
Roman history. A necessary prelude, therefore, to the political
thought of Polybius is to review briefly the traditional, literary,
history of the Roman constitution and to examine such indications
of political thought as can be found in the scanty fragments of his
predecessors. Both of these tasks are difficult.

The origins of the Roman state are veiled in an obscurity from
which neither the myths set down in later ages nor the spade of the
modern archaeologist will ever rescue them. Apart from scattered
references in the surviving literature of the Republic, the earliest
literary accounts of the origins of Rome which afford anything like
a complete picture date from the period of Caesar and Augustus.

They occur in such writers as, preëminently, the Roman Livy and, secondarily, the Greek Dionysius of Halicarnassus and Diodorus Siculus. Behind these authors extended nearly two centuries of historical writing in Rome since the first identifiable historical author, Fabius Pictor. Fabius, though a Roman, composed in Greek a history of Rome which extended from the mythical Aeneas to his own period, that of the second Punic War. Behind Fabius in turn lay some interest in Roman history on the part of Greek writers. Aristotle is said to have included the institutions of Rome among the studies made by himself and by his pupils in preparation for writing his *Politics*.[1] According to Dionysius of Halicarnassus, certain Greek historians in the period of Alexander's immediate successors, the *Diadochi*, that is, at the beginning of the third century B.C., included Roman history incidentally in their accounts.[2]

Upon what sort of written or oral materials these Greek and Roman writers drew for events before their own times has been the subject of much learned discussion. It seems likely that they had available lists of magistrates, of increasingly dubious validity for the earlier period, some sort of annual notes on significant events kept by the priests, archives which contained laws, senatorial decrees, treaties, and the like in questionable completeness, records of the public careers and achievements of distinguished men as preserved either on public monuments or by their descendants, and a rudimentary oral or written tradition of the period of the kings, merging into myths of the actual foundation. It is now generally agreed that the sack of Rome by the Gauls in the early fourth century B.C. did not wreak such destruction of early written records as the skeptical historians of the last century supposed.[3]

It is equally clear, however, that these raw materials for history were incomplete and often not fully intelligible to the later writers and that, where they depended on family records or oral tradition, they had been subject to considerable distortion in favor of individuals, of families, or of Rome herself. Moreover, the earliest historians were completely under the dominance of the Greek

approach to history. Greek historiography tried to trace the foundation of cities and institutions to specific founder heroes or lawgivers. If Rome was to be accepted as a civilized rather than a bar-
barous state, she too must be shown to be of Greek descent and to
have some connection with the beginnings of Greek history in the
epic period. Thus, for instance, very early in the conscious literary
historiography of Rome, there appeared the myth that the Romans
were descended from a Trojan hero, Aeneas, who had made his
way to Italy; that the site of Rome had even before his arrival been
settled by refugees from Greece and was visited by Herakles in
his wanderings; that the city of Rome itself had a specific founder-
hero, Romulus; that its institutions could be attributed specifically
to Romulus himself or to one or another of his six successors as
kings; and even that these institutions had in some cases been consciously imitated from Greece. It is not necessary here to consider
the skepticism which prevailed during the nineteenth century concerning such traditions of early Roman history or the trend among
recent historians to accept, on the basis of archaeological evidence
and the study of comparative institutions, the main outlines of the
ancient accounts.[4] Polybius and Cicero accepted the traditions as
generally historical and based their conclusions about the nature
of the Roman government on them.

The literary version of Rome's early history was, therefore,
probably established in its main outlines by the time of Polybius.
It placed the foundation of Rome by Romulus in the middle of
the eighth century B.C. and portrayed its primitive society in a
form familiar in early Greek history, that of a group of clans based
on blood relationship. The elders of the clans formed a council or
senate and there was a king whose rule tended to pass by descent
but who had, apparently, to be approved by some form of popular
election in an assembly based on the clans, the *comitia curiata*. It
is not improbable that the kings sought confirmation from this
assembly of their more important political and judicial decisions or

legislative enactments. Thus the ultimate sovereignty of the people was apparently explicit from the beginning of the Roman state.

A sharp class distinction appeared in early Rome which is not paralleled in Greece, though Greek writers compared it to the existence of certain noble families at Athens called *Eupatrids*. This is the distinction between patricians and plebeians, the origin of which is very uncertain; nor does it affect the present discussion since it had lost all practical meaning in the time of Cicero. Public and religious offices were originally held only by patricians; the patricians alone knew both secular and sacred law. The plebeian had to attach himself to a patrician to assure himself of proper representation in civil and religious matters. His dependent relationship involved him in the performance of certain duties toward his patron and constituted for the poorer plebeians a real condition of subordination as clients of their patrician patrons.

A second distinction between the early Roman city-state and the Greek lay in the strongly military character of the former. Though the most primitive assembly was by clans, that which became really effective at the end of the regal period was an assembly by the military companies or centuries into which the whole levy of the people, the legion, was subdivided. Furthermore, the power of the Roman king was conceived of as a military command, an *imperium*, a term whose origin and meaning is much disputed. The *imperium* was peculiar to the king and in addition he had a general control expressed by the vaguer word *potestas*, a term which also covered the powers of such lesser officials as may have existed to assist the king in his civil and military duties. According to tradition, the growth of Rome and its increasing warfare led, toward the end of the monarchy, to a reform of both the military and the civil organization. The military character of Sparta's government had been imposed on her at a specific crisis in her history, the second Messenian War, about 610 B.C., and was attributed to a specific lawgiver, Lycurgus. The Romans, perhaps under the influence of Greek patterns of historiography, similarly traced their reform to the sixth king, Servius Tullius, but even tradition did not make him a fundamental "lawgiver" in the Greek sense. He simply improved on existing military institutions. His reform of the military organization, which divided the army into companies called "hundreds," *centuries*, and assigned service on the basis of wealth, in *classes*, became also a political grouping. The assembly of people under arms and arranged by classes and centuries, the *comitia centuriata*, displaced the original assembly by clans, the *comitia curiata*, as the principal organ for the expression of popular sovereignty in election, legislation, and jurisdiction on appeal from executive judgments. Whether this change took place before the end of the monarchy or during the first century of the Republic remains uncertain. The innate conservatism of the Romans appears in the fact that though the election of the chief magistrates was transferred to the assembly of the centuries, the grant of the chief power of command, the *imperium*, continued to be made by an atrophied assembly by clans, represented in the historical period by thirty attendants of the magistrates, or lictors, one for each of the traditional thirty clans. The subordination of the organization and functioning of the state to defense, the requirement of military service from all citizens, and a strong sense of discipline and obedience, which extended even to the relation between father and family, were all characteristics of the later Roman state.

Besides the organization by family connection and that by military service, Rome from the beginning showed an organization by wards,. called *tribes*. These at first numbered four, but as the state extended territorially new tribes were added until in the middle of the third century B.C. they reached thirty-five. At that time, about 241 B.C., it was apparently felt either that there were tribes enough or that to extend them further would make it impossible for members to reach Rome for meetings. Even previously, membership in a tribe once established had come to pass by inheritance. Thereafter new citizens were enrolled in the existing tribes. As membership in an Athenian deme became after Cleisthenes' reform in 508 B.C. the essential designation of a citizen, so the Roman always included his tribe in his full name.

At what date the tribal assembly, or *comitia tributa*, of the whole people first appeared was uncertain. But at the beginning of the Republic, the plebeians are traditionally pictured as already having an assembly of their own, a *concilium plebis*, from which patricians were excluded and whose decisions, *plebiscita*, were not recognized by the state as law, *lex*, binding on the whole people. This plebeian assembly was organized by tribes, as against the clans or centuries of the official assemblies. Moreover the plebeians had their own officers, *tribunes*, whose name is presumably connected with *tribe*, though there always seem to have been fewer tribunes than there were tribes, perhaps initially only two and never more than ten. The plebeians also possessed their special temple of Ceres on the Aventine, with its caretaker, or *aedile*. The appearance at so early a date of a state within a state is a unique phenomenon for which no adequate explanation can be derived from the ancient literary sources or securely achieved by modern scholarship. The existence of the organized plebeians became a major factor in the early history of the Republic and a continuing influence on Roman political thought and action. Specifically, the achievement of full political rights by the plebeians meant that eventually the whole people came to be organized by tribes for political purposes. Whether this occurred through the inclusion of patricians in the plebeian assembly or by the development of a parallel assembly of the whole citizen body is uncertain. At any rate, the tribal assembly of the people, the *comitia tributa*, became coequal in the third century with the assembly of the centuries and was, in fact, the chief organ for legislation and for elections of magistrates other than the chief ones whose primarily military character required the *imperium*.

The transition from a life kingship to an annual magistracy was completed in Athens and was partially achieved at Sparta during the seventh century B.C. At Rome, according to tradition, it was interrupted by the intrusion of foreign rulers who attempted to change the character of the kingship. The first of these, the fifth king, was named Tarquin and supposedly came from the Etruscan city of the same name, Tarquinii, toward the end of the seventh century B.C. His father was reputed to have been a Greek refugee from Corinth. Tarquin changed the character of the Roman monarchy from an elective and limited tribal chieftainship to an absolute and hereditary rule. In some respects his emergence parallels that of the tyrants in Greek cities during the same period, but the similarities are perhaps due to the influence of Greek models on Roman historiography. Rome was by no means so far advanced politically, socially, or economically as were the Greek cities, in which the new commercial and industrial classes supported energetic individuals in overthrowing the dominant landed aristocracies.[5]

Tarquin's successor, Servius Tullius, may have been of Latin blood but he had been brought up in the royal household, and he married the widow of his predecessor.[6] Despite the admiration with which the later Romans regarded him as the presumed reformer of their military and civil organization, he does not seem to have been less monarchical than his predecessor. He was succeeded by a son or grandson of Tarquin the First. The second Tarquin, the Proud, conducted himself in such an autocratic and high-handed manner that the Romans revolted and ejected Tarquin himself and his supporters.

The reigns of the last kings did three things for Rome. Tarquin the First introduced into her religious and constitutional practices many Etruscan elements, such as prophecy by means of an examination of entrails, the magisterial seat, lictors, and similar trappings. Servius Tullius placed her political and military organization on a new footing. And Tarquin the Proud made the name of king so hated that naked monarchy would ever thereafter be impossible at Rome. But these reigns did not change the fundamentally Roman character of the constitution or its orderly development.

The conservative genius of the Romans appears nowhere more clearly than in the fact that though they had disposed of the monarchy, they did not change the nature of the supreme power of the state. The Romans showed a faculty which the Greeks, for all their ability at philosophic abstraction, did not have. The Romans conceived of power as separate from office, *imperium* or *potestas* from *magistratus*, whereas the single Greek word *arche* covers both. With the expulsion of the kings the Romans reduced the term of the supreme magistracy from life to a year and installed two occupants, the consuls. But they neither divided the *imperium* nor, theoretically, placed any limit upon its exercise. Each consul exercised the full *imperium*; so far as possible the two were kept physically separate to avoid conflict and when they were together they alternated in preëminence. The equal possession by each consul of the traditional full *imperium* resulted in a curiously negative feature of the Roman constitution. Balance and control were not secured by delimitation of function so that each might be fully competent in his own sphere. Rather, when two officers of equal competence disagreed, either could prevent the other from acting so that nothing could be done until the conflict was resolved.

The constitutional history of the early Republic is dominated by the so-called struggle between the orders — the fight of the richer plebeians to achieve political and social equality with the patricians and to free the poorer among them from dependency upon their patrons and from the abuse by the patricians of their legal and economic advantages. Many aspects of this struggle recall the similar struggle in Athens during the sixth and early fifth centuries B.C. The provision of a written code of laws by the Decemvirs about 450 B.C. paralleled the publication at Athens of the codes of Draco and Solon around 600 B.C. The gradual opening of magistracies to the plebeians recalls the gradual opening of the archonship at Athens to all citizens. The fight of the plebeians for protection from arbitrary imprisonment for debt and for the redistribution of land repeats two of the reforms of Solon. The right of appeal to the popular assemblies in capital cases suggests Draco's substitution of legal procedure for the ancient right of private blood vengeance. Such parallels forcibly impressed later Roman historians. Indeed, the account of the early struggle has undoubtedly taken on the colors of Greek history and political thought, from which were borrowed the current formulas for political strife during the later Republic at a time when ancient precedents were being adduced, recast, or even invented to support contemporary political programs.[7]

The struggle for equality between all citizens was far more prolonged in Rome than in Athens and never in fact completely resolved. It traditionally began in 494 B.C., when the plebeians seceded from the city in protest against the abuse of magisterial power by the patricians. Only slowly and by a succession of protests did they secure recognition of legal, political, social, and economic equality. Modern scholarship tends to accept the tradition that the laws of the Twelve Tables, the foundation of Roman civil law and the "magna charta" of equal rights for all, were codified and publicly posted in the years 451–449 B.C.[8] Yet the proper procedure to invoke the remedies provided by these laws was not published until 304 B.C., by a follower of the liberal censor Appius Claudius, the aedile Flavius. Traditionally, the struggle is supposed to have been settled by a series of laws passed in 368 B.C., after ten years of debate, by the tribunes Licinius and Sextius. One of these is said to have required that one consulship annually should be reserved to the plebeians. Yet the consular lists indicate that the patricians almost regularly held both consulships during the next two decades. Livy, faced with this inconsistency, states that in 342 B.C. a new law guaranteed one consulship to the plebeians and permitted them to hold both in any given year. Even so, Roman conservatism was such that a pair of plebeians did not hold the consulships of the same year until 172 B.C. And two plebeians were not censors together until 131 B.C. However, in the eighty years following the legislation of Licinius and Sextius, the plebeians consolidated their position. In addition to the tenure of such high offices as the dictatorship, censorship, consulship, and praetorship, they secured admission to the colleges of religious officials, the pontiffs and the augurs, by a law of the tribune Ogulnius in 300 B.C. Even so, in any civil or religious magistracy, the patricians throughout Roman history retained a titular superiority over their plebeian colleagues. A final success was achieved by the plebeians in 287 B.C., when a Hortensian law made decisions of the plebeians, *plebiscita*, binding on all citizens, including the patricians who had, apparently, previously claimed to be exempt from them. Thus plebiscites became fully equal to laws of the whole people and are, in fact, indistinguishable from them in the later Republic. This law probably completed the equalization of the assembly of the tribes with the assembly of the centuries in legislative matters and left to the centuriate assembly only the peculiar prerogative of electing the magistrates who held the *imperium*, the consuls and praetors.[9]

The Hortensian law marks the end of the "struggle between the orders," the conflict between patricians eager to retain their monopoly of political, legal, and religious control and the plebeians fighting for equal rights. The plebeians had achieved their main objectives: full equality in the popular assemblies, access to office, knowledge of the law, and protection of the legal and economic rights of ordinary citizens against the arbitrary exercise of magisterial power or unjust oppression by wealth and privilege. Thereafter the nature of the internal conflicts in the Roman state was altered. A new aristocracy arose, based on wealth and privilege. Despite the theoretical right of any citizen, patrician or plebeian, to hold office, only those with means, leisure, and a considerable political following could achieve it. Thus office became a prerogative of a narrow group of prominent and well-to-do families, both patrician and plebeian. Since tenure of a magistracy generally meant inclusion by the censors in the senate, these families constituted a quasi-hereditary senatorial aristocracy. Even more exclusive were the group of senatorial families who secured an almost monopolistic control of the highest offices, the consulship or its equivalent. These, according to the most generally accepted modern view, constituted within the senatorial aristocracy a narrower group of "noble" families. Only exceptionally did a "new man," an outsider like Cato the Elder, Marius, or Cicero, break into the charmed circle of this plebeio-patrician "nobility."

The plebeio-patrician aristocracy was enabled to retain the control of public affairs formerly exercised by the patricians because popular sovereignty as expressed in the Roman assemblies was limited merely to voting on matters brought before them by the appropriate magistrates, normally after prior consideration in the senate. There was no debate from the floor and only those could address the assembly or be candidates for election who were accepted by the presiding magistrate. Furthermore, in the Roman assemblies decision was reached by a majority of the voting groups, whether centuries or tribes; the vote of the individual counted only in settling the vote of his group. Thus the well-to-do could control a majority of voting groups by controlling within sufficient groups a majority of individual votes. It is possible that had the inner development of the Roman state been allowed to continue under peaceful conditions after 287 B.C., the liberalization which found expression in the far-sighted views of such leading families as the Valerii, the Horatii, and on occasion the Claudii would have continued. But just at the time when the struggle between the orders had finally been stabilized by typically Roman, conservative, patriotic compromises, Rome entered upon a century of fresh wars. The Pyrrhic and Punic Wars eclipsed in magnitude those which had won for Rome the supremacy of Italy south of the valley of the Po. They imposed such a strain on the state that little opportunity or energy remained for internal constitutional growth. The scope and complexity of the problems which the wars presented were such that inevitably control and initiative had to be assumed by the senate. In general, the popular assemblies acquiesced in the leadership of the nobles.

The growth of the Roman government as pictured in the ancient literary sources closely paralleled the Greek concept of constitutional history. A simple pastoral society of patriarchal clans under a tribal monarch degenerated into tyranny, against which both nobility and commoners revolted. A conservative aristocracy of patricians became oligarchical and was overthrown after a long struggle by the "democratic" plebeians. Fortunately for Rome, the assemblies did not go to the extremes of Greek democracies but accepted the wise leadership of the new aristocracy of patricio-plebeian nobles. The resultant compromise seemed, as will appear presently, very like the Greek ideal of a mixed constitution.

Just as this stage of development was achieved and Rome emerged as one of the great powers of the Mediterranean world, there appeared the second of the factors which influenced Polybius' interpretation of Rome's constitution. The new national self-consciousness, aroused by contact with Greek culture in south Italy, revealed itself in the surprisingly rapid creation of literature at Rome, written both in Greek and in Latin, but, even in Latin, closely modeled on Greek patterns. This early literature has for the most part perished; only some twenty-one comedies of Plautus survive in whole or in part. These afford no material for the history of Roman political thought. Of the early historians, in whom might have been found some attempt to explain, if not to justify, the rise of Rome to world domination, only the merest fragments are preserved in later citations and references. Any impression, therefore, of the reflections of contemporary Romans concerning Rome's emergence on the scene of world affairs must be drawn from the somewhat more fruitful, but still scanty, remains of two great epic poems which were composed during this period of national trial and triumph.

The first epic was by Naevius. He may have been a Campanian by origin but he had fought for Rome during the First Punic War.

Naevius made this struggle, which lasted for twenty-three years, from 264 to 241 B.C., the subject of a poem in the native Italian accentual meter called Saturnian. At some point in his poem, he introduced a digression on early Roman history which contained, probably from Greek sources, an account of how Aeneas came from Troy to Italy.[10] Unfortunately, research, as presented most recently by Warmington in the Loeb Classical Library, has been able to collect from ancient citations only sixty-six complete or incomplete lines and a few further references. These are cited in part by commentators on Virgil but mostly by late scholars to illustrate archaic usages. It is impossible, therefore, to hazard any guess as to Naevius' attitude toward Roman politics. Two fragments refer to the unwillingness of troops, presumably Roman, to abandon a post of danger or to desert others in danger.[11] They suggest an emphasis on the virtues of loyalty and discipline. Naevius also wrote two tragedies on Roman topics, one on Romulus and one on the contemporary victory of Marcellus over the Gauls at Clastidium in 222 B.C. It has been assumed, probably with justice, that Naevius' composition of epics and tragedies on contemporary events shows a strong feeling among the Romans of the period that they were living in an epic and heroic age, worthy of the literary treatment which the Greeks had largely reserved for myths of gods and heroes. Yet it should be remembered that tragedies on contemporary themes were not unknown in Greece. During the Persian Wars, Phrynichus and Aeschylus had written tragedies on such events of their own day as the sack of Miletus and the victory of Salamis.

The *Punic War* of Naevius stood for the Romans as an admired monument of antiquity. Cicero makes Brutus point out the debt of Ennius to it and the commentators on Virgil show where he in turn borrowed from it.[12] But it may be suspected that the poem was little read in later ages; certainly Cicero, who frequently quotes Ennius, does not quote the *Punic War*. The *Annales* of Ennius, indeed, completely overshadowed Naevius' epic, even though the later poet omitted the First Punic War because of his predecessor's work. Ennius came from the south Italian town of Rudiae in Calabria; he claimed Messapian descent and may have received a Greek education at Tarentum. He is said to have been equally at home in Greek, Oscan, and Latin. He served in the Roman army in Sardinia at the end of the Second Punic War and was brought thence to Rome by the conservative Cato, then quaestor. One late writer even claims that Cato, the foe of Hellenism at Rome, learned Greek from his protégé. When Ennius came to Rome in 204 B.C., he might just have known Naevius, who is said to have been exiled at about that date because of his attacks on certain nobles.[13] Ennius was a versatile genius not only linguistically but intellectually. He may properly be regarded as the real founder of Roman literature, despite the work of Livius Andronicus, Naevius, and his own older contemporary Plautus. He excelled in all forms of literature, in epic, in tragedy, in comedy, in philosophy, and even in miscellaneous light verse on current themes, to which the Romans gave the name of "satire" and which they claimed as their own invention. He associated with the most distinguished Romans of his time, particularly with the liberal, Hellenizing group which gathered about the great Scipio, conqueror of Hannibal.

Like Naevius, Ennius tried his hand at tragedies on Roman subjects, a *Rape-of the Sabines* and probably an *Ambracia* on the capture of that town during a campaign conducted by his patron Nobilior against the Aetolians in 189 B.C., in which the poet himself took part. For the purpose of the present discussion, however, Ennius' most impotant work was his *Annales*, an epic on Roman history from its mythical beginnings practically to the time of his death, in 169 B.C. Although Livius Andronicus, Naevius, and Plautus had already adapted Greek meters to Latin in their plays, the two former had preserved the native Italian saturnians for epic. Ennius took the step so significant for the growth of the Latin epic, that of writing in the meter of Homer, the dactylic hexameter. Warmington gives 565 lines or parts of lines from the *Annales*.

While the majority of these, as in the case of Naevius, are quoted either by commentators on Virgil, to prove his borrowings, or by grammarians to illustrate rare words and constructions, nevertheless a fair number are preserved because of their literary quality. Some of these last occur in such later Roman scholars as Aulus Gellius of the second century A.D., but most of them are found in Cicero, who had an intense admiration for Ennius.

Ennius opened his poem by claiming that Homer had appeared to him in a dream and stated that by transmigration, including the intermediate stage of a peacock, his soul had migrated into the body of the Italian poet.[14] Ennius then began his account of Rome from the fall of Troy. It is clear, particularly from the long fragment preserved on the auspices taken by Romulus and Remus at the founding of Rome, that Ennius emphasized the divine favor which presided over Rome's destiny from the beginning. Nor was the direct intervention of the gods confined to the mythical period, since one reference to a speech of Jupiter is placed in the book dealing with the war against Pyrrhus. Ennius perhaps awarded to Pyrrhus more nobility of spirit than was his due in the famous speech in which the king released his Roman prisoners without ransom. In general, however, the fragments begin at about this point to show the second cause to which Ennius attributed Rome's greatness, namely, the virtues of both state and individuals. First among these was Roman steadfastness, particularly in adversity, as exemplified by the self-devotion of Decius Mus at Asculum or in the speech in which Appius Claudius the Censor urged the senate not to come to terms with Pyrrhus. In a later fragment, Ennius remarked in a phrase imitated by Virgil that fortune is given to the brave, though elsewhere he recognized the variableness of fortune, particularly in war. But the most famous expression of Roman steadfastness occurs in the description of Fabius Maximus the Dictator, who "alone by his cautious policy saved the state for us and did not prefer rumors to safety so that thereafter even until now his glory shines more and more." Closely connected with steadfastness was discipline, of both commander and soldier. The third characteristic which made the Romans superior to others in Ennius' mind was their moral character. He expressed this in a famous line which Cicero used to introduce his assertion of the same characteristic: "The Roman state stands firm on ancient morals and men." [15] Finally it was the desire for glory which urged the Romans to deeds of boldness. Glory figures not only in the just-quoted passage on Fabius Cunctator but also in lines possibly from a speech of Scipio Africanus before the battle of Magnesia in 190 B.C.: "Now is the day when the greatest glory is set before us, whether we live or die." In the surviving fragments of the *Annales*, therefore, the greatness of Rome is traced to divine favor and to the virtues of steadfastness, discipline, moral character, and the desire for glory. Nothing is said of the form of the Roman state as such; the emphasis is on the heroic deeds and noble character of individuals and of the people as a whole.

Thus the stage was set for the adaptation of Greek political theory to the Roman government. The traditional history of the Roman state portrayed the emergence of a conservative democracy, in which the people accepted the leadership of the nobles and in which the three traditional forms of government were represented, monarchy in the magistrates, aristocracy in the senate, and democracy in the assemblies. Each element theoretically had some control over the others, but in fact direction lay with the nobles, who monopolized the magistracies, and therefore membership in the senate, and held the initiative in the assemblies. The excellence of this constitution, and particularly the harmonious loyalty of all elements to the good of the whole, had not escaped the notice of writers like Naevius and Ennius. It was clear to them that Rome's success had been due to the virtue of her citizens as expressed in their government and military achievements.

VI

POLYBIUS: THE MIXED CONSTITUTION
ADAPTED TO ROME

TWO YEARS AFTER THE DEATH OF ENNIUS, THERE CAME TO ROME
a Greek who was the first, so far as we can tell, to attempt a philosophic consideration of her constitution. Polybius was the son of a
leading statesman in the Achaean League in Greece. He himself,
by taking part in the affairs of the League, had become grounded
in statecraft and imbued with an intense interest about what made
for success in the sphere of politics. When he was in his early thirties, in 168 B.C., the Romans defeated Perseus of Macedon at Pydna.
In the following year, despite her previous alliances with the
Achaeans and their neutrality in the recent conflict, Rome arrested
a thousand leading citizens of the League. These unfortunates were
deported to Italy, and, since there was no provision for the deten-
tion of prisoners by the state, they were entrusted to prominent
families and to various Italian communities. They were held without trial for fifteen years, at the end of which time only three
hundred survived to be restored.

Rome's brutal act had one good result. Polybius, one of the
prisoners, was assigned to the household of Aemilius Paullus, the

victor of Pydna. There he became intimate with the sons of Paullus, particularly with the younger, who had been adopted by a son of the great Scipio. This youth, who eventually became the final conqueror of Carthage and of the Spanish stronghold of Numantia, is known to history either as Scipio Aemilianus or as Africanus the Younger. The families of his father and of his adopted father had long been known for their liberal politics and for their interest in the culture of the Greek world, a culture whose introduction into Rome was, according to the conservatives like Cato, having most deleterious effects upon the minds and morals of the young. Polybius saw that Rome was destined to become one of the most powerful states in the Mediterranean, if not the most powerful. He realized that although the Romans had defeated Carthage, Macedonia, and Syria, his fellow Hellenes still regarded them as uncivilized barbarians whose meteoric success might, through the operation of unpredictable Fortune, be followed by an equally sudden disaster. Polybius claimed that neither of these impressions was true. The Romans whom he knew were far from uncivilized and in fact the myth was already pretty well accepted that they were descended from Greeks and Trojans as well as from aboriginal, barbarian Italians. Moreover, Polybius felt certain that Rome was in Greece to stay and that the Greeks had better realize that her attainment of the status of a great power within the space of a century had been due not to the fickle goddess Chance, or *Tyche*, but to the institutions and character of the Romans themselves.

Polybius therefore determined to describe Rome's conquest of the Mediterranean and to explain it. His *History* would not only serve to convince the contemporary Greek world that Rome's rule was inevitable, and probably preferable to the existing state of continuous unrest and warfare. It would also serve the purpose which had become standard for historical writing since Thucydides, that of teaching men how politics worked and how best to manage public affairs. In forty books, Polybius covered the period from 220 to 168 B.C. He included a brief prefatory treatment of events since the outbreak of the First Punic War in 264 B.C. and a later supplement on events down to the destruction of Carthage and Corinth in 146 B.C. Unfortunately, only five books survive complete. From the remainder, long extracts were made for an encyclopedia compiled for a Byzantine emperor of the tenth century A.D. Polybius was also used extensively by Livy and is frequently cited on specific points by other ancient scholars. While, therefore, it may not be possible to recover his historical thought in its entirety, its general character must be reasonably well represented by the surviving portions of his *History*.

Polybius, next to Thucydides, shows the keenest insight of any ancient historian into fundamental historical processes. Like Thucydides, he determined to handle only a limited period of history, which constituted in his eyes a unity, rather than to trace the rise of Rome from her beginnings. He took an even wider view of history than did Thucydides, who had brought peoples other than the Greeks only incidentally into the scope of the Peloponnesian War. Polybius prided himself on his recognition that the events of his time formed a universal nexus and that he must consider the histories of all the Mediterranean countries, even though at any given moment these were not directly relevant to his main subject. He was no historian of the study. As a young man he had himself participated in politics and diplomacy and in later life he accompanied Scipio both to Carthage and to Spain. At Rome he mingled freely in the society of the nobles who as magistrates, commanders, ambassadors, or simple senators dealt from day to day with the internal and external affairs of state. He had for his age advanced and humane concepts of public and private conduct. He was, for instance, the first ancient historian explicitly to condemn the looting and destruction of works of art as such. He recognized virtue and courage wherever he saw it, even if in a Galatian barbarian, but he did not, as did some of his Hellenistic contemporaries, idealize either the barbarians or the Greeks or the Romans. He was as ready to condemn the Romans for cruelty or for folly as he was Philip

of Macedon. Since he lived to the ripe age of eighty-two, it is not
unlikely that his opinions changed with the passage of time. At
any rate, some critics have sought to detect various strata of revi-
sion in his work and especially to argue that initially he attached
more importance to the operation of Chance, or *Tyche*, in history
than he did later.

Throughout his history Polybius emphasized the excellence of
Rome's constitution as a major factor in her success. Particularly,
he paused at the great defeat of the Romans by Hannibal at Cannae
in 216 B.C. and devoted almost a whole book to the Roman political and military system. Though of this book only excerpts are
preserved, these apparently represent the major portion of the contents. The preserved section of his preface to the book is worth
quoting because it gives so clearly his general purpose. The translation is that of W. R. Paton in the Loeb edition: [1]

"I am aware that some will wonder why I have deferred until
the present occasion my account of the Roman constitution, thus
being obliged to interrupt the due course of my narrative. Now,
that I have always regarded this account as one of the essential parts
of my whole design, I have, I am sure, made evident in numerous
passages and chiefly in the prefatory remarks dealing with the
fundamental principles of this history, where I said that the best
and most valuable result I aim at is that readers of my work may
gain a knowledge how it was and by virtue of what peculiar
political institutions that in less than fifty-three years, nearly the
whole world was overcome and fell under the single dominion
of Rome, a thing the like of which had never happened before.
Having made up my mind to deal with the matter, I found no occasion more suitable than the present for turning my attention to the
constitution and testing the truth of what I am about to say on the
subject. For just as those who pronounce in private on the characters
of bad or good men, do not, when they really resolve to put their
opinion to the test, choose for investigation those periods of their
life which they passed in composure and repose, but seasons when

they were afflicted by adversity or blessed with success, deeming
the sole test of a perfect man to be the power of bearing high-
mindedly and bravely the most complete reverses of fortune, so it
should be in our judgment of states. Therefore, as I could not see
any greater or more violent change in the fortunes of the Romans
than this which has happened in our own times, I reserved my
account of the constitution for the present occasion . . .

"What chiefly attracts and chiefly benefits students of history
is just this — the study of causes and the consequent power of
choosing what is best in each case. Now the chief cause of success
or the reverse in all matters is the form of a state's constitution;
for springing from this, as from a fountain-head, all designs and
plans of action not only originate, but reach their consummation."

Polybius then described briefly the three traditional forms of
government, each in its good and bad manifestations, which were
discussed in the first chapter, namely, kingship and monarchy, as
he contrasted them in place of the usual monarchy and tyranny,
aristocracy and oligarchy, and democracy and mob rule or ochloc-
racy. He reviewed the rise of the state from the family and its
progression through the various good and bad forms much in the
manner of Plato, to whom he refers. At this point, he interjected
a remark that the Roman constitution after its slow rise to perfection was sure to change for the worse some day, a theme to which
he returned at the end of his discussion. He then praised the constitution of Lycurgus at Sparta because that famous lawgiver fore-
saw that a simple constitution is soon perverted and therefore combined in his mixed constitution the best features of the three simple
types. Lycurgus thus ensured a longer duration for liberty at Sparta
than was recorded elsewhere. Polybius pointed out, and this became
a significant point in favor of the Romans, that they achieved the
same result not by the rational reforms of an individual but by
the discipline of many struggles and troubles in which they always
chose the best in the light of experience gained in disaster. Polybius
held that if one looked to the *imperium* of the Roman consuls, the

constitution was monarchical; if to the senate, it appeared aristocratic; and if to the ultimate sovereignty of the assemblies, it seemed
democratic. He supported this view by a brief analysis of the functions of each part, and then showed how they were actually inter-
dependent and could not function without one another's support.
He concluded that this careful balance and interdependence made
all three elements strive together effectively for the common good.

After a long description of the Roman military system, and
particularly of the Roman camp, Polybius compared the Roman
constitution with various Greek ones. He dismissed Thebes because
her success had been due not to her constitution but to the ability
of two individuals, Pelopidas and Epaminondas. He discounted
Athens because of the fickleness and inconstancy of her population, who rose to heights in moments of danger but lost their advantages in periods of tranquility. He also eliminated Crete because
of its dishonest and unjust public policies. The constitution of
Sparta he found admirably suited for internal liberty and stability
but that of Rome was far better for the attainment of power over
other peoples. The constitution of Carthage, originally admirably
mixed like that of Rome, had begun to decay because the chief
voice in deliberations had passed to the masses, whereas at Rome it
still rested with the senate. Likewise, the Carthaginians depended
on mercenaries, who fought from self-interest, whereas the Romans
had a citizen, and therefore a patriotic, army. Polybius concluded
this section by showing how the Romans inspired their citizens to
gain a reputation for valor by the public honors which they bestowed on the brave. Particularly in their funeral ceremonies, they
extolled the exploits and offices of the ancestors of the deceased
as well as his own. At Rome, also, improper money-making was
frowned upon, particularly the acceptance of bribery. Finally, the
Roman religion inculcated what Polybius regarded as a salutary
superstition, one which made the mere word of a Roman more de-
pendable than the witnessed oath of a Greek. Such were the political
characteristics to which Polybius attributed Rome's success. Her

admirably balanced mixed constitution was the result of historical evolution, tested by experience. It left control in the hands of the senate. Her army was disciplined, patriotic, and stimulated to valor by the recognition accorded to bravery. And her religion instilled into her individual and public conduct trustworthiness, *fides*.

Polybius has been blamed both for having misunderstood Aristotle's concept of the nature of the "mixed polity" and, on the other hand, for having misrepresented the character of the Roman government by interpreting it in terms of the orthodox Hellenistic theory of the mixed constitution, to which its resemblance is claimed to have been purely superficial. On the first count, Charles H. McIlwain, after allowing that Polybius probably did not know the *Politics* of Aristotle directly, nevertheless concludes that "there is a fundamental difference between the checks and balances within the highest governmental organs of the state which to Polybius constitute the greatest merit and the secret of permanence in the mixed constitution of Sparta and to a smaller extent of Carthage, but above all of the Roman state, on the one hand; and on the other, the *fusion* of political *principles* which characterized the government under the supremacy of the middle class in Aristotle's *Polity* as set forth in Book III of the *Politics*." [2]

On the second count, critics hold that Polybius, by comparing the Roman government to the orthodox mixed constitution of Hellenistic theory, obscured the essential fact that all power at Rome in his day rested with the senate. The magistrates in reality were subservient to the senate because they came from it and would hesitate to go against its wishes. The senate dominated the assemblies not only directly by controlling the introduction of public business and by the nomination of candidates for office but also indirectly by the preponderating influence over the voting which senators could exert through their clients and dependents. It might be said in defense of Polybius that both he and the liberal Romans with whom he associated probably would not have regarded such aristocratic control as harmful so long as it was exercised in the interests of the state. That the wiser element should make the ultimate decisions was, indeed, regarded as essential to the stability of the mixed constitution.

Even with respect to the stability of the mixed constitution, Polybius is not wholly self-consistent. While generally in the sixth book he regards the mixed constitution as immune from the tendency present in each of the good simple forms to degenerate into its bad counterpart, he does at some points suggest that there is a cyclical sequence of constitutions, rather than a balancing off of good and bad. It has been suggested by some scholars, and denied by others, that this inconsistency is one of the evidences of one or more revisions of the work. On this view, he began by accepting the theory of the stable mixed constitution from Dicaearchus and seeing its realization in the Roman government as he found it under the enlightened leaders of the mid second century. In the following years he saw this enlightened sense of Rome's responsibilities toward the outside world give way to a cynical imperialism. At the same time he witnessed the inner corruption of the aristocracy and the stirring of popular resentment which culminated in the Gracchan movement. Scipio Aemilianus, gazing at the ruins of Carthage in 146 B.C., quoted with clear reference to Rome Hector's lines from the *Iliad* that "the day will come when sacred Ilium shall perish, and Priam and the folk of Priam of the ashen spear." Similarly, Polybius felt that the Stoic theory of a cyclical succession of constitutions, perhaps expounded by Panaetius during his visits to Rome in the forties and thirties, better suited the facts as they now appeared to him. This may be the explanation of Polybius' inconsistency. Or, as a historian primarily concerned with the nexus of events rather than with political theory, he may have unconsciously used both theories at once. It is, after all, not impossible to conceive of a theoretical balance of opposites, in which the mixed constitution occupies the central position, and at the same time to see in history a cyclical succession of these forms.[3]

None of the foregoing inconsistencies compares to the most

surprising weakness in Polybius' political speculations. As has been suggested in the previous chapters, the theoretical or philosophical justification for government, whether of the city-state or of larger forms, had become a familiar problem for classical and Hellenistic thought. Yet Polybius affords almost no indication of this type of speculation. He implied, to be sure, that Rome's rule was acceptable to the Italians because of her trustworthiness and generally just government. He remarked in connection with the adherence of the Macedonians to the false Philip, the pretender Andriscus who started the fourth and last Macedonian War, that they were foolish to prefer such a hateful man to the beneficent rule of the Romans.[4] Finally he suggested in his later books that Roman morals were declining and her policy was becoming more selfish. But nowhere in the existing portions did he attempt an extensive philosophic justification of her rule beyond his explanation of the excellencies of her constitution.

Discussion on this last topic does not, however, seem to have been unknown at Rome even in Polybius' own day. Cicero in the third book of his *de Republica* placed in the mouths of Philus and of Laelius a debate on the relation of justice to government, the basic theme of Plato's *Republic*. Philus defends the position which the sophist Thrasymachus had maintained in the first book of Plato: that government cannot be carried on without injustice, that there is no natural justice, and that rule should benefit the ruler. Laelius, the older friend and counselor of Scipio Aemilianus, upholds the cause of justice in government. Good reasons have been advanced for considering that these two points of view were actually maintained at Rome in the circle of Scipio by the visiting Greek philosophers Carneades, head of the Platonic Academy and a skeptic, and the Stoic Panaetius.[5] Carneades came to Rome with two other philosophers on an embassy from Athens in 156 B.C., and seems to have created quite a furor because of his pragmatic and skeptical analysis of government.[6] Panaetius first visited Rome in the late forties and again in the early thirties of the second century B.C.

He apparently held that the ideal human society should be, as earlier Stoics had maintained, universal and without lesser subdivisions. However, he admitted that as a practical matter, lesser political organizations were necessary for the security of life and property. He agreed with Plato that the best form of political organization was the city-state and he accepted the mixed constitution as the most stable for such a state. Cicero definitely states that Panaetius discussed practical problems of government with his Roman friends and it is noteworthy that the five fragments of Panaetius' political thought in a recent edition of his remains are all quotations or references by Cicero. Thus it is likely that such discussions as Cicero imagines in the *de Republica* at least represent the conflict between Carneades' "sophistic" argument that government depends on injustice and Panaetius' orthodox view of the city-state with a mixed constitution as based on natural reason, law, and justice.[7]

During the third and second centuries B.C., the awakening of Roman literary self-consciousness was inspired by her achievement of a position of world power and was conditioned by her admiration for and adoption of the superior culture of Greece. From this Hellenization there developed two trends in Rome's political thought. Her own earliest writers saw in her successes the fulfilment of a divine destiny by a historic process which depended on the virtues of the Romans as individuals and as a state. The Greek who most seriously studied her constitution, Polybius, found that it represented the achievement through this historic process of the balanced form of mixed constitution in which control rested with the wise aristocrats. Thus, on the one hand, the Romans were regarded as destined for world rule by divine favor of the gods and their own moral fiber. On the other hand, the development of the Roman government toward a form capable of imperial responsibilities was stunted because thinking Romans were convinced that their city-state form of government had realized the ideal mixed constitution advocated in orthodox Greek political thought. They could not break through the limitations of this theory to some more ecumenical concept of government. As the next chapter will show, various other factors, such as the desire of the nobles to retain the power and privilege which they enjoyed under this constitution, the traditional distrust of any sort of monarchical aspirations, and the selfishness of the urban populace once they saw that empire benefitted them, helped to hinder the development of any broader theory or practice of government. But basically, the failure of Hellenistic philosophy to propound a concept of government adapted to an ecumenical state meant that the Romans had no real choice other than the orthodox theory of the city-state to which to conform their political thought. A century of civil war was necessary to break the cramping intellectual domination of this traditional point of view. In the end, a successful government of the Roman world was shaped not by the practical Caesar, who would have abandoned the orthodox theory entirely, but by the traditionalist Augustus, who compromised between it and empire. Thus Cicero stood at the intellectual crossroads between republic and empire:

VII

CICERO'S WORLD

THE WORLD INTO WHICH CICERO WAS BORN WAS RENT BY POLITICAL strife and armed conflict. Polybius had been even more right than he could have foreseen when he felt that the balanced Roman constitution of the second century was fated, like all things mortal, to change for the worse. He saw personal ambition replacing the sense of public duty and licentious manners corrupting the traditional virtues. He realized that Roman policy was being increasingly directed toward her own self-interest, particularly the self-interest of the senate, and less and less guided by principles of equity toward her allies and subjects, not to say toward other powers. Unfortunately, no comments survive from Polybius concerning the movement of the Gracchi, which he lived to witness. But he undoubtedly shared the distrust which Scipio the Younger is said to have felt toward the methods, if not the aims, of his nephews. The forces which first manifested themselves in the movement of the Gracchi and which were finally to undermine the constitution admired by Polybius were the result of four major trends in Roman politics during the second century B.C.[1]

The virtues which Polybius so praised in the Romans had been maintained by the force of public opinion in a small and closely knit community. When the well-to-do came in contact with the freer customs and greater luxury of the Greek East, those who had no inner conviction of morality sloughed off the restraints of the narrow Roman conventions and indulged themselves in new-found freedom, not to say license. They soon discovered that outside of Rome no one could challenge them if they abused for their own benefit the power which conquest gave them. Thus the senatorial class became more than ever concerned with retaining within their families public office, which opened the way to wealth and power, and with enriching themselves. At the same time, they were jealous of any challenge to the control of their class as a whole, of any individual who attempted to gain too much power for himself. Commanders in the field, once victory was won, had to submit to ratification of their settlements by commissions sent out from the senate. Even when a panel for hearing complaints of provincials against governors, the *quaestio de repetundis*, was instituted, it became merely another instrument for calling to heel a governor who had stepped out of line, and for protecting a governor who stood in well with his fellow senators.

The second trend arose from the first. Senators of ability and ambition sought to further their own careers in the face of the restraints imposed by the senatorial opinion and practice. An obvious and natural recourse for a commander or politician who was balked by the senate was to appeal in the one case to the troops under his command in the field, or in the other, to the popular assemblies at Rome. He naturally had to offer a *quid pro quo*. The result was that the troops looked more and more to their commanders, rather than to the state, to further their interests, and the people became more and more the followers of the demagogue who made them the most lavish promises.

The selfishness of the upper classes encouraged the two further trends. In the first place, the senate disregarded the interest of the average Roman citizens and alienated public opinion at Rome. In the second place, it treated the Italian allies with disrespect and disregard for their treaty rights. There is a great deal to be said for applying even as early as the second century B.C. the explanation for the fall of Rome shared by three modern economic historians of Rome, Tenney Frank, Michael Rostovtzeff, and Fritz M. Heichelheim.[2] This explanation is, in fact, Plato's, namely, that the corruption of the city-state begins when the aristocracy becomes an oligarchy and substitutes self-interest for public interest. Or, to paraphrase Lord Acton, power tends to corrupt and the more absolute the power, the more absolute the corruption.[3]

These four disruptive trends, concealed beneath the tranquil surface of the senatorial government during the second century B.C., found their first — and violent — outlet through the well-meaning efforts of idealistic political reformers. As is often the case, these reformers came not from the masses but from the very senatorial class against which their reforms were directed. They were Tiberius and Gaius Gracchus, the two sons of an upright senator who had distinguished himself by what was rare at the time, honorable dealings with the Spanish barbarians against whom the Romans had been conducting intermittent warfare for nearly a century and whom they generally treated with the same disregard for honor that the white men displayed toward the Indians in the New World. The mother of the youths was Cornelia, daughter of Scipio Africanus and aunt by adoption of Scipio Aemilianus, who also, by marrying her daughter, became brother-in-law of his cousins. Cornelia, early left a widow, employed Greek philosophers as tutors for her boys. Tiberius, the elder, became convinced that the evils of the times would be cured if the social and political teachings of Greek philosophy were realized by a return to the traditional form of the Roman city-state.[4] When he attempted to put his ideas into practice as tribune in the year 133 B.C., he at once aroused the jealous hostility of the rich senators, whose position and pockets his reforms touched closely. After the senators had failed to block the reforms by peaceful means, they stirred up a riot in which Tiberius was slain. Ten years later, from 123 through 122 B.C., his more intense and realistic brother Gaius, also as tribune, sought both to avenge his brother and to achieve an even more ambitious scheme of democratization. He in turn died in a civil tumult stirred up by the senate.

Later Roman historians liked to point out that these riots occasioned the first shedding of blood by civil strife in Rome since the days of Coriolanus, over four centuries and a half earlier.[5] It was bad enough thus to release the pent-up passions which in the next century would more than once make Rome's gutters run red. It was worse, however, to point the way for less principled, more demagogic men to gain their selfish ends by appealing to the mob against the traditional control of the senate. Cicero, a man of peace and order, blamed upon the Gracchi the breakdown of what he regarded as the ideal form of government at Rome, that which had prevailed during the second century. He was relatively blind to the faults of the aristocracy during this period, which had given rise to the four disruptive trends already described. And he regarded the substitution of demagoguery for leadership by the best as the prime weakness of government in his own day. For this he blamed the Gracchi, not realizing that they were only the occasion, that the cause lay in the tensions within the city-state created by the responsibilities of empire.[6]

The Gracchan movement brought into the open another conflict besides that between the mob and the senate. As has been indicated, the Italian allies were treated during the second century less and less as partners of Rome and more and more as subsidiaries. Not only did they bear more of the burdens and get fewer of the rewards of conquest; even at home, Roman officials treated them with arbitrary and harsh disregard of their treaty rights. During the Gracchan decade, certain liberals had attempted to meet the just grievances of the allies but had failed in the face of conservative, senatorial opposition. A revolt of Fregellae was ruthlessly suppressed in 125 B.C. Discontent simmered throughout Italy for the next thirty years. Finally, the younger Drusus tried in 91 B.C. to secure the granting of Roman citizenship to all Italians. Again the senate blocked this wise and liberal move. Patience was at an end and the Italians broke into an open revolt which, from the Latin word for ally, *socius*, is known as the "Social War." There was a short but bloody and hard-fought struggle, and the Romans were forced to grant citizenship to all communities south of the valley of the Po before the bulk of the Italians laid down their arms. And remnants of the allied armies continued the struggle until Sulla in 82 B.C. put an end to all fighting in Italy.

The significance of the Social War is obscured for the casual student of Roman history because it became merged in the rivalry for power between Sulla and Marius. Yet the revolt made more fundamental and more permanent changes in the character of the Roman state than did the transitory innovations of the Marians or the reaction under Sulla. The early Roman state had been generous in the extension of its partial or full citizenship and in the terms under which it made alliances with other communities. This generosity had paid dividends during the war against Hannibal, when the Italians preferred Rome's hegemony to Punic domination. But during the second century B.C., Rome had laid increasing demands on the allies for military assistance and had given them less share in the rewards of overseas conquest. As Athens had converted her hegemony over the Delian League into an oppressive domination, so Rome gradually became the master rather than the leader of Italy. The Social War forced Rome to abandon this preferred position in Italy and to admit all communities to equality and a common citizenship. Moreover, the upheavals created throughout Italy by the Social and concomitant Civil Wars finally destroyed the integrity of surviving local cultures, like the Etruscan and Samnite, which were already weakened by centuries of contact with the dominant Latin culture. Italy entered upon a period of rapid Romanization that corresponds to the cultural standardization which she has experienced in modern times since her political unification in 1870. Local peculiarities and dialects did not wholly disappear and local pride remained strong, but Italy was no longer a conglomerate of diverse races and languages. Thus was created a feeling throughout Italy that whatever the local differences and traditions, all were Romans and all had participated in the conquest of the world. Augustus was later to build his imperial government upon this sentiment, in opposition to the ecumenical and monarchical ideas of Caesar and Antony.

The unification of Italy by the extension of Roman citizenship was, however, disastrous for the effective working of the Roman constitution as a city-state. Citizenship had now been spread far beyond the geographical limits within which its active exercise in the Aristotelian sense was possible. When Cicero spoke before the Roman assemblies in the middle of the first century B.C., he addressed only a tiny proportion of the total citizen body and that increasingly the least desirable. In consequence of her position as capital of the world, Rome had drawn to herself large numbers of slaves, who were freed by indulgent masters. Veterans and others who could not make a success of normal living tended to congregate in the capital in hopes of a handout from the government, or in order to sell their votes to the highest bidder. Life in the overgrown and jerry-built capital could not have been very enviable; water and food supplies were barely adequate, police and fire protection practically nonexistent. The rich lived in their elegant mansions and villas and went out only if surrounded by retainers and clients; the poor made themselves as inconspicuous as possible or joined one of the gangs organized by rival demagogues to intimidate the public.[7] It is no wonder that Cicero, despite his upbringing in a small town, was not a democrat when it came to dealing with the Roman assemblies. Thus the transformation of the Roman electorate from a rural peasantry into an urban proletariat only accentuated the difficulty created by the extension of citizenship beyond the feasible limits of active participation in the assemblies. Roman citizenship was no longer "orthodox" in the sense that privileges were balanced by obligations. It was moving toward the imperial concept of a favored position in a world state, in which privilege did not involve corresponding duties. This was one of the major respects in which the Roman city-state constitution proved increasingly unsatisfactory as a form of government for an empire. Yet Cicero never seems fully to have appreciated this difficulty.

A second consequence of the Social War was to afford greater opportunity in such unsettled conditions right at Rome's gates for the revolt of ambition against the restraints of class and tradition. The growth of the empire during the second century had, as already indicated, fostered this revolt. In the early part of the century, Scipio Africanus had enjoyed unlimited powers and attained a brilliant position of leadership by his conduct of the Punic and Asiatic wars. In 187 B.C. he was called to account by his opponents in the senate. Though he haughtily refused an accounting for his actions, he did not attempt to dispute the predominance of the senate by an appeal either to the troops or to the mob. He simply retired from Rome. In contrast, at the end of the century, in 107 B.C., Marius, a fellow townsman of Cicero and a self-made man, appealed from the senate to the people to secure for himself a military command against the rebel African chief Jugurtha, the same chief who is said to have remarked that at Rome everything was for sale, including the votes of senators.[8] Marius soon found a rival in one of his own subordinates, the aristocratic Cornelius Sulla. These two men converted the Social War into a struggle for personal supremacy at Rome. Marius was perhaps the better general but he was the less astute politician and was driven into the arms of the extreme demagogues, successors of the Gracchi. It was he and his colleagues who began the grim practice of wholesale proscriptions of their political enemies, a practice which Sulla ruthlessly visited upon them when he gained control. The death of Marius and Sulla's final victory over both the democrats and the remnants of the Italian revolution at a battle before the Colline Gate of Rome in 82 B.C. restored political mastery to the conservatives. Sulla put through a reactionary program aimed to curb the powers of the assemblies, of the tribunes, and of the magistrates and commanders in favor of the senate.

But the ruthlessness of Sulla's own conduct and the greed of his subordinates alienated sympathy from his regime. When he retired in 79 B.C. to die shortly thereafter, a reaction set in which soon found a leader in one of his own former subordinates, Gnaeus Pompeius. Pompey's family perhaps originated in Picenum, in the northeast of Italy.[9] At least for several generations it had owned large estates in this area and had been the outstanding family. Pompey's father, Gnaeus Pompeius Strabo, was the first member to attain the consulship in 89 B.C., and thus to secure admission to the highest ranks of the Roman aristocracy. Pompey himself, as a young man, had received important commands and magistracies in other ways and at earlier ages than law or tradition prescribed. He began his career under Sulla, but after Sulla's retirement he emerged as a leader of the opposition to the conservatives in power and allied himself with the rich Crassus, who, though likewise a senator, supported the interests of the financiers. In his later career, Pompey followed a similarly wavering course, directed not by principle but by his own ambition and vainglory. Though he ultimately became the bulwark of the conservatives against Caesar, he, no less than his successful rival, contributed to the ultimate disruption of the traditional constitution. The conflict between Pompey and Caesar was as much one between two rival claimants for sole power as between the constitution and a monarchical "leader," a *Duce* or *Führer*.[10]

The emergence of outstanding political leaders of the sort just described led to a division of the senate between two points of view; those who felt that the whole senatorial order should stand together and those who hoped to better their own position by attaching themselves to ambitious leaders. This alignment did not develop into a party organization in the modern sense. It is true that, on the one hand, the great senatorial families had their followings of clients, of freedmen, of countryfolk from their estates, and of other hangers-on. On the other hand, ambitious individual senators organized regular gangs who were to some extent sworn to loyalty to their leader and who were regularly paid and often armed. But political competition was limited to the senatorial class and did not, as in a modern state, extend downward to the ordinary voters, who simply followed their leaders or voted for the measure which promised them the most, without any conscious adherence to conflicting "party platforms." It should be remembered that in the Roman constitution political initiative rested with the magistrates. The quaestorship, which since the time of Sulla had admitted to the senate, gave no real opportunity for political self-expression. Hence the politically effective higher magistracies, including the tribunate, the tool of demagoguery, were held by persons already admitted to the senate. The senate, both directly through the magistrates and indirectly by its control of the electorate, could generally determine who might proceed through the career of public office, the *cursus honorum*. Equestrians, however wealthy and prominent, exercised no direct political leadership. They could at best exert indirect pressure by their friendship or financial dealings with senators. Nor did the Roman constitution permit of the emergence of a real popular leader, a man of the people. Those senators who became demagogues, like the Gracchi, Marius, or Caesar, did so only by breaking away from the "party line" of the senate after they had attained a higher, or curule, magistracy.

Modern scholars have shown that a factor far more important than principle in determining political alignments within the senate was family connection. There was a constant rivalry for prestige and power among the great families, a rivalry expressed in marriage, divorce, adoption, and other methods of cementing family alliances. In particular, there existed two main groups within the senate. On the one hand were a group of families for which tenure of the higher public offices had become a hereditary prerogative. These families, whose members had held the consulship or its

equivalent, constituted the "nobles," *nobiles*. Inferior to them were
the families which had never gone beyond the praetorship or some
lesser office. The intrusion into consular rank of a person in whose
family there had never previously been a magistrate was so rare
that these "new men," like Cato the Elder in the second century
B.C. or Cicero in the first, did not constitute a third group. This
division accounts in part for the two points of view or factions
which Cicero defined within the senate. On the one hand, the
optimates, the conservatives, thought of themselves as the "best
people." They stood for the closed corporation of the aristocratic,
"noble" families and its vested interest in public office and provincial command, with all the legimate or illegimate profit that these
implied. The *populares*, on the contrary, sought for political power
by catering to the Roman mob; they pretended to carry on the
democratic traditions of the Gracchi but actually they were often
self-seekers who desired by direct appeal to the assemblies to promote personal ambitions at the expense of the general interests of
the noble families. The two factions must not be thought of as
well-defined parties; they were simply informal groupings knit
together by self-interest, family alliance, or political and social obligations. Their lines were always shifting. Between the extremes of
the two points of view, many senators were reasonably disinterested, well-meaning, and public spirited. These, and like-minded
equestrians or even ordinary citizens, Cicero called the *boni*, the
"good men." With his naturally conservative sympathies, he undoubtedly found more such on the optimate, or "right," side than
on the popular, or "left." [11]

It is, indeed, often charged that Cicero began his political career
as a supporter of the *populares* and the little men in an attack on
vested interests, but that when he himself was taken into the aristocratic fold, he abandoned his liberal views and became as staunch
a conservative as any of the noble *optimates*. This view does scant
justice to Cicero. As has been shown, his whole background and
upbringing predisposed him toward an equestrian and Italian point

of view as against a narrowly noble and Roman one. It was natural, therefore, that in his early career he should support the liberal movement which was seeking to free the constitution from the conservative strait jacket in which Sulla had confined it. In particular, it was natural for Cicero, the man of words and of peace, to be dazzled by the brilliant military career of his contemporary, the liberal leader Pompey, for whom the path of success had been so extraordinarily easy. Pompey's meteoric rise through military success resembled that of Cicero's fellow townsman of an earlier generation, Marius. In the case of both, Cicero's admiration for their dazzling but temporary achievements blinded him to the permanent evils which they wrought upon the state by their conceit and political obtuseness.[12]

In Cicero's eyes, one of the most disastrous results of the Gracchan movement was to bring into the open the conflict of interest which had developed behind the scenes between the two elements who constituted the "upper classes" at Rome, namely, the senators and the equestrians, particularly those who were well-to-do. This conflict had its roots in rivalry for the riches which acquisition of an empire had made available to Romans in a position to exploit them. This exploitation was not, as it might be in a modern empire, exploitation of economic resources or development of industry and commerce. Neither senators nor equestrians constituted an industrial or a commercial class in the modern sense. Industry on any large scale was unknown to the Greco-Roman world. Even the exploitation of resources by agriculture and farming remained very simple. Both senators and equestrians did, as will appear presently, participate in the general financing of economic ventures. But direct participation in commerce or in the details of finance always remained undignified in the eyes of the Romans, even more than it had for the Greeks of higher social standing, who looked down on the so-called "banausic" occupations.[13]

Rome was indeed not a natural center for commerce and industry, such as had been Athens, Corinth, and Carthage, not to

speak of the famous trading centers of Asia Minor and Syria. At
Rome, and generally throughout Italy, agriculture was regarded as
the only respectable means of livelihood. The commerce necessary
for the support of the urban population and for the luxuries desired by the wealthy was left in the hands of foreigners or freedmen or the Greeks of South Italy. The "Roman traders" mentioned as active in Asia Minor when Mithridates occupied it in
88 B.C. and attested by inscriptions from Delos for the second and
first centuries B.C. must have been Greeks from South Italy and
others who had acquired citizenship.[14] Similarly, the operations of
banking and exchange, which had been developed to a high degree
during the Hellenistic period, remained for the most part in the
hands of non-Romans. There must have been many parallels in
Cicero's day to the career of the fabulously wealthy parvenu Trimalchio, as described a century later by Petronius. Trimalchio
had come to Italy as a slave and had been freed. He made an immense
fortune by his varied ventures in commerce and finance. He sought
the cachet of respectability by investing in land, living off his rents,
taking an active part in the affairs of his municipality, and sporting
a ring similar to the gold one reserved for equestrians. But Petronius' satire and the scorn which his characters feel for Trimalchio's
display show how difficult it was for such a self-made man to secure
social recognition.

Despite the prejudice against trade, commerce, and banking,
the governing classes found ways to take advantage of the great
opportunities for profit which were opened up to them by the
expansion of Rome's empire. The Roman state had no civil service
adequate to handle the affairs of an empire. When a senator went
out as governor of a province he received from the state scarcely
more staff than a younger senator, elected to the office of quaestor
and representing the treasury, and perhaps a few clerks. But a
wealthy senator was surrounded by numerous dependents, ranging
from friends to clients. He had a staff of skilled freedman and slave
clerks to handle his personal affairs. Naturally he took an entou-

rage of such dependents and clerks with him to his province. Since he was absolute master of the funds of the province during his command, since his young quaestor would hardly report any irregularities of a governor whose relation to him was likened by the Romans to that of a father to a son, since the governor would account only to the senate on his return, and since his fellow senators would not be too critical of one who took advantage of opportunities for which they hoped in their turn, it may readily be imagined that not only the governor but all his entourage expected to profit from their provincial service. Cato the Younger incurred ridicule rather than sympathy when, after he had carefully accounted for the funds from Cyprus, which he annexed, he lost all these accounts through shipwreck. Cicero prided himself on leaving for his successor the profits of his province of Cilicia, rather than pocketing them. Catullus, a lyric poet contemporary with Cicero, complained bitterly that the parsimonious character of Memmius, whom he accompanied to Bithynia, sent all the entourage home with nothing but cobwebs in their purses. Hence it was considered normal for a governor, even when he was not a Verres or a Caesar, to line his own and his staff's pockets at the expense of the provincials.[15]

In addition to such direct profits, the provinces afforded another, more indirect, source of gain. Since the Roman state had no adequate civil service, it had recourse to contracting with private individuals for the performance of many public functions, such as the construction of roads, aqueducts, and other public works. When it became necessary to collect taxes on a large scale in the provinces, the state naturally adopted the same system. Despite the abuse and criticism to which this system gave rise, it was not in itself an unreasonable solution. The contract, usually let by the censors every fifth year, assured the state of a revenue against which it could budget in advance. Also the contract, based on an average yield of the province where the tax was a tithe, gave the contractor a reasonable percentage of profit. However, the sums involved were so large that only the very wealthy could afford to bid for the contracts and even they generally had to form partnerships to do so. But senators were not permitted either by law or by tradition to sully themselves with finance; like the English nobility of the eighteenth and early nineteenth centuries, they remained a landowning aristocracy. Hence the opportunity to profit from this new field of investment passed to the equestrians, to those who, like Cicero's friend Atticus, had accumulated fortunes but preferred the profits of private enterprise to the honors of public service. Nevertheless, despite the restrictions of law and of public opinion, senators secretly invested funds in the great equestrian partnerships. In consequence, the profits from tax contracting offered occasion both for collusion between the two groups and for conflict — collusion when the senatorial governor wished to help an equestrian group in which he or his friends had invested, and conflict when the demands made by the tax gatherers on the provinces restricted the greed of the governor and his friends.

The chief profit in tax contracting did not come from the contract itself; the percentage of proceeds kept by the company was strictly defined and a bad year might make it impossible for the province to meet its taxes. However, the provincial communities often did not have funds in hand to meet immediately their tax quotas. They were then forced to borrow in anticipation of their own collections and they borrowed from the same wealthy partnerships which held the tax contracts. The rates charged on such loans were also limited by law, but the governors would wink at violations and would support the tax contractors in demands for exorbitant interest. Cicero as governor of Cilicia in 52 B.C. inherited a case of this sort, in which a company was attempting to collect from the town of Salamis in Cyprus an interest four times that permitted by law, namely 48 percent a year. The company refused to accept any payment on principal until the town could pay the whole of the principal and interest. The noble senator Brutus, a silent partner in the company, intervened with Cicero to assign troops to help the representative of the company to extort the money. Cicero refused to permit more than the legal 12 per cent per year but equally did not press a settlement of the case, and undoubtedly his successor was more compliant toward the company.

During his tribunates, Gaius Gracchus attempted to break the nascent alliance between governing and financial classes by changing the character of the panel before which provincials could bring charges of extortion against rapacious governors. Since the senate controlled foreign affairs, this panel was set up in the first place, in 149 B.C., as a special committee of the senate, presided over by a praetor, to hear such cases. Gracchus, however, initiated a law by which the list for the panel should be composed of equestrians. Thus the governor who milked a province so that the tax companies could not make their profits would be liable to prosecution by his victims before a jury whose sympathies he had also alienated. It is uncertain whether Gracchus acted in what he conceived to be the interest of the provincials or simply in order to further his own democratic ends by splitting the opposition. It is equally uncertain how many, if any, other panels for other crimes were involved in his change, since Sulla later extended and regularized this type of legal procedure for several different crimes affecting the state. In 81 B.C. Sulla definitely restored solely senatorial membership on all the panels. Hence, when Cicero began public life in Rome, the question whether membership on all of these panels, or *quaestiones*, should be senatorial or equestrian was a burning political issue. In 70 B.C., Cicero prosecuted successfully Verres, a notoriously corrupt governor of Sicily, before a senatorial panel as constituted by Sulla. In his opening speech, he called attention to the widespread criticism of the senatorial juries. He thus prepared the ground for the compromise which the democratic consuls of that year, Pompey and Crassus, effected as part of their program to undo the reactionary measures of Sulla. Thereafter the panels were composed one-third of senators, one-third of equestrians, and one-third of a slightly lower financial class, the *tribuni aerarii*.

This compromise finally settled the issue of the composition of the juries, not only in the court on extortion but also in the various other courts which had been instituted. But it did not solve the fundamental issue of the rivalry between senators and equestrians. The two groups would from time to time present a united front against demagogic attacks on property and vested interests, such as the revolutionary movement of Catiline or the measures by which Caesar sought to increase his prestige by favoring the masses.[16] But for the most part, rivalry continued bitter for the profits of empire and appeared openly in such cases as the senate's refusal in 63 B.C. to confirm Pompey's arrangements in the East, which favored the equestrians, and refusal in the late sixties to release the equestrian companies from tax contracts which bad harvests had rendered unprofitable. Such issues were decided by motives of self or class interest and not for the good of the state or of the provincials. Cicero was to devote much of his active political career to the attempt to heal this breach.

The sixty years which elapsed between the Gracchi and Cicero's speech against Verres had thus produced an extraordinarily complex political situation at Rome. This served as a background to Cicero's political program and philosophy. The various elements in the situation had their origins in disruptive trends produced by the expansion of the Roman empire during the second century B.C. But Cicero did not realize this. He blamed the confused and disunited condition of government in his own day on the Gracchi, whose attack on the aristocratic, senatorial control of the state had unleashed forces previously held in check by respect for the authority of the senate. These forces, or trends, may arbitrarily be assigned to three areas. In the provinces, greed and ambition led generals to appeal to the troops to support them against the senate and also brought the interests of senatorial governors into conflict with those of equestrian financiers. In Italy, extension of citizenship and the proletarianization of the masses in Rome had rendered popular government a sham behind which rival factions within the senate conducted their struggle for power and prestige. And in Rome, the aristocracy was divided not only by the division within the senate between *optimates* and *populares* but by that between the senatorial and equestrian orders. Cicero was conscious of all of these problems. But his upbringing and intellectual sympathies predisposed him to look at them in terms of the orthodox theory of the city-state with its mixed constitution. His failure to transcend this point of view typifies the inability of ancient political thinkers to provide an adequate theory for an ecumenical form of government.

VIII

CICERO'S POLITICAL CAREER AND PROGRAM
THROUGH HIS CONSULSHIP

MARCUS TULLIUS CICERO, SON OF MARCUS, WAS BORN IN 106 B.C. IN the town of Arpinum.[1] Arpinum lies some sixty miles south of Rome among the Volscian mountains in the valley of a river anciently called the Liris and in modern times the Garigliano. Arpinum had been captured at an early date by the Samnites. It passed under Roman domination and received the partial citizenship called "Latin" in 305 B.C. Full citizenship, which meant the right to vote and to hold office at Rome, was granted in 188 B.C. At that time the inhabitants were enrolled in the Roman tribe called *Cornelia*, which, in consequence, was Cicero's tribe. Arpinum must have been typical of most of the towns of central Italy. In Cicero's youth there must still have survived a strong local loyalty; it is not unlikely that the Samnite speech, Oscan, was spoken if not in the Romanized town, since Cicero never indicates that he knew it, at least in the neighboring countryside. It was certainly used in Pompeii until Sulla settled a colony of Romans there after he captured it in 89 B.C.[2] Arpinum was not a Roman colony but a *municipium* which enjoyed its own form of government, akin to the

Roman but still a reminder of the original independence of the town.

Arpinum probably remained loyal to Rome during the Social War of 91–88 B.C. But her Samnite antecedents must have created sympathy for the griefs and ambitions of the allies. Moreover the resulting integration of the Italian communities into the Roman state created a concept of double citizenship which even the Hellenistic Leagues had not evolved. Cicero was fully conscious of this concept; he comments specifically on Cato the Elder's loyalty both to Tusculum and to Rome. He himself had a warm affection for his ancestral estate on the Fibrenus just outside Arpinum. Yet he realized that the larger concept of patriotism was that to the common state, a concept which may go back to Panaetius and the Stoics but to which Cicero gave a Roman tinge of selflessness and duty. In the *de Republica*, and more particularly in the *Tusculans* and the *de Officiis*, love of country is described as overriding all other affections and as demanding that subordination of self to duty which the Romans called piety, *pietas*. Moreover, in his own career, Cicero managed to combine his belief in Rome and her imperial destiny with a realization of the importance of the local life and traditions of the Italian communities. He became a member of Rome's ruling class and dealt with her imperial affairs on a world scale; yet he was always sympathetic with the concerns and problems of the Italian communities and never hesitated to work for the interests of their inhabitants. His patriotism was Roman, but it was Roman in an Italian sense; for him, despite his admiration for Greek culture, the Romano-Italic peoples were superior to other peoples. Finally, he remained loyal to the old Roman constitution though he saw dimly that it was inadequate for imperial needs.

Cicero's personal background had a second important influence on his political thought. His ancestors were well-to-do farmers and his grandfather had built up his property to a capital value which qualified him as an equestrian. During the second and first centuries B.C., the equestrians became, as has been said, less and less landowners, such as had been Cicero's family, and more and more financiers. The senators remained a landed aristocracy with a monopoly of public office. Cicero's equestrian background was one of landed, not commercial or financial, wealth. He entered upon a senatorial career. His loyalty might well have lain with the landed aristocracy of which he was a member. But he never lost his sympathy for the equestrians and one of the cardinal aims in his political program was that of healing the breach which the Gracchi had created between these two classes. Even as a young man, with his way to make in the courts at Rome where the senate then reigned supreme, he particularly defended the interests of the equestrians as well as of the smaller Italian townsfolk. When he himself had made a success and had become a member of the senatorial aristocracy, he did not forget his youthful background.

Furthermore, Cicero's most intimate friend and confidant throughout his life, the man to whom the bulk of his surviving correspondence is addressed, was the prominent equestrian, Titus Pomponius Atticus. Atticus represented the best type of equestrian. He came of a wealthy and old Roman family. In his boyhood he studied with Cicero under a distinguished and charming Epicurean, Phaedrus. Unlike Cicero, he remained loyal to the tenets of this philosophy. He spent much of his youth in Athens to avoid involvement in the civil wars — hence the name *Atticus*. Throughout his life he prudently stood aside from public affairs and thus remained on friendly terms with all the conflicting personalities of the period.[3] He used his great wealth to promote literature, not without profit to himself, since he maintained a staff of slaves to copy and publish Cicero's works and, probably, those of other authors. He was a loyal and devoted friend. He bore patiently with Cicero's moods, both boastful and despondent, and he handled his personal affairs, including Cicero's sometimes difficult relations with his wife. With such a friend, Cicero could not go counter to the equestrian interests, however closely he became involved with the senatorial nobility.

To turn to a third element in Cicero's personal background, his grandfather had been active in local affairs at Arpinum. But his father was a man of retired and studious disposition. Cicero therefore came by the two great interests of his life through natural inheritance. He devoted himself to a career of public office and regarded this as his chief glory; yet he felt that success in public life must rest on a broad and thorough education, not on a specialized training, and whenever he was precluded from public life, he had recourse to the second of his interests, the study of rhetoric and philosophy. Few men have so successfully combined an active life in the service of the state not merely with a broad general culture but also with voluminous and significant literary production.

Thus Cicero's birth in a small hill town and his family background gave him a sympathetic understanding of the sentiments of the Italians and particularly of the equestrians; he did not have the social and political advantages of an aristocratic senatorial connection but he had in compensation a broader, less class-conscious point of view. He entered upon public life imbued with the traditional concept of the active community in which all elements work together for the common good and in which wealth and eminence impose obligations of disinterested public service. Cicero was as eager to be well off as the next man, but there is no evidence that he used either his private practice as advocate or his tenure of public office to enrich himself in any improper way.[4] Finally, his studious father bequeathed to him a broad and humanistic concept of education. Education should make a whole man; it should not be narrowly vocational. And even in the midst of public affairs, the truly educated man should never lose interest in the pursuit of knowledge. Cicero played a not insignificant role in the events of one of the great periods of transition in the history of Western Europe. But he made his enduring contribution to Western culture by adapting to the Latin tongue and the Roman genius the finest thought of the Greeks in the fields of rhetoric, ethics, religion, and philosophy.

Cicero came to Rome in early manhood amid an atmosphere of war, civil strife, and political anarchy. It must have seemed unlikely that the Roman state could resist the various disruptive forces which were combined to tear it apart. In the second of his preserved speeches, Cicero in 80 B.C. defended a certain Roscius from the small town of Ameria against a charge of murdering his father. The charge was brought ·by Roscius' cousin who, with the connivance of a freedman of Sulla, had gotten possession of the property of the deceased. Thus Cicero was by implication attacking a creature of the powerful dictator. Cicero ostentatiously drew a sharp distinction between the acts of the underling and the ignorance thereof on Sulla's part.[5] He won his case and continued to plead in the courts for nearly a year. In 79 B.C., however, reasons of health, as he was later to claim, forced him to take a vacation. It may be suspected, also, that he felt that absence from Rome might be politically discreet.[6] He went, as did all Romans who desired to complete their education, to Greece and the Aegean. There he studied rhetoric under Molo of Rhodes and philosophy under Poseidonius, the successor of Panaetius as head of the Stoic School. Poseidonius professed the same political views as had his predecessor; that is, he too had tempered the universalist position of the early Stoics by adherence to the orthodox theory of the city-state and its mixed constitution.

Cicero returned to Rome in 77 B.C. He was still a small-town lawyer who had gained some reputation in the courts at Rome and he had only equestrian rank without strong political connections to give him a start on a public career. He succeeded, however, in being elected to the lowest of the magistracies, the quaestorship, for the year 75 B.C. and was assigned as financial assistant to the governor of Sicily. He gained such popularity there that five years later the Sicilians selected him to prosecute their extortionate governor, Verres. Verres, who had ruled the province as propraetor from 73 through 71 B.C., boasted that he must govern his province for three years to get money enough to pay his lawyers, to bribe the jury, and to have something left for himself.[7] The details of this famous case are well known. After the opening accusations, Verres went into exile rather than stand further trial and suffer an obviously inevitable condemnation.

In the two speeches which Cicero actually delivered, that by which he vindicated his right to prosecute and that which led Verres to flee, and also in the five further speeches which he later published to elaborate his charges against Verres, Cicero showed his familiarity with the problems of provincial government. He condemned Verres for his outrageous abuse of power and his complete lack of a sense of responsibility for the provincials or for the interests of the Roman state. Throughout his later career, in his speech on behalf of Pompey's command against Mithridates, in his defense or accusation of other governors, and in his own administration of Cilicia in 52 B.C., he came closely in contact with the problems of empire. His attitude was always "enlightened" but he never transcended the limitations of Roman nationalism and of Greek political theory. He felt that Rome had a responsibility toward her subjects to rule them well; in the *de Officiis*, he spoke of her rule as "the protection of the world rather than empire." [8] But he never conceived that a form of government might be evolved which would place all inhabitants of the empire on equality or that the Roman constitution, if its former excellence could be revived, would not prove adequate for the government of the world. Hence his speeches and letters, valuable as they are for the historical problems of the Roman empire, make no contribution to the evolution of a theoretical basis for an ecumenical state such as Rome was in fact creating.

In the Verrine case, Cicero's success against the current leader of the Roman bar, Hortensius of the conservative party, brought him into great prominence. It marked him as a champion of equity for Rome's subjects and an imperialist who had the interests of the state and of the governed at heart. It aligned him against the selfish aristocrats who saw in public office only a chance for personal aggrandizement. It identified him with the more liberal and patriotic group in the senate and particularly with the equestrians. Cicero had pointed out to the senatorial panel that not only Verres but the integrity of the senatorial class as a whole was on trial. In the same year, 70 B.C., the consuls Pompey and Crassus, also representing the liberal and financial elements, completed the removal of the reactionary restrictions placed by Sulla on the organs of government other than the senate.[9] Yet Cicero's tone was never one of hostility to the senate as a whole, but only to the selfish, vested interests. He was equally opposed to the extreme demagogues who wished to make the will of the assemblies supreme. He already was urging the subordination of the advantage of any class to that of the state.

Cicero attained the next step in his official career, the aedileship, in 69 B.C. Three years later, he became praetor and was allotted charge of the court on extortion, the scene of his success against Verres four years previously. It was as praetor that Cicero spoke before the tribal assembly in favor of a bill introduced by the tribune Manilius. Manilius proposed that the assembly bestow upon Pompey an unusually extensive command against Mithridates, king of Bithynia, who for a second time had occupied Asia Minor. In supporting this bill, Cicero allied himself with the popular faction in the senate and more particularly with the equestrians against the conservative nobles. Pompey's earlier career had, as already pointed out, been a succession of extraordinary commands and of opposition to the senate. In the previous year, 67 B.C., he had received from the assemblies an extensive command against the pirates who were harassing the eastern Mediterranean and had displaced a conservative commander named Metellus. The present bill substituted Pompey for the conservative general Lucullus, who had lost the confidence of the troops in Asia Minor. The bestowal of both commands by the assembly was contrary to the senate's claim that it should allocate provinces and armies and handle foreign affairs generally. By this speech, therefore, Cicero definitely identified

himself as a supporter of Pompey, the *populares*, and the equestrians.

In the following year, 65, Cicero began to canvass for the consular elections which would be held in the summer of 64 B.C. for
consuls to take office on the first of January, 63. The extreme conservatives, now joined by the scheming politicians Crassus and
Caesar, threw their weight against Cicero and in favor of two noble
candidates. One was the weak but presentable Antonius, younger
son of a distinguished orator of the early part of the century who
had befriended Cicero and uncle of the more notorious Mark Antony. The other was a dissolute but apparently forceful patrician
named Catiline. Just before the election, Cicero was able to prove
in a public speech unusual corruption on the part of his rivals. He
himself placed first by the unanimous acclaim of all the voting
groups, the *centuriae*. Antony came in a bad second to be his colleague; and Catiline failed in this, his second, try for the consulship.

It is well to pause at this point and consider Cicero's political
position at the pinnacle of his career, since this was as important
a factor as either Greek political theory or Roman history or his
own background in shaping his thought. Cicero was what in Roman
politics was called a "new man," the first of an equestrian family
to attain the consulship. He boasts that he was almost the first such
in living memory. Moreover, he had attained all the offices in his
career at the minimum age allowed by law.[10] This represented no
mean achievement for one who was not a noble. Moreover, Cicero
had made his own way chiefly by his success as a pleader in the
courts and as a speaker before the assemblies; he had no glamour of
military achievement to recommend him. In a speech on behalf of
Murena, during his consulship, Cicero contrasted the popularity
of the soldier, Murena, with the lack of publicity which faces the
jurist and said that only the orator can compete with the military
man. Similarly, in the speech for Plancius of 54 B.C., Cicero said
that though the prosecutor Laterensis had served the state well in
the provinces, Plancius had won out in the election to the aedileship

because he spent his time in the Forum, before the public. When Cicero campaigned for the consulship in 64 B.C., his brother Quintus composed for him a brief manual on campaigning for office. Quintus reiterated the need for the candidate to be constantly in the public eye cultivating the good will of all classes. Certainly Cicero had created his own popularity in this way. Nor was he identified with any of the great or small political factions in the state for his success; rather he had placed certain factions under obligation to himself and alienated others.[11]

As the political situation deteriorated during the sixties, Cicero had come to realize that those who a decade previously had seemed to be liberals were proving to be in fact as selfish and ambitious as their opponents and that in particular Crassus and his henchman Caesar were simply using popular support to gain control of the state. His brother Quintus had advised him in 64 B.C. to stand in with the *optimates* and to persuade them that his "popular" speeches, presumably with particular reference to that on the Manilian law, were directed chiefly to win the support of Pompey.[12] During these years, Pompey was, in fact, gaining new glories in Asia and was free from political involvement at Rome so that Cicero's admiration for him remained undimmed. But Cicero himself had now attained political leadership. Since he was committed neither to the *optimates* nor to the popular faction, he served as a rallying point for all those who wanted a stable government, free from factional rivalry and corruption.

This rivalry and corruption came to a head during Cicero's consulship in a conspiracy organized by Catiline, whose ambition to secure the consulship and use it as a means of securing political power for himself had been so frequently balked. The details of the conspiracy need not be set forth here. But it should not be dismissed too readily as a minor episode of political unrest which Cicero magnified for his own self-glorification. Catiline appealed to real causes of discontent among the Roman mob, among the Italians, still uneasy from the Social War, and among the veterans whose claims had been inadequately recognized by the state. Almost certainly, Catiline's conspiracy had the hidden support of Crassus and Caesar, who hoped to use him to promote their own schemes. It has often been questioned whether Catiline's conspiracy was as serious as Cicero made it out to be. Any man is, however, justified in regarding as serious a plot to murder him in his own bed. It has also been questioned whether, had Catiline succeeded, the course of the downfall of the Roman Republic would have been seriously altered. Such speculation cannot be answered because too many insoluble "ifs" are involved. At all events, Cicero, supported by Cato the Younger, finally secured from the senate support for the death penalty for those conspirators who were arrested in Rome. Catiline himself was slain in a bitter battle near Fiesole. Cicero was later to suffer for carrying out the senate's recommendation of the death penalty and for allying himself with the conservatives against those, like Caesar, whose own ambitions led them to sympathize with Catiline's "popular" aims.

In the speeches against Catiline, Cicero first publicly expounded his political program. This was the natural result of his character, upbringing, and earlier career. It received its precise formulation as a result of his recent political experiences. The program contained three "planks." The first was what Cicero defined as *concordia ordinum*. *Ordo* was a technical term for either the senatorial or the equestrian class; it did not include what the Victorians called the "lower orders." Already both in his prosecution of Verres and during his praetorship in a defense of Cluentius on a murder charge, Cicero had appealed for unity between senators and knights. *Concordia*, or in Greek, *harmonia*, had been an ancient ideal in the politics of the city-state. The political struggles at Athens in the late fifth and fourth centuries B.C. gave the concept, also expressed in Greek by the world *homonoia*, "like-mindedness," prominence as a necessary element in political stability. *Homonoia* was even used to express the desired union of the Greeks against the Persians. At Rome the settlement of the struggle between the patricians and

plebeians in 367 B.C. had been commemorated by a temple erected
in the Forum to Concord.[13] Cicero felt that stability in the state
depended on the propertied classes. If only the unanimity could be
restored which had existed before the Gracchi had set financiers
against landowners, the constitution would again operate in its
traditional fashion. On the occasion of Catiline's conspiracy, the
better elements among senators and equestrians rallied to his support. As has been said, his previous career had identified him with
both these groups. Hence he could boast that during his consulship
this part of his program was attained. He was to lament during the
succeeding twenty years that the concord then realized was not
maintained.

The concord between the leading classes needed backing by a
wider public. This Cicero found in the agreement of all good
men, *consensus omnium bonorum*. All right-minded men, whether
senators, knights, or ordinary citizens throughout Italy, would rally
to a moderate platform if only the senate and equestrians got
together. Cicero identified the *boni* with solid citizens who owned
property and who therefore opposed the various proposals of the
extremists to do something for the discontented. One such pro-
posal was a new distribution of public land to the poor. This was
first proposed in 63 B.C. by a creature of Crassus and Caesar, a
tribune named Rullus. Cicero succeeded in blocking the bill of
Rullus. But Caesar, as consul in 59 B.C., carried out a similar distribution. Another demagogic measure, the distribution of free
grain, was put through by Clodius during his tribunate in 58 B.C.
The extreme of a revolutionary redistribution of property had
been aimed at by Catiline. Cicero prided himself on the support
of the *boni* against such proposals. This support failed to prevent
his exile in 58 B.C. at the hands of the popular faction, lead by the
tribune Clodius and with the tacit consent of Pompey, Crassus, and
Caesar. When Cicero returned to Italy in midsummer of 57 B.C.,
the *boni* flocked from all sides to welcome him back. But this popular enthusiasm was only momentary. Thereafter Cicero found only

disappointment and disillusion in his hopes for moderate opposition to Caesar's extremism. Both Cicero's advocacy of Pompey from 52 to 48 B.C. and his condemnation of Antony after Caesar's assassination in 44 B.C. were in effect appeals to the *boni* to rally around the traditional constitution.

The program of harmony between the senatorial and equestrian classes and of the support of the traditional constitution by all good men required strong leadership to buttress it against the generals on the one side and the demagogues on the other. This leadership Cicero sought in the senate as a whole — in its authority. *Auctoritas* was one of the abstract concepts, like *imperium*, to which the Roman attached extraordinary importance. It had specific uses in Roman politics which connected it closely with the senate. During the early Republic, the patricians had had to approve any legislation which came before the popular assemblies. While the substance of this control was later rendered void by requiring that this *auctoritas patrum* should be given in advance, before legislation was even proposed, the form survived as a piece of Roman constitutional traditionalism. Moreover, if the senate, whose decrees were always simply advisory to the magistrate who consulted it and not binding save by custom, passed a decree which either was blocked by intercession of a tribune or lacked validity on some technical ground, the decree remained on record as an *auctoritas senatus*. In general, *auctoritas* was that quality in an individual or body which made others obey even when, in the English sense, he or it had no legal authority over them. Cicero felt that the leadership in the state should rest with the senate. Its *auctoritas*, sustained by the equestrians, would command the respect and agreement of all men of good will.[14]

The political program advocated by Cicero as consul was, therefore, a natural result of his background, character, and career. His youth at Arpinum inculcated in him the traditional Roman concepts of public duty and gave him a point of view which was Italic rather than narrowly Roman. His family was identified with the equestrian class but, being propertied rather than financial, was also sympathetic with the senate. His father had encouraged him in a career of study with the result that he not only made a success as a public speaker but also became deeply imbued with Greek philosophy. A youth passed in a period of bloodshed and warfare revealed to him the selfish ambitions of the office-holding group, whether these sought power by maintaining their vested interests as a class or by appealing as individuals to the appetites of the troops or the voters. Cicero himself, though he lacked family connections, wealth, or military glory, attained the highest position in the state through his own efforts as a public speaker and his own ability to win votes without bribery or corruption. He became the natural leader of those moderate and liberal-minded elements who felt that security and stability would return only if the ancestral constitution were restored. This restoration could be achieved on three conditions. All propertied persons, the *boni*, must guard against socialistic and anarchistic movements aimed to benefit the underprivileged and discontented. The upper classes, both senators and knights, must unite against demagogic leaders. And the senate as a whole should direct affairs rather than any individual military or political figure vested with unconstitutional powers. Cicero's program for practical politics was in fact to restore the Roman constitution of the second century B.C., which Greek political theorists had identified as a close approximation to the ideal mixed constitution. It rested on the three requisites of the *consensus bonorum*, the *concordia ordinum*, and the *auctoritas senatus*.

IX

THE DOWNFALL OF THE REPUBLIC

CICERO HAD APPROACHED THE END OF HIS YEAR AS CONSUL, 63 B.C., conscious that he had saved the state with the support of the better elements among senators and equestrians. A grateful populace had hailed him as Father of his Country, *Parens Patriae*. Cicero was perhaps the first to receive this title in any semiofficial fashion. *Pater Patriae* was later to be conferred officially by the senate on Caesar, Augustus, and succeeding Roman emperors.[1] Cicero might well have expected to rest on his laurels as an elder statesman, one of the foremost men in Rome who were looked upon as first citizens, *principes*. He hoped for leisure and public respect, *otium cum dignitate*. And he felt that the concord of the senatorial and equestrian classes which he had engineered might continue to enjoy the support of all right-minded people, the *consensus omnium bonorum*, and be guided by the authority of the senate, the *auctoritas senatus*.

But there were signs that the elements which had backed Catiline were not defeated. Even before the conspiracy, Caesar had raised the question of the decree by which the senate presumed to declare martial law and suspend the ancient right of citizens to

appeal to the people, the so-called *senatus consultum ultimum*.
During the second century B.C., no national emergencies had occurred of sufficient gravity to necessitate the appointment of a
dictator. In fact, the last recorded instances of recourse to this office
are at the time of Hannibal's invasion of Italy.[2] When the Gracchan
disturbances necessitated police control in Rome, the senate was
unwilling to revive the old-fashioned dictatorship. In the case of
Tiberius Gracchus, it legitimized his assassination by declaring that
he had been a public enemy. This put him outside the traditional
guarantees which protected a citizen from the arbitrary exercise
of magisterial power. Against Gaius, the senate went even further.
It not only declared him a public enemy while he was still alive
but also instructed the consuls to see that the state received no
harm.[3] This emergency decree afforded a device by which the
consuls could proceed against citizens without subjecting themselves to the traditional right of appeal to the assemblies. In the
year 100 B.C., the senate had recourse to the same tactics to empower
the consul Marius to get rid of his former ally, the demogogic
tribune Saturninus. Saturninus was in fact slain in a riot instigated
by the senators.

Now, in 63 B.C., nearly forty years after the event, Caesar
brought to trial an elderly senator called Rabirius on the charge
that he had participated in the riot in which Saturninus had been
slain without appeal to the people. Caesar revived an ancient procedure, the details of which need not detain this discussion, in order
to ensure that the case was heard before the popular assemblies
rather than in the special court which Sulla had established to hear
cases involving violence. Though Cicero defended Rabirius and,
apparently, secured his acquittal, Caesar's move made it abundantly
clear that popular sentiment ran strongly against the senate's method
of dealing with demagogues by the "last decree." Yet Cicero had
acted against Catiline in virtue of such a decree, followed by a vote
in favor of the death penalty.[4]

It was a convention of Roman constitutional procedure that

when a magistrate reached the end of his term of office, he must lay it down in a ceremony called an *abdicatio*.[5] Consuls customarily at this time took an oath that they had conducted themselves honestly in office and also delivered a speech justifying their actions. The tribunes interposed a veto against a speech by Cicero on the occasion of his *abdicatio*. Cicero therefore altered the customary oath to include a statement that the state had suffered no harm during his year of office. This incident gave another indication that opposition to Cicero's handling of the Catilinarian conspiracy was not dead.

Late in 62 B.C., Pompey returned from the East full of conquests. The arrangements which Pompey made for organizing the East as a system of provinces directly ruled by Rome or of client states under Roman protection set the pattern for the practical organization of the Roman empire under Augustus. Yet Pompey as little as Cicero could see beyond his practical arrangements to their implication of the necessity for a new political theory whereon to construct an ecumenical state which would be something more than the imperialistic rule of the Roman city-state over other cities, tribes, or kingdoms.[6] Cicero looked to Pompey hopefully as the leader of the moderate party and supported him in his request for a triumph and for confirmation of his Eastern settlement. But Cicero failed to recognize the opportunity for a new interpretation of Rome's mission. For him, Pompey and his conquests would simply serve to cement the alliance of senators and equestrians and to promote his own program. The conservatives, however, blocked Pompey's triumph for a year and never confirmed his arrangements or rewarded his veterans.

In December of 62 B.C., just as Pompey arrived, a scandalous piece of gossip spread abroad in Rome. A scion of the aristocratic Claudii named Publius had disguised himself as a woman and attended certain religious ceremonies which were held in the home of the wife of the chief religious official, the *pontifex maximus*, and which were open only to reputable matrons. The *pontifex maximus* was Caesar and the scandalmongers said that Publius was having an affair with his wife Pompeia. Publius, like many of the young aristocrats, had been seeking favor with the popular party in order to get ahead faster than was possible under the conservative routine. The conservatives, supported by the general feeling that the pollution of the rites boded ill for the state, brought Publius to trial before a special court. Caesar, however, refused to support the prosecution. He simply divorced his wife with the famous remark that Caesar's wife must be above suspicion. Publius curried favor with the people, organized gangs, and bribed his jurors with money reputedly supplied by Crassus. He presented as an alibi that he had been at Interamna, forty-five miles from Rome, on the day of the ceremonies. Cicero testified that Publius had called on him in the city that very morning. Nevertheless, Publius was acquitted by the corrupted jury. And Publius vowed vengeance on Cicero.

Cicero felt that things were going from bad to worse. Late in 61 B.C., the equestrians, with Cicero's support, asked the senate to reduce their payments on their tax contracts because of bad harvests in Asia. But the conservatives blocked the request. Thus soon the *concordia ordinum* fell to pieces. Though Pompey remained friendly to Cicero, he put on airs suitable only to an Eastern potentate. Caesar had been praetor in 62 B.C., governed further Spain as propraetor in 61, and now, in 60, campaigned successfully for the consulship of 59. He and his patron Crassus, who had been consul with Pompey in 70 B.C., drew the vainglorious and disappointed general into an informal agreement by which each was to secure what he wanted — Caesar the consulship and a command, Crassus the reduction of the tax contracts, and Pompey confirmation of his arrangements and the reward of his veterans. In December of 60 B.C., Caesar indirectly approached Cicero, apparently with the idea that the orator could persuade the senate and people to accept this program. But Cicero, to his credit, refused to compromise his principles and sacrifice the constitution to a gang. The realization of the program of the so-called "First Triumvirate" does not concern Cicero's political thought directly; suffice it that each member got what he wanted, and that the award to Caesar of a command in Gaul was destined to shape the future not merely of Rome but of Europe.

Cicero remained aloof from active politics during the year of Caesar's consulship, despite his grief over the collapse of all for which he had striven. His enemy Publius, in order to qualify for the tribunate, for which plebeians were ineligible, had himself adopted by a plebeian named Fonteius. Caesar, as *pontifex maximus*, presided at the "curial" ceremony before thirty lictors, and Pompey, an augur, took part. As a plebeian, Publius adopted a spelling that represented the pronunciation of the name Claudius by the uneducated, namely "Clodius." By this name he was thereafter known. He was elected to enter the tribunate on December 10, 59 B.C.[7] Early in the following year, he secured the passage of a law which provided the penalty of exile for anybody who had caused the death of Roman citizens without a regular trial. Caesar did not oppose this extreme and retroactive legislation against Cicero. He even publicly claimed to have resisted the execution of the Catilinarian conspirators as illegal. Pompey withdrew from Rome to a country villa and refused to intervene on Cicero's behalf. Actually all three masters of Rome, Pompey, Caesar, and Crassus, wanted to have Cicero out of the way while they completed their plans for controlling the state. Also they desired to demonstrate the futility of opposition to their program. Though the equestrian order and other *boni* attempted to arouse public opinion for Cicero, Clodius' strength was such that Cicero did not dare abide a trial to test the law and fled from Rome in March, 58 B.C. Clodius at once enacted a bill exiling him by name.

Cicero spent an unhappy seventeen months in Thessalonica and Dyrrachium, across the Adriatic. His letters show a degree of despair and a lack of self-control which have exposed him to severe criticism, particularly in view of the Stoic fortitude which he preached in his philosophical works. But allowance must be made

for the fact that his letters were personal, addressed to his closest
intimates and not intended for the public; that all that Cicero had
valued in life was swept away so that even suicide seemed preferable
to continued exile; and that the Latin temperament is more given to
extremes of feeling and expression than is that of Northern peoples.
Meanwhile, agitation for his recall went on at Rome. Gangs of his
supporters, Sestius and Milo, had frequent and violent encounters
with those of Clodius. In one of these, Quintus, Cicero's brother,
was pulled from the speakers' platform, the *rostra*, by the Clodians,
severely beaten up, and left for dead. The recall of Cicero now had
the approval of Caesar, who was in Gaul, and of Pompey; perhaps
they felt that he had been chastised enough, perhaps that Clodius
was getting out of hand. At any rate, in August of 57 B.C. the consul
Lentulus, with the express support of Pompey and various distinguished nobles, secured the passage by the assembly of centuries of
a bill recalling Cicero. He had a triumphant landing at Brundisium
and progress through Italy which culminated in a unique popular
reception at Rome.

Fourteen speeches are extant which Cicero delivered between
57 and 52 B.C. These suffice to show that he was not entirely in
retirement. Most of them deal with matters arising from his exile.
He thanked the senate. He argued that he should get back his
house, which Clodius had had confiscated and used as the site for
a temple to Liberty. He defended those who had supported him,
like Sestius, and he attacked his enemies, for instance, Piso, one of
the consuls of 58 B.C. who had permitted his exile. Immediately
after his return, he perhaps hoped to separate Pompey from Caesar
and to win him back to moderate policies. But any prospect of dissolving the triumvirate was defeated when it was renewed in north
Italy, at Luca, in April of 56 B.C. Again the detailed arrangements
do not directly illuminate Cicero's political thought. Ties of family
alliance were established between the triumvirs, and both Pompey
and Crassus got military commands, the former in Spain and the
latter in Syria, which would give them forces equal to Caesar's.

Cicero realized that against such a combination of power a program of moderate senatorial government was hopeless. Outwardly he made his peace with the triumvirs, particularly with Caesar, since he had never lost his admiration for Pompey. His brother Quintus and his friend the lawyer Trebatius joined Caesar's staff in Gaul on Cicero's recommendation. Despite these signs of reconciliation and despite his own speeches, Cicero knew that he was in fact in retirement, that he now counted for little in active politics.

Throughout his career, Cicero had been an author as well as a statesman, and not merely an author in the sense of publishing his own speeches. As a young man he had, like most educated Romans, written poetry.[8] He had also begun to publish on rhetoric. But the years from 57 to 52 B.C. witnessed a great increase in his output in poetry, in rhetoric, and in philosophy. During this period he composed his great treatises on the education of the orator, the *de Oratore*, and, more pertinent to the present discussion, on the best constitution, the *de Republica*. References in letters to Atticus and to his brother show that he began to write the latter work, *On the Commonwealth*, in the spring of 54 B.C. and a letter to Atticus and one from Caelius to Cicero, both of 51 B.C., indicate that by then the work was finished and before the public.[9]

In 52 B.C. Pompey secured the passage of a law by which five years were to elapse between the tenure of an urban magistracy and a provincial governorship, instead of their being successive in the traditional fashion.[10] It therefore become necessary to provide for the provinces during the ensuing five years from ex-magistrates who had not yet been governors. Cicero, who never liked to be away from Rome, had in 63 B.C. surrendered his claim to Macedonia to his colleague Antonius to win the latter's support against Catiline. He was therefore sent, much against his will, to govern Cilicia in southern Asia Minor. It appears from his letters that he was a good governor. He performed his functions dutifully; he conducted a campaign against some hill tribes; he refused to burden the provincials with extra work to collect wild animals for friends to display at Rome; he resisted the unjust demands of Brutus and the company of equestrians in which he was interested to collect more than their due from the town of Salamis in Cyprus; and he made no undue profits for himself or for his entourage. But his heart lay in Rome, as his urgent letters to his friend Caelius, begging for news, show. Despite Cicero's interest in the provincials, he had no concept of Roman politics in an imperial sense nor did he realize that Rome's real future was being shaped not in the Forum but in the provinces. Cicero left his province at the earliest date allowed by law and hastened back to Rome. He landed at Brundisium late in the fall of 50 B.C. to find civil war imminent.

The close agreement between the triumvirs, as renewed at Luca, had been based on a careful balance of power. This was dislocated by the death of Caesar's daughter Julia, the wife of Pompey, in 54 B.C. and by the defeat and death of Crassus at Carrhae in Syria in 53 B.C.[11] Pompey had drawn closer to the conservatives. Caesar must have seemed remote in Gaul, though he had his agents active at Rome on the popular side. During 53 B.C., rioting organized by the rival gangs of Clodius and Milo prevented any consular elections and resulted finally in a street brawl soon after New Year's Day, 52 B.C., in which Clodius was killed.[12] The senate then vested Pompey, who already held a proconsular command over Spain, with extraordinary police powers in Italy. Two months later it secured his election as consul for 52 B.C. without a colleague. In his consulship, Milo was brought to trial and Pompey surrounded the court with armed guards, ostensibly to prevent disorder but in fact to intimidate the court. Cicero, grateful to Milo for aiding his recall from exile, alone dared to undertake his defense. But even Cicero's nerve failed, despite his once proud boast, "Let arms yield to the toga." [13] He spoke ineffectively and the desired condemnation was voted. Milo went into exile at Marseilles. Later in the year, Pompey signalized his rapprochement with the conservatives by selecting as colleague in the consulship the noble Metellus Scipio, whose daughter he had married after the death of Julia.

It had been agreed, either at Luca or thereafter, that Caesar could campaign in absence during the first half of 49 B.C. for the consulship in 48. His election was naturally a foregone conclusion if this agreement stood. He could therefore proceed directly from the judicial immunity of his proconsulship to that of the consulship without becoming a private citizen and being exposed to legal attack by his enemies. Pompey, still unwilling to make an open break, now tried by various underhanded tricks to secure the termination of Caesar's command before he entered upon his consulship on January first, 48 B.C. When these maneuvers failed, he tried to get the senate to vote that Caesar should surrender part or all of his troops. Caesar reasonably asked that Pompey should do the same. Finally, late in 50 B.C., after all negotiations had failed, the consul Marcellus appealed to Pompey to "save the state." Caesar still offered to treat on anything resembling parity but Pompey's stubborn conceit prevented him from agreeing. Early in January of 49 B.C., the senate passed an emergency decree which entrusted the state to the new consuls and to the proconsuls, which meant in effect to Pompey. Caesar led his troops from his province of Cisalpine Gaul, that is, the Po Valley, across a little river which formed the frontier of Italy proper, the Rubicon between Ravenna and Rimini. He thus violated the provision of the law of Sulla on treason which forbade a general to bring troops into Italy under arms except as necessary for a triumph.

The rights and wrongs of Pompey and Caesar in causing the outbreak of civil war and the detailed course of that war do not concern this discussion. Cicero had not participated in the final debates in the senate before the break because he had retained his command, in hopes of receiving a triumph for his victory over the Cilician tribesmen. In normal times this might have been granted to him, since many generals had through the courtesy of their fellow senators triumphed for equally slight successes. But Cicero's claim was submerged by the more important problems which faced the senate. In the meantime, in accordance with the traditional restriction, so long as he retained his military *imperium* he could not cross the sacred limit of the city of Rome, the *pomoerium*, to attend meetings of the senate. When Pompey abandoned Rome, for the strategic reason that the bulk of the forces on whose loyalty the senate could count were concentrated in the eastern provinces, Cicero realized the political folly of thus surrendering to Caesar what was in fact the symbol of rule, the capital. He therefore at first refused to accompany the Pompeians to Greece.

Cicero would not, however, return to Rome and to Caesar. His loyalty still lay with the traditional republican constitution which he had consistently espoused since he entered on the political stage. Cicero is often accused of having become increasingly conservative after he attained the consulship and of having identified his interests with those of the *nobiles* rather than of the liberals. His support of Pompey and the reactionaries is adduced as evidence that he had lost his early breadth of view and opposition to the selfishness of the old aristocracy. Cicero's letters at this period show how conscious he was of the personal and political weaknesses both of Pompey and of the senators with him.[14] But when it came to a choice between those who, however inadequately, supported the constitution and those who were attempting to overthrow it, Cicero felt no hesitation. His ideals remained the same; the background had shifted. There no longer existed any middle ground of liberalism. To be politically effective, Cicero had to join one of two extremes. On the side of Pompey and the senate, there was still hope of striving for a real and harmonious commonwealth. Caesar offered only the consummation of the revolution which the generals on the one side and the demagogues on the other had for half a century been waging against the authority of the senate.

Caesar realized the need to win over to himself men of repute because his cause was still that of the extremists and the mob. He therefore wooed Cicero. Eventually, in March of 49 B.C., the two met. Cicero refused to withdraw from his support of Pompey and the senate. In the summer he left Italy for Greece and late in the year accompanied Pompey to Dyrrachium, the port across the Adriatic from Brundisium where he himself had spent the later part of his exile. But the disunion and selfish bitterness which he witnessed among Pompey's supporters disgusted him. He did not participate in the final withdrawal to Thessaly and the disaster of Pharsalus in August of 48 B.C. He returned in October to the Italian port Brundisium, where he waited nearly a year for Caesar's return. He still held his military command in hopes of a triumph by Caesar's gift. When Caesar visited Italy briefly in September of 47 B.C., he received Cicero at Tarentum and with characteristic generosity let bygones be bygones, but the triumph was forgotten.

In the spring of 46 B.C., Caesar defeated the most important surviving republican force at Thapsus in Africa. The figurehead of republican opposition, Cato the Younger, committed suicide at Utica. The only remaining opposition gathered about the sons of Pompey in Spain. Caesar had been elected to the dictatorship in the fall of 49 B.C., to the consulship for 48, and to the dictatorship for the second time in the summer of the same year, after Pharsalus. This dictatorship had continued into 47 B.C. since no magistrates were elected until the last three months of that year, when Caesar again held the consulship. After the battle of Thapsus, he received a dictatorship for ten years, like that which had been exercised by Sulla under the guise of putting the constitution back into order. Later offices bestowed on Caesar added little to the absoluteness of his power.

Naturally, under so monarchical a rule there was no place for senatorial government and the exercise of Cicero's influence. Cicero appeared little in public and spoke only to secure pardon for such opponents of Caesar as Ligarius, a Pompeian, Marcellus, the consul of 51 B.C., or Deiotarus, king of Galatia. In these speeches, and particularly in the last two, Cicero set before Caesar ideals of public conduct which he hoped that the dictator would display. In the speech for Marcellus, Cicero proposed to Caesar a positive program of restoring the peace and safety of the state, with the suggestion that this would mean a return of constitutional government.[15] The later speech for Deiotarus harped on clemency and perhaps by implication attacked the reports that Caesar meant to become king. Caesar's intention to retain absolute control undoubtedly became increasingly clear between the time of these two speeches, whatever the truth behind the reports that he aimed at monarchy.

During these years, also, personal sorrows crowded about Cicero. His brother and his nephew, both called Quintus, deserted the Pompeian cause for Caesar and took occasion to malign and traduce Cicero, who behaved very well throughout the quarrel. The brothers were apparently reconciled, probably because Quintus saw that Cicero enjoyed Caesar's favor. Late in 47 or early in 46 B.C., Cicero finally divorced the wife to whom he had been married for more than thirty years. Terentia undoubtedly had her faults, but she had also taken care of his affairs during his exile. In later life, affection between the two apparently wore thin. It is perhaps not for moderns to pass judgment on Cicero in this matter, since the Romans of the later Republic looked on marriage and divorce from a more mundane point of view. Cicero shortly thereafter married and quickly divorced a rich young lady called Publilia, who was his ward. This was again not an exceptional act from the Roman point of view. During the brief marriage, Cicero had suffered a loss which touched him deeply. His daughter Tullia, to whom he was devoted, died early in 45 B.C. Cicero never entirely recovered from his sorrow at her death. At the moment he shrank from contact even with old and tried friends like Atticus, so that the presence of a young wife must have been more than he could bear.[16]

Distress over public affairs and personal sorrow turned Cicero more than ever before to philosophy. The years between 49 and 44 B.C. saw the bulk of his production; it was probably during these years that he worked on a sequel to the *de Republica*, a discussion of laws, the *de Legibus*. He also completed shortly after Caesar's death three books on "duties," the *de Officiis*, which is, with the possible exception of the *de Legibus*, his last surviving treatise.

Caesar's program cut to the very heart of senatorial privilege and of the preferred position of Roman citizens in the Mediterranean world. He ran the government singlehanded, admitted anybody whom he chose to the senate, extended citizen rights widely, and advanced plans for a general equalization of all inhabitants of the empire. A group of senators, including both selfish conservatives and doctrinaire republicans, formed a plot to assassinate him. If they considered including Cicero, they probably felt that he was too old to be useful and too high-principled to agree to murder, even under the guise of tyrannicide.[17] The immediate result of the deed, on the Ides, or fifteenth, of March in 44 B.C., was not what the republicans expected, namely, an automatic return of the traditional constitution. The Roman mob, aroused by Caesar's lieutenant Antony, turned against the assassins. Most of them, including their leaders, Marcus Junius Brutus and Gaius Cassius Longinus, fled from Rome. The bulk of the senators, instead of resuming the direction of the state, awaited the turn of events. Cicero himself was rejoiced by the removal of Caesar and attempted to negotiate between Antony and the assassins to secure a peaceful resumption of constitutional government.

A new factor was introduced into the situation when Caesar's heir, his great-nephew Gaius Octavius, returned from Greece to claim his inheritance. He was only eighteen and Anthony tried to dismiss him cavalierly. But with surprising insistence, Octavius asserted his rights and, in accordance with his testamentary adoption by Caesar, took the name Gaius Julius Caesar Octavianus. For the next sixteen years he is commonly called Octavian. Antony, by his intransigence, also forced Marcus Brutus and Cassius to flee from Italy to the east. Finally in the autumn, he so angered Cicero that the orator made a slashing attack upon him before the senate. This was the first of the fourteen orations which Cicero delivered against Antony during the ensuing year, and which are called, after those of Demosthenes against Philip of Macedon, the *Philippics*.[18] Antony left Rome to attempt to dislodge one of the assassins,

Decimus Brutus, from Cisalpine Gaul. Octavian raised a force among Caesar's veterans in Campania and forced the senate to send him north to support the two consuls, who had already led forces in pursuit of Antony. Cicero supported the acceptance of Octavian by the senate in the hope that he might be used and put aside.[19] Octavian and the consuls forced Antony to withdraw from the seige of Decimus Brutus in Mutina. But in two battles during April 43 B.C., the consuls were slain. Antony withdrew towards Narbonnese Gaul, where Lepidus held a considerable army. Though Lepidus had professed loyalty to the senate, he now claimed that his Caesarian troops would not fight against Antony, so he came to terms, as did the other governors in the west. In the late summer of 43 B.C., Octavian also joined the coalition.

The three leaders, Antony, Lepidus, and Octavian, moved on Rome. In November they were invested by the assembly with dictatorial power like that which Sulla and Caesar had held for restoring the constitution, except that the power was now given to three men. Thus the so-called "Second Triumvirate" was not, like the first, simply an informal agreement between its members but was a legally recognized, if unusual, college of extraordinary magistrates. The triumvirs did not show the tolerance which Caesar had displayed toward his opponents. Like the earlier masters of Rome, Marius and Sulla, they purged their enemies in a series of proscriptions. One of the first heads demanded by Antony was that of Cicero. The elderly Cicero tried flight but was overtaken near Formiae. He bravely offered his neck to the soldiers sent to behead him. On that seventh of December of 43 B.C., with his family broken up, the state for which he had so long striven surrendered to bloodthirsty tyrants, and his own strength exhausted, it must have been preferable to die rather than to live longer amid the ruins of all that he had held dear.

During the twenty years from his consulship until his death, Cicero had consistently striven to stem the forces which were carrying the traditional constitution headlong into ruin. He has often been charged with inconsistencies and political trimming during this period. Opinions may differ on this point and his judgments were undoubtedly not always wise, particularly his loyalty to Pompey. But his great failure was his inability to see beyond the traditional political ideas which he derived from Greek thought, Roman history, and his own career. He had ample opportunity to understand the problems of empire. He stood for good and enlightened government. But he could not conceive of government in terms other than those of the traditional city-state with its mixed constitution and its aristocratic control. Hence for him the world state must be either a monarchy or, as he preferred, the dominance of the Roman city-state over its conquests. Whether or not Caesar was a genius or an opportunist, he undoubtedly saw more clearly than did Cicero the true nature of the problem set by Rome's empire. Yet the point of view expressed by Cicero was so strong that it not only defeated Caesar; it molded the final form of the Roman imperial government. Later ages forgot Cicero's leadership of the republican cause and expression of its ideal in their admiration for the Stoic hero of the downfall of the republic, Cato the Younger.[20] Cato figures even in the Augustan poets as the embodiment of Roman steadfastness. To that extent, Augustus laid claim to the heritage of Cato as well as of Caesar. But his compromise between the need of an imperial administration and the preservation of the republican constitution appears to have been inspired by Cicero. Cicero could hardly have foreseen that his political ideals would thus be realized by that one of the triumvirs whose desertion of the senatorial and republican cause must have appeared to him most reprehensible.

X

CICERO'S POLITICAL THEORY

CICERO'S PERIODS OF CREATIVE WRITING WERE, AS APPEARED IN THE last chapter, those in which he was politically inactive. Of the three treatises which primarily set forth his political theory, the *de Republica*, or *On the Commonwealth*, dates from between 54 and 52 B.C. The *de Legibus*, *On the Laws*, may date from the same period, but there is reason to think that it was more probably completed in the last year of his life. Likewise, the *de Officiis*, *On Duties*, was written after Caesar's assassination. Cicero's political treatises must be read against the background of the downfall of the republic, the defeat of all his beliefs and loyalties. Yet these beliefs and loyalties remained unshaken and relatively unaffected by contemporary events. Cicero blamed the troubles of his times on the ambition, corruption, and weakness of individuals and on the decay of the moral and political standards which he believed to have characterized the men of the Scipionic circle and the constitution of the second century B.C. He failed to see that behind these faults, serious as they were, lay the fundamental impossibility of governing an ecumenical empire with a government suited to a self-contained city-state. He remained true to the orthodox theory of the mixed constitution as expounded by Plato, Aristotle, and their successors and, according to Polybius and Panaetius, best exemplified in the Roman government because this represented the achievement of national virtue and intelligence, working themselves out in the slow forge of history, and not the creation of any one brilliant individual.

Cicero was predisposed by temperament, education, and his own career to be a traditionalist. His threefold political program of the sixties — the harmony between senators and equestrians, the support of the state by all men of good will, and the guiding authority of the senate — had completely failed during the fifties. His experiences during that and the next decades almost convinced him that the true republic could never be restored in contemporary Rome. Plato, under similar circumstances, had constructed his ideal state entirely in the realm of theory. He had laid its foundations squarely on the moral character of the individual. Cicero turned back to an actual past and derived his ideal from the period which he regarded as most nearly perfect in Roman history, the second century B.C. Moreover, he based his political ideal on Roman history and tradition. Plato's state and its laws are characteristically Greek, but they do not specifically represent any one Greek city. They derive equally from historical fact and from logical theory. Cicero's state is strictly fitted for Rome and carefully tailored to the Roman constitution.

Cicero's *de Republica* was one of his works which did not survive the Dark Ages. Its existence in its entirety in the later Roman empire is attested by the use made of it at the beginning of the fourth century by Lactantius, particularly in his *Divine Institutes*, and a century later by St. Augustine, particularly in his *City of God*. Citations in such late commentators and grammarians as Nonius Marcellus of the fourth century might have been derived from earlier excerpters or directly from the complete text. At the beginning of the fifth century A.D., the scholar Macrobius used the final portion of the *de Republica*, the vision of Scipio with which,

in imitation of Plato, Cicero closed his account, as the basis for a
learned discussion of the afterlife. The popularity of Macrobius'
commentary on the *Somnium Scipionis* preserved this portion of
Cicero's text throughout the Middle Ages. Until 1820, only these
various quotations and references served to perpetuate the treatise.
In that year the librarian of the Vatican, Mai, later a cardinal, discovered that a medieval copy of a commentary of St. Augustine
on the Psalms had been written on leaves of parchment which had
previously been used and then erased, thus becoming what is called
a palimpsest. The underwriting proved to be portions of the text
of the *de Republica*, written during the later Roman empire in the
fourth or fifth century A.D. Unfortunately, the later scribes had not
reused the leaves in their original sequence or even employed all of
them. Thus the task of reconstituting the text of the *de Republica*
necessitated piecing together in what seemed to be the right order
those portions which were preserved and supplementing them by
the citations or paraphrases available in other authors. The result
affords probably only a third of the original text and that in unequal
distribution. The bulk belongs to the first three books; the last three
are, except for Scipio's dream, represented by scanty fragments.

The general concept of the work is derived from Plato's *Republic* but its form is different. Plato's dialogue is for the most part
really a monologue by Socrates, interrupted by frequent remarks
on the part of his auditors to give the impression of a fairly lively
interchange. Cicero's dialogue takes rather the form of long set
speeches, each presenting a point of view uninterruptedly. This
form was traditionally attributed to Aristotle, though none of that
philosopher's dialogues survive to prove that this departure from
the Platonic model originated with him. Cicero assigned the main
role in his dialogue to his ideal statesman, Scipio the Younger. He
imagined that a group of friends gathered at the country estate of
Scipio during the Latin holidays in 129 B.C. In that year the dissen-
sions started by Tiberius Gracchus were still harrassing the state.
Toward its end, Scipio himself was to die under circumstances

which gave rise to a rumor that he had been poisoned, presumably in connection with his attempt to abolish the land commission established by Gracchus. The imminence of Scipio's death, hinted at once or twice in the dialogue and strongly implied in the vision at the end, naturally makes his role more dramatic.

The work was divided into six books, to each pair of which Cicero prefaced an introduction in his own person. The first introduction defends the life of the statesman, particularly as exemplified by his own career. His characters are then introduced in a discussion of a recent astronomical phenomenon. The talk shifts naturally to the troubles in the state and thence to a request that Scipio expound the ideal commonwealth. The first book contains Scipio's discussion of the three pure forms of the state and their degenerations, of the balanced or mixed constitution composed of all three, and of the Roman state as an illustration thereof. Scipio supports this final thesis in the second book by tracing the historical growth of the Roman state toward this ideal balance.[1]

Cicero's second preface argues that the highest quality of man is reason, that the noblest function of reason is statesmanship, and that the best expression of statesmanship must be founded on justice. Philus then debates with Laelius on the nature of justice. Philus upholds the utilitarian view that government must be based on injustice, or the interest of the ruler. Laelius rebuts with the traditional Platonic view that justice is an absolute virtue, necessary in any government which is to be called good, and that therefore government must be in the interest of all, of the commonwealth.[2] The fragments of the fourth book indicate that the discussion dealt with social classes, maintenance of moral standards, and the education of the young, including the place of literature therein.

Cicero opened the fifth book with a preface about the interdependence of the character of the Roman state and the virtues of her leading men. He used as his text the line of Ennius cited in an earlier chapter: "On ancient customs and heroes the Roman state stands firm"; *Moribus antiquis res stat Romana virisque.*[3] According

to the few remaining bits, Scipio went on to expound the nature
of law and the need for its enforcement. He then considered the
training of leaders of the state, with particular emphasis on the
stimulus of honor and glory. The sixth and last book, also largely
lost, treated the qualities and duties of the statesman and the value
and reward of his labors. This discussion culminated in the allegor-
ical vision, already mentioned, which Scipio claimed to have had as
a young man when he visited the Numidian chief Masinissa. In the
vision, Scipio the Elder escorted his grandson through the heavenly
spheres to prove to him two things: how petty are human effort
and achievements when seen under the guise of eternity, and how
true reward and glory will come for the just statesman in the afterlife, because a just life on earth fosters man's immortal spirit and
enables it after death to rise closer to the eternal spirit that guides
the whole universe.

Cicero's conscious imitation of Plato would suggest that he proceeded directly from the *de Republica* to his study of the actual
laws necessary for his ideal commonwealth. Internal evidence has,
in fact, been adduced to show that already in 52 B.C. he was working
on this second treatise, the *de Legibus*. But he does not seem to have
completed it in 44 B.C., when he published his *de Divinatione*, so
that the *de Legibus* may have been cast in its present form after
Caesar's death.[4] Only the three first books survive, and there are
gaps in these. Since Macrobius quotes from the fifth book, critics
debate whether there were in all six or even eight. Cicero regarded
"the Athenian stranger" of Plato's *Laws* as the philosopher himself.
He therefore made the characters of his own treatise himself, his
brother Quintus, and his close friend Atticus. Just as Plato had laid
his scene in the Cretan countryside, so Cicero laid his in his native
Arpinum on his ancestral estate.[5]

The talk begins with a mention of Cicero's poem on Marius.
His companions urge him to use the leisure of old age to write
history. He says that writing history indeed requires leisure and
that if he can withdraw from active pleading and become only a

legal consultant he might have this leisure. They feel that he will never free himself from the courts but ask him nevertheless to expound the general principles and laws suited to the ideal commonwealth which he had described in the *de Republica*. Cicero first argues that law is right reason in ordering and forbidding. Since right reason is inherent in nature herself and is shared by all men, law proceeds from nature; that is, behind human law lies natural law. Moreover, this natural law is the source of justice. Hence justice is not simple conformity to statute law, which may be good or bad, and is not merely the utilitarian good of the government, but must be referred to a natural standard of the honorable. Both the just and the honorable must be sought for their own sake. This suggests a consideration of the nature of the highest good which is broken off by Quintus, who urges a return to the subject of law. Cicero concludes the first book with the Socratic statement that the highest wisdom is to know thyself, that is, to know the image of God within oneself and thence to recognize the divine and eternal in all the universe.

The second book opens with a discussion of Cicero's love for his native Arpinum. Cicero makes the statement already alluded to as significant for the spread of Roman citizenship. He remarks that Italians like himself have a double citizenship, that of the town of their birth and that of Rome. But, he says, in their affection that fatherland must stand first in which the name of commonwealth testifies to the citizenship of all together.[6] The discussion of law is then resumed by a summary of the preceding book. Cicero amplifies the definition of law as the exercise of natural reason in commanding and forbidding by stating that it is the distinction between things just and unjust. Law is the essential element without which there is no state. Law in this sense is again the expression of natural reason or of the mind of God; it is not simply the specific and transitory statutes established or repealed by human agencies. Thus the basis of law must be belief in and respect for the gods from whose universal reason it proceeds.

After so Platonic a preface, Cicero prescribes the regulations
concerning worship in the ideal state. He devotes the rest of the
book to justifying them either from Roman tradition or from Greek
legislation or from Plato's prescriptions. The combination of sources
is noteworthy, particularly for the emphasis laid on Roman traditional practices and for the statement that the laws of the Twelve
Tables derived in part from Solon's legislation at Athens. Significant
also is the importance attached to the control exercised over the
conduct of public business by the augurs in virtue of their interpretation of the will of the gods. Cicero denies the position which is
expressed by the modern apothegm that "religion is the opiate of
the people." [7] He claims that history supports the reality of the
revelation of the will of the gods to men through signs and
omens.[8]

The third, and last surviving, book discusses the magistrates.
Magistrates should govern in conformity with the law. In fact, the
magistrate is a speaking law and the law a silent magistrate. Cicero
reasserts his belief that government is essential to a state and to the
universe and that it proceeds from God through the universe to the
world about us and to mankind. Hence monarchy arose and when
this proved unsatisfactory, magistrates were necessary. They must
know the limits of their authority and the citizens must obey their
proper commands. Here Cicero repeats Aristotle's principle that he
who obeys must expect in turn to rule and that he who rules must
remember how in a short time he must himself obey. The detailed
regulations concerning the magistracies follow closely the Roman
pattern. Most interesting is the discussion of the tribunate. Quintus
maintains that its institution meant the decline of the weight, the
gravitas, of the optimates and the growth of the power of the mob.
Cicero admits that the tribunate, like any other office, may be abused
but claims that its institution gave the people a sense of their importance and liberty and therefore made them more willing to yield
to the authority of the leading citizens, the principes. He states that
his own exile was not really the work of the villain Clodius but a

step necessitated in the public interest because of the crisis in the state. He fails to convince either Quintus or Atticus.

Later Cicero argues that the senate must serve as an example to other citizens not because of the penalties imposed by censors but through the character of its members, a condition which he admits to be far from true in his own day. But, as in the fifth book of the *de Republica*, he holds that the character of the leaders, the *principes*, determines the character of the whole state. From this topic, he proceeds to that of balloting. He would prefer open voting but realizes this is impossible, because it makes the mob feel too subject to the aristocracy. On the other hand the secret ballot gives too much scope to bribery and corruption. Cicero proposes a compromise; he would have written ballots which would be available for inspection by the citizens of highest rank, the *optimates*. Again he fails to convince Quintus and Atticus, who regard the introduction of the secret ballot as the ruin of aristocratic control. Atticus pays high tribute to Cicero when he states that the best government, the *optima res publica*, was that which Cicero had established in his consulship, namely, one in which control was vested in the best men, the *optimi*.

The *de Officiis* deals primarily with moral problems, or "duties." But Cicero, like Plato in the central books of the *Republic* and Aristotle in his *Ethics*, maintained that the moral quality of the individual and his actions could be judged only in so far as he and his acts contributed to the state and the common good. The basically social character of Cicero's ethics justifies a brief discussion of the *de Officiis*. The first book in particular lays down broad principles concerning the origin of society in the natural instincts of man and concerning justice in society. These principles coincide with the views expressed in his *de Republica* and his *de Legibus*. As in the earlier works, Cicero is eclectic. Though he later claims to be an Academic, he here states that Academic, Peripatetic, and Stoic political and ethical theories in a large measure coincided since all were derived from Socrates and Plato.[9] Cicero follows his regular procedure of applying Greek theories to Roman experience and of illustrating his points by examples drawn from both Greek and Roman history. His method figures particularly in the first two books, where in almost every case parallel Greek and Roman instances are cited. The third book begins in the same way but becomes more purely Roman as the discussion works into specific, almost legal, problems of choice between expediency and moral duty.

Cicero addressed the *de Officiis* to his son Marcus. Since the Roman father was expected to concern himself with his son's education, Cicero wrote in his own person throughout. There is no pretense of dialogue or of other than a contemporary setting. The work abounds in personal allusions and references to events of the times. Cicero especially inveighs against Caesar's ambition. The dictator, by seeking his own rather than the common good, had put an end to the "Republic," the commonwealth. Cicero, having thus lost any opportunity for public service, had taken refuge in study and writing. The new, monarchical, administration had acted unjustly both to citizens and to allies. It represented the consummation of the revolution begun by the demagoguery of the Gracchi and by the military ambition of Sulla. This criticism of the "tyrant" arose not from Cicero's personal feeling that he had been put aside but from his sincere devotion to the traditional constitution.[10]

In the first two books, Cicero followed closely a treatise by Panaetius on moral duty, entitled in Greek *Peri tou kathekontos.* The first book deals specifically with moral duty, or what Cicero denotes as the "honorable," *honestum.* Society arises because of a natural instinct in men but must be brought to perfection by the exercise of the intellectual virtue, wisdom, and the three moral virtues, justice, courage, and temperance. In fact, those characteristics which distinguish man from the other higher animals, reason and speech, make possible social organization. Hence of all the associations which man's natural gregarious instincts create, associations of friendship, family, and society, the state has first claim on his moral duty. Moral duty stems from the four virtues upon which the state depends and principally from justice, since as Plato showed justice alone can give moral value to the other three virtues. That is to say, they are moral only in so far as they aim at the common rather than at private good. Cicero spends some time on courage. He argues that, however worthy may be bravery on the field of battle, courage displayed in civil activities may also preserve the state, as Cicero's own consulship had proved. Courage must be free from self-seeking, vindictiveness, anger, and pride. Cicero then treats temperance. This virtue concerns itself with what is fitting, namely, the decorous or *decorum*. By self-control, the moral action is fitted to the situation and to the individual. Everyone has two endowments, his common humanity and his particular abilities. Moral actions must suit individual abilities and circumstances but should be motivated by interest in the common good. The discussion of propriety leads into a consideration of social behavior which is not primarily political. Toward the end of the book, Cicero reiterates the preëminence of justice among the virtues. He holds that from a moral point of view theoretical wisdom or speculation is less significant than practical wisdom as evidenced in actions, whose moral value depends on justice or the concept of the general good. He concludes that "in choosing between moral duties, that type comes first which is involved in human society.[11]

The second and third books concern more directly moral choice by the individual. The second book ostensibly treats the expedient, called the "useful" or *utile*. It opens with a condemnation of the present ills which had arisen from subordinating the common good to personal ambition. Cicero then discusses at length various things which appear to be expedient, such as friendship, reputation, generosity, and the like, but which really depend for their ultimate validity upon their correlation with justice. Thus in a choice between actions ostensibly expedient, it will be found that a moral decision can be reached by consideration of their bearing on the common, rather than the personal, good. Cicero himself added the third book because Panaetius had not considered the conflict of moral duty, the *honestum*, and expediency, the *utile*. Though the book has been called more independent than the others and much inferior to them, it seems rather to show signs of haste and lack of finish, which might well be true of a work written in the last crowded year of Cicero's life.[12] The first part develops the topic much in the same style that characterizes the earlier books, with both Roman and Greek examples. But the latter portion becomes simply a listing of possible conflicts, not strung on any connecting theme, very legal in tone, and illustrated primarily from Roman history. The book concludes rather abruptly with an attack on the Epicurean exaltation of pleasure. The general answer has, however, been made clear, namely, that when expediency runs counter to moral duty, it is no real expediency. As in the earlier books, moral choice must subordinate the advantage of the individual to the good of society.

The political theory of Cicero as expounded in the *de Republica*, *de Legibus*, and *de Officiis* forms a consistent whole. It agrees with the political program which he developed during his active career, sought to achieve during his consulship, and maintained as an ideal throughout the succeeding decade of discouragement. In him the merging of the Hellenic and Italian cultures was complete. For two centuries this merger had been in process. The age of Cicero and of Augustus witnessed its full flowering. It endured for two further centuries before it began again to separate into its original components. In political theory, the merger meant, as has been said, the application of the Greek theory of the mixed constitution to the Roman government. Cicero was not the first to make this application. Polybius had introduced into Rome the political theory which Plato, Aristotle, and the Peripatetics had worked out. Panaetius and his pupil Poseidonius had broadened its ethical base as applied to Roman rule. The Stoic justification for rule also went back ultimately to Plato. But the Stoics had failed to solve the dichotomy implicit in Plato, namely, that the state on the one hand is an expression of human nature and natural order in the universe and on the other hand derives from the transcendental idea of justice. For the Stoics, the perfect state would be an expression of universal reason and would therefore embrace all mankind and be guided by a supremely rational ruler, or rulers, who would be "animate law" so that written codes would not be necessary. Since ideal virtue and the ideal state were manifestly unobtainable, the later Stoics admitted the importance of approximate morality and of the city-state governed by written law as an expression of reason.[13]

Cicero made an important advance. He bridged the gap between the ideal good, or transcendental justice, and practical moral duty, or the politically expedient, by an appeal to Roman legalism. Law at the lowest level expresses reason and justice in a particular human society. But particular law codes contain common principles, which are inherent in the nature of society generally. Since society is based on man's participation in the reason which permeates the universe, law common to all human societies derives from the natural law based on universal reason and justice, and hence on God. In this way, human actions cease simply to be expedient and become moral duties, prescribed in accordance with general principles based on universal and divine reason. Law, not the arbitrary will of a fallible human monarch, becomes the surest expression in society of these general principles. And politics is not the art of the possible, but the organization of society on rational principles. Both theory and experience had proved to the satisfaction of Greek and Roman political philosophers that even if, ideally, reason could find expression in a single or a few philosopher kings, in practice monarchy and aristocracy as well as democracy were likely to degenerate into government for the interest of the ruler rather than of the commonwealth. That form of government was most likely to be stable and to endure which combined the three pure forms in a mixed constitution and which, added Cicero, operated in accordance with law. The Roman government and Roman law had historically realized this best constitution.

Cicero made another significant contribution to the merger of the Greek theory of the mixed constitution with the Roman government. His political program had called for the harmonious coöperation of the well-to-do equestrians and senators, the support of all right-minded citizens, and the guiding authority of the senate. But practical experience showed Cicero that the whole senate was too large a body to act of its own initiative. Traditionally, it had followed the lead of one or more outstanding members. In the halcyon days of the second century B.C., the magnanimous Scipio the Younger had been so prominent that his influence, his *auctoritas*, prevailed throughout the state. He had truly been first citizen, *princeps*. In Cicero's own day, other such *principes*, himself and Pompey included, singly or jointly had led the senate. In this concept of the first citizen, the *princeps*, whose moral character and political wisdom commanded universal respect and who used his talents to serve the state, not personal ambition, Cicero found the answer to the need for leadership. Sulla, Caesar, and the Second Triumvirate perverted their military might, their extraordinary grants of power, and their control over the electorate to further their own ends at the expense of the Republic. Their success meant revolution. Cicero's concept of the single *princeps*, or several *principes* acting in harmony, made possible the adaptation of the mixed constitution to an imperial government.[14]

Cicero's concept of society, under Stoic influence, was more generous than had been that of Plato and Aristotle. He realized that government must be for the good of all citizens, which meant in his day all Italians, and not simply for the benefit of the governing class or monarch. He also realized that Rome's empire depended on her regard for the interest of her allies and subjects. But there were two limitations on his breadth of vision of the common weal. Despite his handling of provincial cases in the courts, he never included the provincials within the Roman state; he probably regarded them simply as an extension of the noncitizen classes whose presence was implicitly necessary for the maintenance of the city-state of Greek political experience and theory.[15] Secondly, he did not perceive that the extension of Roman citizenship to all of Italy had made the traditional city-state impossible; it meant that popular sovereignty in fact was vested in the Roman mob and that the bulk of Italian citizens were disenfranchised. On these two counts he was as blind as had been Plato and Aristotle to the impossibility of reconciling the orthodox theory of the city-state with the practical needs of imperial government. His career in the courts, assemblies, magistracies, and senate at Rome and his lack of interest in any provincial appointment made him feel that the form of government in which he had succeeded so brilliantly would itself be successful if it could be purified from the corrupting influences of noble narrowness, demagogic disunion, or military ambition, and restored to the patriotic virtue which it had displayed in earlier ages. If Cicero's concept of enlarging the mixed constitution by the leadership of a first citizen or *princeps* was to be fruitful in adapting the republic to the empire, his inability to take with Caesar an ecumenical view of membership in that empire descended as a hindrance to the effectiveness of the eventual adaptation. When finally citizenship was extended to all inhabitants of the empire in the early third century A.D., it was too late; already the mixed constitution had given way to oriental absolutism.

Cicero may be accused of lack of originality in his political theory. He may be compared to his disadvantage with Caesar, in that he was simply confirmed by his own political experience in his devotion to the traditional Roman constitution, whereas Caesar had the genius to see that Rome's imperial mission demanded an imperial government. But the Greeks and Romans attached less importance to originality as such than do moderns. For them, the advance of speculation along lines already laid down was a significant achievement. If Cicero had done no more than synthesize and put into Latin the results of the application of Greek political theory to the Roman constitution, he still would have made a great contribution to Roman thought.[16] But his treatises can lay claim to being more

than mere textbooks. They interpret political theory in the light of
experience, both the nation's and his own. The conclusions which
Cicero drew from this interpretation were to a large extent a confirmation of the orthodox theory of the mixed constitution. With
hindsight, it is easy to find faults with this conservatism. Yet the
ideal for which he strove was no mean one. It was to preserve the
sovereignty of the commonwealth, which the Romans denoted by
the word "liberty," *libertas*, and a sound government aimed at the
common good.[17] This ideal he saw being swept away by contemporary disorders in favor of an arbitrary, tyrannical dictatorship.
If he failed to recognize the new possibilities in Rome's imperial
mission, he nevertheless pointed the way for Augustus to realize
these possibilities by compromise rather than by revolution. The
Augustan compromise combined the inheritance of Caesar, concealed monarchy, with that of Cicero, the restored Republic guided
by the authority of its chief citizen, *Respublica restituta* and
auctoritas principis.

XI

CICERO AND AUGUSTUS:
PRINCIPATE AND RESTORED REPUBLIC

Cicero was executed in december of 43 b.c. for some fifteen years thereafter, Rome lacked a constitutional government. The only authority was that established by law for the Second Triumvirate in November 43 b.c. These years found Rome filled for a second time with proscriptions, bloodshed, confiscations, and civil war. First the triumvirs defeated the republicans under Brutus and Cassius at Philippi in 42 b.c. Then Octavian spent several years putting down the last of the sons of Pompey, Sextus, who had seized Sicily as a base of operations and was in control of the sea. Upon the defeat of Sextus in 36 b.c., Lepidus, the third triumvir, attempted to assert himself. But his troops deserted him and Octavian forced him into retirement. In the meantime, Antony in the East had been ensnared more by the possibilities of power than by the charms of Cleopatra, queen of Egypt. Cleopatra sought to use Antony's Roman troops to reëstablish the Eastern empire of the Ptolemies. She persuaded Antony to play the double and dangerous game of remaining a Roman magistrate and at the same time becoming a Hellenistic monarch. As relations became more strained between

Antony and Octavian, the latter turned for support to the sentiment of Italy and the western provinces. Finally, in September of 31 B.C., the rival forces of East and West met at Actium on the west coast of Greece. Antony and Cleopatra, defeated, fled to Egypt. There on the approach of Octavian they committed suicide. Once again, as in the days of Sulla and Caesar, the Mediterranean world knew a single master who had won his way to the top by arms and through blood and whose career to date seemed the negation of constitutionality.

Octavian presents a psychological riddle which will probably never be solved. He appeared on the Roman scene at the age of only eighteen. By cool-headed and cold-blooded political maneuvers, he won both the inheritance of Caesar and the support of Cicero. Yet he dropped his republican pretensions when interest dictated a union with Antony and Lepidus, and he acquiesced in, if he did not actively promote, the proscriptions of which Cicero himself was a victim. He put away his wife Scribonia, reputedly on the very day on which she bore him a daughter. This was perhaps not too extreme by contemporary standards. But he forced a distinguished senator, Tiberius Claudius Nero, to divorce his wife Livia who had already borne him one son and was about to bear another. Octavian himself then married Livia in indecent haste.[1] Writers of later generations have preserved stories which portray Octavian as a jester toward the gods, heartless toward his associates, and wanton in his habits. This dark picture of the young Octavian may preserve to some extent malicious misrepresentations of his actions by contemporary enemies. In political dispute, the Romans did not spare the personal characters of their opponents. Certainly Octavian handled his political career with a cautious self-interest which may have been ruthless when ruthlessness was necessary but which seems always to have regarded public opinion. In a city where everything became a matter of public gossip neither irreligion nor immorality would have passed unnoticed. Moreover, Octavian remained faithful until death to the wife whom he had so precipitately married early in 38 B.C.

During the nearly forty-four years that elapsed from the battle of Actium until his death at the age of seventy-six on August 19, A.D. 14, Octavian established a form of government which brought two centuries of peace and prosperity to the Roman world. His achievement so impressed succeeding generations that despite the changes and interruptions which dislocated the political continuity of western Europe, later monarchs derived their titles from those which were bestowed on Octavian. At the same time, he so won the respect and affections of the inhabitants of the empire that both during his life and after his death they honored him as no later ruler was to be honored. The Romans of the declining empire could wish their rulers no higher fortune than to be more fortunate than Augustus, better than Trajan: *felicior Augusto, melior Traiano.*[2]

Modern historical scholarship has generally followed the picture of Octavian given by Tacitus and Suetonius, who wrote at the beginning of the second century A.D. John Buchan, for instance, makes him out to have been calculating and selfish, a man who realized that for propaganda purposes he must veil his absolutism behind a popular front. Ronald Syme's *Roman Revolution* gives an even more cynical portrayal of him as the ward boss who made good and adopted a garb of respectability to cover his past. Yet it may be questioned whether even if a ruler can fool part of the people part of the time, he can fool all of the people all of the time; that is, whether so successful a political and personal achievement as was that of Octavian could rest upon a fraudulent base. That problem, however, is not of direct concern to the present discussion.

Julius Caesar had run foul of two sentiments, the selfish interests of the nobles and the feeling of superiority of the Italians to the rest of the world. To these may be added a third, particularly represented by Cicero, namely, the belief in the orthodox theory of the city-state as applied to the Roman constitution. To all of these sentiments, Caesar's plans for an ecumenical government responsible to him alone and in which everyone else would be equally a subject did violence. When the jealous nobles assassinated Caesar, Antony, who took up his plans, even further outraged Italian and Roman national feeling. He, unlike Caesar, openly made himself into a Hellenistic monarch, though the name of king had for centuries been anathema to Romans. He also presumed to dispose of the provinces of the Roman people as he personally saw fit. His cavalier treatment of his wife, Octavian's sister Octavia, and his affair with Cleopatra, whom he seems to have married without dissolving his previous marriage to Octavia, also deeply offended Roman moral feeling and national pride.[3]

Octavian learned his lesson from the mistakes of Caesar and Antony. As the term of the triumvirate drew to a close, he suppressed more and more any outward reference to it. When the break with Antony came, Octavian secured election to the consulship for 31 B.C. and appealed to Italy and to the western provinces to take an oath to support him against the renegade. Thus he based his leadership no longer on an extraordinary *imperium* but on a constitutional magistracy supported by the psychological appeal of a religious oath. He continued to hold the consulship through 23 B.C. But in his own record of his achievements, called the *Res Gestae Divi Augusti* or, from the city of Ankara in Turkey where an inscribed copy was first discovered, the *Monumentum Ancyranum*, he attributed his control of the state during the years immediately following Actium not to any legal power or magistracy but to "universal consent," *per consensum universorum potitus rerum omnium.*[4] This phrase recalls Cicero's concept of government with the support of the *consensus bonorum.* In the year 27 B.C., Octavian offered to resign all his offices but the senate refused and a compromise was worked out which gave due recognition to the sentiments by offending which Caesar and Antony had come to grief. This compromise at least outwardly could be called a "Restoration of the Commonwealth," a *Respublica Restituta.* The term *Respublica* had become identified with the traditional government of the Senate and Roman people. Cicero's idealization of this government in his *de Republica* undoubtedly did much to establish the concrete denotation of a phrase which had previously connoted the general commonwealth under any form of government. In gratitude for this settlement, the senate formally conferred on Octavian the new title of *Augustus*, by which he has since been known. Octavian now shed the last element of his original, private name and replaced it with his new honor, to become *Imperator Caesar Augustus*. The three elements of this name, which exactly parallel those of a normal Roman name, like Marcus Tullius Cicero, deserve a moment of consideration.

The word *imperator* indicated originally the holder of a military command or *imperium*. In the early republic, it had become customary for a successful general to be saluted by his troops as *Imperator* and to retain this as a title at least until his triumph. During the first century B.C., recipients of such salutations retained the title permanently as what the Romans called an *agnomen*, or honorific epithet, an addition to their regular three names. Michael Grant, in his book *From Imperium to Auctoritas*, concludes from a study of some rare bronze coins issued between 46 and 44 B.C. by the sons of Pompey after their father's death that they regarded him as having possessed this title in some peculiar capacity. They spoke of themselves as *Imperator filius*, that is, not "the son of the *Imperator*" but "*Imperator* the Younger." In the same way they perpetuated Pompey's *agnomen* of *Magnus*, "The Great." As was pointed out in an earlier chapter, Pompey received an unusual *imperium* for his war against the pirates and for his campaign against Mithridates, namely, a command equal to that of the governors of the provinces over which he was given control. In 57 B.C. it was proposed, though not carried, that he be given an *imperium* superior to those of governors of any province from which Rome drew her grain. In consequence of the conference of Luca in 56 B.C., he was awarded the command of Spain but permitted, contrary to precedent, to remain in Rome and govern by deputies, or *legati*. And in 52 B.C. he held a sole consulship, in fact a revival of the originally monarchical *imperium* and a disguised dictatorship. In all these ways, as well as by his outstanding victories, Pompey might have been regarded as an exceptional *Imperator*. Sextus Pompey went a step further and prefixed *Imperator* to his name in the form *Imperator Sextus Magnus*. Noteworthy in this form is the abandonment of the gentile name of *Pompeius* and the use of *Magnus* in its place.[5]

Octavian improved on the Pompeian usage by abandoning his adoptive personal name *Gaius* in favor of *Imperator* but in retaining the family *cognomen* of *Caesar*, with all that it meant in connecting him with the great dictator. Thus *Imperator* became for him a personal name. During the period of the triumvirate, it probably retained its connotation of his unusual command. After 27 B.C. it tends to vanish from the coins. Hence it is possible, though not certain, that thereafter he regarded it simply as his official first name, without further connection with his *imperium*. Certainly he added after his names and among his ordinary titles separate numbered salutations for his victories. None of Augustus' immediate successors used *Imperator* as a *praenomen*. Presumably they felt that it had a personal connection with him as well as that, in the words attributed to Tiberius, it meant command over troops and not leadership of citizens.[6] Nero, who first revived its use, prefixed it to his personal name. It is with this revival that the term became a title rather than a name. As such it has been used continuously; witness the modern derivative "emperor." In conclusion, therefore, the retention of *Imperator* by Augustus as his first name, whether or not directly connected with his retention of any unusual command or *imperium*, presented him to the public as the commander-in-chief of the armies.

Caesar became, as has already been indicated, almost the name of a new *gens*.[7] There were other *Iulii* and the new master of Rome wanted only members of his own family to share in a connection with the ruler. Possibly he expected the House of the Caesars to become a dynasty like that of the Ptolemies, Seleucids, or Antigonids. Certainly his attempt in arranging for the succession to combine a family relationship to himself with grants of imperial powers indicate that he was not blind to the influence over the public mind of a hereditary claim to rule. It is equally significant that in indicating his paternity, after the Roman fashion, he did not call himself "son of Julius" but "son of the deified one," *divi filius*. Since Romulus, only one Roman, Caesar, had been deified, so the person meant could not be in doubt. This superhuman paternity encouraged the tendency evident at all levels of society to regard Augustus as endowed with divine power if not actually a god himself.[8]

The name *Augustus*, granted to Octavian in 27 B.C., had theretofore been an epithet reserved for the gods. The senate considered calling Octavian *Romulus* because he had refounded Rome. But it finally settled on the new title, with its divine overtones not only of one who was increased or exalted but also of one who, like a god, brought increase and prosperity to others through the peace which he had established. Under the republic, such honorific titles as *Africanus*, *Felix*, or *Magnus* had been bestowed formally or informally, and had been placed by their recipients after their full Roman names. The titles had also descended in the recipients' families. Sextus Pompey was perhaps the first to take the further step of substituting *Magnus*, the title which he inherited from his father, for the family name *Pompeius*, unless the coins mentioned above show simply an abbreviation of his name by the omission of *Pompeius*. When the young Octavius entered into the family of Julius Caesar by posthumous adoption, he had, in the customary fashion, taken his adoptive father's name but retained his original family name in the derivative form by which he is generally called during the period of the triumvirate, *Octavianus*. Scipio the Younger had kept his natural father's family name in the form *Aemilianus*. But Octavian now determined to slough off the last evidence of his status as a private individual. Instead of adding *Augustus*, he substituted it for *Octavianus*. Thus his three names indicated that a new family had come into being, the *Caesares Augusti*, of which the founder was the deified Julius and he himself, the *Imperator*, was the second member.[9]

The names adopted by Augustus as his personal designations show, therefore, a deliberate attempt on his part to set himself apart from other humans, to eliminate all trace of his original private status, and to make himself into the representative or founder of a dynasty of Caesars who were permanently connected with victorious command, who were descended from a deified ancestor, and who were themselves more august than ordinary mortals. While the form of Augustus' name remained purely Roman and while precedents for his substitution of titles for personal names could be found in the later republic, and particularly in the career of Pompey, the great champion of the Senate and Roman People, nevertheless the real precedents for the suppression of his original personal names in favor of official or hereditary ones is to be sought in the Hellenistic monarchies. In this way, as in his concern with the succession, Augustus showed clearly that he meant the position which he had created to be a permanent part of the Roman constitution and that he realized, as Caesar had, that some such monarchical figure was a necessary focus for the government of Rome over her Mediterranean subjects.

If, then, Augustus conceived that the Roman state needed a permanent and controlling individual at its center properly to fulfill its imperial function, the question may well be asked whether he could boast, either sincerely or insincerely, that he had restored the Republic, since "Republic" meant, as has been stated, the sovereignty of the Senate and Roman People and the actual direction of affairs by the Senate. In answer, several points may be made. In 27 B.C., Augustus, outwardly at least, withdrew from any extraordinary powers which he had previously possessed and received from the senate the specific function of governing those provinces which still required the presence of considerable military forces. On the model of Pompey, he was allowed to appoint delegates, *legati*, to command these provinces and armies on his behalf while he remained at Rome. Whether or not he was also granted a command superior to those held by the senatorial governors of provinces over which he did not have direct control is much disputed. Certainly if he did have such a *maius imperium*, as it would have been called, he used it as seldom as possible and only when an emergency seemed to require his immediate intervention. Moreover, apart from his retention of *Imperator* as a first name, he suppressed all reference to his military command, or *imperium*, in his official titles. And even *Imperator* was little used after 27 B.C. on the coinage. He does not even call himself *proconsul*, a title which his governorship of provinces might have justified. Augustus made every effort to put behind him the arbitrary and military means by which he had come to power. He knew that one of the causes for the collapse of the republic had been the rivalry of ambitious men who commanded armies devoted to them personally rather than to the state. He saw that the only safeguard against this danger was to concentrate the command of the troops in the hands of a single continuing commander-in-chief. But he did his utmost to guarantee that his successors, like himself, should derive their command from the state, represented by the senate, and should exercise it as servants, not masters, of the commonwealth.

Augustus, by ceasing to hold the consulship annually after 23 B.C., made a wise move toward further conciliating senatorial prejudice. Many senators felt that they came of far nobler and more ancient stock than he did. They were understandably irked that they should be inferior to him. Had he continued to monopolize one consulship annually, he would have excluded many nobles from an office to which they felt that they had a hereditary right.[10] Augustus was wise enough, warned by Caesar's mistake, to recognize this pride of position and to withdraw from apparent competition with the nobles. Indirectly he exercised certain controls over the careers of senators so that no one could get ahead if he disapproved. But there is little evidence that he used these controls for any other purpose than to see to it that those who rose to the highest offices were not unworthy of them. At least outwardly the traditional system of elections remained in force. Augustus also catered to tradition by conducting several revisions of the senate in the course of which those who had gotten in improperly during the period of Caesar and the triumvirs were persuaded to withdraw or were stricken from the lists. Thus its numbers were reduced from nearly a thousand to the six hundred established by Sulla. Augustus did all in his power to stimulate the senate to active performance of its function as the body in which public policy could be debated and shaped.

If the senate failed to play its part, the reason for this was not, as Tacitus implies, that Augustus left it only a show of liberty, but rather that whether he would or no, his personality and his opinions were bound to dominate. This became particularly true when, with the passage of time, he became an almost legendary elder statesman in a body most of whose members were his juniors and few of whom had been active in politics at a period when he did not dominate the state. Also, the conditions of peace and prosperity which Augustus created afforded no challenge for ambitious and public-spirited men. There was an increasing temptation for the senators to go through the motions of a public career but actually to sit back and let the emperor handle the administration while they enjoyed themselves. The compromise which Augustus reached with the sentiments of senatorial pride and the belief in the orthodox theory of the city-state was in no sense, as Mommsen maintained, a sharing of power between equals. Sovereignty rested ultimately with the "Senate and Roman People," the traditional term for the corporate body politic. Augustus restored the senate to its ancient position as the aristocratic and guiding element in this corporate body. Augustus himself was simply an agent assigned specified powers by the Senate and Roman People to fulfill certain assigned functions. If in the end the servant became master, this occurred because it is only human nature to resign the conduct of affairs to one who has the will, the ability, and the means for effective decision and execution.

Augustus apparently felt that something was lacking to him when, after 23 B.C., he had no official contact with the Senate and Roman People other than as commander of various provinces. He had already received various privileges which stemmed from the tribunate. As a patrician, he could not be tribune and in any case it would have ill become his dignity to be one of a college of ten, the other members of which were young men on the second rung of their official career. He therefore used the Roman device of separating competence from office, and had conferred upon himself a "tribunician power." This *tribunicia potestas* connected him sentimentally with the champions of popular freedom in Roman history. He became the last in the long line of those who had fought for the interests of the plebs against the patricians, the masses against the nobles. This power entitled him to bring motions before the senate and legislation before the assemblies and to intervene in the administration of justice to defend the lowly. The major political and social reforms which Augustus attempted were effected by laws passed in the assemblies. The fact that these were known as Julian laws, *leges Iuliae*, shows not only that he himself moved them in virtue of the tribunician power but that when he thus acted in a popular guise he preserved the Julian name and all its associations with what the dictator had sought to do for the Roman people. Augustus also did much to ameliorate the condition of the Roman masses, by providing them with food, amusements, and public buildings, and by reorganizing the administration of the city of Rome. His policy throughout the empire was to maintain the Roman citizens in a preferred position and to extend their privileges only charily to non-Romans. The tribunician power was given great prominence by Augustus in that he numbered the years of his control of the state by it. The actual powers and privileges

which it entailed he might have received separately or exercised
informally. Its importance, therefore, lay not in any concrete
addition to his position but in the sentimental aura with which it
surrounded him. It represents his compromise with the third of
the sentiments which had opposed Caesar and Antony — the feeling
that the Romano-Italic conquerors of the empire were entitled to a
preferred position therein.

In the record of achievement which Augustus left to be inscribed in front of his tomb, the *Res Gestae* already mentioned,
he says that after 27 B.C. he was only the equal in power of his
colleagues in various offices but excelled all in authority: *post id
tempus auctoritate omnibus praestiti.*[11] Since the turn of the century,
students of the Augustan principate have retreated further and
further from the legalistic approach by which Mommsen, in the last
century, sought to base the position of Augustus on specific powers.
They have increasingly traced the source of his control and influence to informal and psychological factors. Chiefly emphasized
among these factors has been his *auctoritas*. It has come to be realized that his control over the state was far wider than his actual
powers would justify and that this control rested on the fact that
what he said carried weight whether or not he had any legal title
to command. Respect for persons of eminence in the state had been
a feature of the Roman constitution since a very early period.
Cicero had attached great importance to the *auctoritas* of the leading citizens, the *principes*. Beginning with Augustus, the number
of senatorial decrees which are mentioned as having been initiated
by the emperor, *auctore Caesare*, steadily increases. It may well be
that the tribunician power was the prime vehicle for the emperor's
auctoritas in this limited sense, though Augustus was granted the
right to introduce motions into the senate independently of that
power. Moreover, his *auctoritas* was far wider in scope than this.
Even if he held an overriding military power, a *maius imperium*,
undoubtedly much that he did to reform administration, to give
instructions to other magistrates and governors not directly re-

sponsible to his *imperium*, and generally to direct and control all branches of the government was accepted simply because of the respect felt toward him, because of his *auctoritas*.

When Augustus himself speaks of his status in his own record of his achievements, he uses the phrase *me principe*, "under me as prince." [12] Just as it is hard for moderns to divest the name *Imperator* of the connotations which cluster around "emperor," so it is difficult not to translate *princeps* as "prince." But the word originally meant simply "first citizen" or "leading man." It had no legal or constitutional significance — even less, indeed, than had the name *Imperator* with its implication of an *imperium*. Augustus, therefore, conceived of himself as first among equals, excelling others not in power but in influence. The terms *princeps* and *auctoritas* are complementary. Both portray Augustus rather as an elder statesman, who constantly exercised his influence for the good of the state, than as a dictator, king, or emperor.

The discussion of the position of Augustus and the compromise which he effected between the need for a monarchical head of the empire and the sentiment which enshrined Rome's republican constitution in the minds of his contemporaries may seem a far cry from Cicero's devotion to the city-state and his relative blindness to the empire. But analogies are at once apparent between the ideals for which Cicero strove and the achievements of Augustus. The oath which Italy and the western provinces took to support Octavian against Antony and the *consensus universorum* which acknowledged his control of the state recall Cicero's rallying of all good men in support of the constitution against Catiline. Augustus, by purging the senate of unworthy members, restored its character as a council of the best men in the state, the *optimi* or *optimates*. He admitted implicitly that to a considerable extent such *optimates* were to be found in the families who had traditionally possessed the wealth and leisure to devote themselves to the public service, the *nobiles*, but he did not close a public career to talent wherever found. Moreover, he finally integrated the equestrian order into

the public service by cutting down on the possibilities of private
tax contracting and by employing the equestrians in his own administration. The equestrian order became, in fact, a training ground
from which under the early Empire the senate steadily recruited
its losses. Thus Augustus achieved the *concordia ordinum*, the
harmony between these two orders.

The "Restored Republic" of Augustus outwardly represented
a close approximation to the ideal mixed constitution of Cicero's
de Republica and of orthodox Greek theory. The magistrates re-
gained the dignity which they had lost in twenty years of civil
war; the senate served as the chief council of state; and the popular
assemblies retained, under careful control, the sovereign rights of
legislation and of election to office. In addition — and here the
parallel to Cicero is most startling — Augustus added to the aristocratic mixed constitution a supplementary element. This was not a
monarch but a sort of prime minister. The fifth book of Cicero's
de Republica is unfortunately so fragmentary that scholars are not
agreed on the exact contents. Certainly Cicero had begun it with
emphasis on the importance of character in the leaders of the state
and had gone on to the principles and objectives necessary for such
leaders.

In a letter to Atticus, Cicero speaks of a *moderator rei publicae*,
a controller of the state, whose aim should be the happy life of all
citizens, *beata civium vita*. Elsewhere he speaks of a *rector et
gubernator civitatis*, a ruler and helmsman of the state. St. Augustine alludes to Cicero's discussion of the education suited for a chief
citizen in the state: *ubi loquitur de instituendo principe civitatis*.
The medieval author Peter of Poitiers, whose fuller text suggests
that he may have had access to the same passage independently
of St. Augustine's allusion, uses the same words: *principem civitatis*.
Whether or not Cicero himself actually used the word *princeps*
in this context has been much debated. Discussion has also raged
over the problem whether he conceived of his *moderator, rector*, or
gubernator as a single chief of state or whether there might be

several at once. It has been pointed out already that elsewhere in his works he speaks often of the *principes civitatis*, referring to the leading men in the senate, or calls an individual leader like Pompey a *princeps*. The safest conclusion seems to be that the fifth book of the *de Republica* followed closely Plato's discussion of the philosopher king and that just as Plato thought that there would be one or at most few who are fully qualified to be trained to this exalted position, so Cicero conceived of his leaders as a limited group but not necessarily a single figure. However, it is clear that he regarded certain figures in Roman history as so outstanding that they overtopped in authority even contemporary *principes*. Such men were his hero, Scipio the Younger, or himself as consul, or Pompey as the leader of the constitutional party against Caesar.[13]

Augustus himself speaks of an embassy sent to meet him by vote of the senate in 19 B.C. and composed of magistrates and other "chief men," *principibus viris*. Suetonius twice refers to Augustus along with other *principes* in the state. Later writers continued to recognize that there might be other "chief men" in the state, even though *princeps* was reserved, in the ordinary parlance, for the emperor himself. Thus Augustus did not mean his principate to be uniquely exclusive; he was an outstanding man in the state but there might be room for others of prestige and influence. Yet he never intended 'that there should be more than one possessed of the plenitude of powers vested in him. The rivalry of the republican *principes* when they exercised power as well as influence had proved disastrous to the state.[14]

A resemblance to Cicero's concept of his *principes* as men of outstanding virtue is the emphasis which Augustus laid on his own virtues. The traditional ones of fortitude, wisdom, valor, and temperance appear in Augustus' own record, the *Res Gestae*, as fortitude, clemency, justice, and piety. These virtues, particularly the typically Roman virtue of *pietas*, are also those which characterize Aeneas in the epic in which Virgil allegorically represented the ideals of the Augustan age. The same or similar virtues recur constantly in the propaganda put out by succeeding emperors. Augustus keenly desired good repute in the eyes of his contemporaries, which Cicero had held out as the highest satisfaction for the statesman. Augustus took great pleasure in testimonials of popular esteem, whether they were embodied in official acts, such as the bestowal on him of the title *pater patriae*, or in the unofficial demonstrations which so often greeted him on his public appearances. Augustus' elaborate directions for his burial and the deification which he was accorded exemplify Cicero's doctrine, in the *Dream of Scipio*, that a great statesman should seek the reward of glory in the memory of following generations and in the afterworld.[15]

The question whether Cicero's *de Republica* had any direct effect upon the Augustan principate has exercised scholars ever since the trend away from Mommsen's views attached increased significance to the republican aspects in Augustus' compromise and to his own presentation of himself as *princeps*. The distinguished German historian of the ancient world, Eduard Meyer, proposed in a book on Caesar and Pompey first published in 1918 that Cicero wrote the *de Republica* definitely with Pompey in mind, since in the late fifties B.C. Pompey had become the leading figure on the side of the senate, the champion of constitutionality against Caesar's drive for one-man power. According to Meyer, Augustus modeled his position on that held by Pompey, that of a leading citizen, a *princeps*, to whom the senate granted special powers to carry out certain functions on behalf of the state. Hence Cicero's influence on Augustus was, in Meyer's opinion, at second hand. Richard Reizenstein, in a paper published in 1917 on "The Idea of the Principate in Cicero and Augustus" maintained that the influence of the *de Republica* on Augustus was direct. Richard Heinze, in 1924, suggested that Cicero's treatise was simply a political program which envisaged, if anybody, himself as the *princeps*. There is truth in all of these positions. Cicero clung to his hope in Pompey despite many disappointments and much dissatisfaction. Pompey's popularity with both people and troops and his support of the senate despite his own unconstitutional powers seemed to Cicero the only hope for the constitution against both the demagogues, like Clodius, and the militarists, like Caesar. Yet when Cicero set the discussion of the ideal commonwealth in the heroic age of Scipio the Younger, he must have meant the discussion to be taken as a general statement of his own political ideal. Even if initially he labored for its realization under Pompey's leadership, the failure of Pompey did not vitiate its general applicability. Cicero's speeches before Caesar suggest that he even hoped that his ideal might transform the dictator into a prince. He could hardly have expected that the young Octavian, cold, self-seeking, and ruthless, would in the end realize so far as was practical his concept.[16]

The ambitious youth Octavian not only deserted Cicero's cause for that of Caesar's successor, Antony, but he even agreed to the execution of his former protector. Yet Plutarch relates how, many years later, Augustus came upon one of his grandsons reading a work of Cicero. The youth, fearful lest this devotion to the great republican would anger the emperor, tried to conceal the roll. His grandfather, however, took the roll, perused it, and said, "My boy, this was a learned man and a lover of his country." Plutarch goes on to say that for the consulship of 30 B.C., following the battle of Actium, Augustus joined with himself Cicero's son Marcus and that during this consulship the senate ordered the removal of the statues of Anthony, abolished the honors voted to him, and decreed that no Antonius should thereafter bear the personal name of Marcus. Thus, concludes Plutarch, the final punishment of Antony was, by divine intervention, left to the family of Cicero. Plutarch's stories, if true, indicate that the mature Augustus repented of the cruelty of the young Octavian. Augustus was, in fact, tolerant of the expression of republican sentiments by such figures as the orator and patron of letters Pollio or the historian Livy.[17] His tolerance is of a piece with his general compromise with the traditional republic. Perhaps the parallels which can be drawn between the "Restored

Republic" with a *princeps* as established by Augustus and the *de Republica* of Cicero are due simply to the fact that Cicero's concept expressed so closely the general pattern both of orthodox Greek political theory and of Roman traditional institutions, as these had come together in the second century B.C. But the rather close similarity between Augustus' position as *princeps* and the fragments of Cicero's fifth book, particularly the emphasis on authority, virtue, and glory, strongly suggest that Cicero's treatise had a direct influence on Augustus. A deliberate use of Cicero would coincide well with Augustus' effort to concilate the republican feelings still strong among senators and other Roman citizens.

Tacitus, writing nearly a century after the death of Augustus, opened his history of the immediately succeeding emperors with a balanced estimate of Augustus. Tacitus' own opinion obviously lay with the critics who accused Augustus of drawing to himself all the functions of laws, magistrates, senate, and people, and of concealing monarchy under the spurious name of a republic. At the death of Augustus, says Tacitus, there were few who remembered the Civil Wars and almost none who remembered the republic of Cicero's time. Just as Cicero looked back to the second century B.C., so the early empire looked back to the last days of the republic as those of freedom ranged against tyranny. Tacitus viewed Augustus in the light of his successors who, according to him, had one common trait, whether they were villains or fools — they all ruled in despite of the senate and usually in opposition to it. Tacitus failed to realize that the abdication of power by the senate, which he regarded as the loss of traditional Roman freedom, *libertas*, may equally have been its own fault. The senate of the empire failed to live up to the responsibilities laid upon it by Augustus. It wasted its energy in petty caviling at an imperial control which its own ineptitude necessitated.[18]

XII

CONCLUSION

THE ROMAN EMPIRE IS COMMONLY DATED FROM AUGUSTUS. FROM
a practical and organizational point of view, however, it developed
continuously from Rome's first expansion overseas, not to say from
her first conquests in Latium itself. Augustus regularized the administration of the empire and made many improvements in the hap-
hazard structure and methods which had grown up during previous
centuries. Undoubtedly he was much influenced by innovations of
Caesar, of Pompey, and of earlier Roman statesmen who had
coped with the problems of empire. He borrowed much, also, from
the practices of the Hellenistic monarchies. But in the main lines
of his organization of the empire, and of society within the empire,
he was conservative. If he administered a block of provinces, as
Pompey had done, in virtue of an unusually wide *imperium*, he
received this *imperium*, and in fact all his powers, from the Senate
and Roman People. He left an equally large block of provinces to
direct administration by the senate, even though he may have
intervened from time to time in the senate's sphere, whether through
his *auctoritas* or because his *imperium* was superior to that of the

senatorial governors or by special request of the senate. He preserved the favored position of Romans and Italians with respect to
other subjects of Rome and he particularly exalted the senate. He
sought to revive the traditional Roman virtues and faiths. In all
of this he was not so much an innovator as a traditionalist; he made
the minimum of alterations and reforms necessary to ensure effective government and to obviate the difficulties which the acquisition of an empire had created for the Roman state.

The preceding chapters have not, however, been concerned to
show in what respect the Augustan empire as an institution represented either a continuation of the past or something new. Nor
have they attempted to trace the sources of Augustus' thought as
regards the solution of problems of organization and administration or even of his own powers. They have been devoted to the
challenge presented to political theory by the *de facto* need of
governing areas larger than the self-sufficient city-state. It has been
their contention that the failure of political thinkers in the Hellenistic and Roman periods adequately to meet this challenge is ultimately more significant than any success or failure in solving the
new needs for government and administration. Thus the historical
background has been presented only in so far as it seems to explain
the development of political theory. Much has been done already to
show the debt of Augustus and the emperors who succeeded him
to previous political experience in ecumenical government; more
undoubtedly could be drawn from both Hellenistic and Roman
sources, particularly indeed from the practical information which
Cicero himself gives concerning provincial matters. These chapters
have tried merely to trace the effect of the political theory of the
city-state on the form which Augustus gave to the constitution of
the Roman world state.

The principate of Augustus came at the end of some five centuries of political thought and experience. Athens first tried to
combine "freedom," in the sense of the self-expression of man as a
political animal through the city-state, with empire. She succeeded

only in establishing the mastery of one city-state over others and in bringing upon all Greece a ruinous war from which neither the people nor the city-state form of government fully recovered. Her historical failure, however, was so overshadowed by her cultural achievement that Greek political thought never escaped from the tyranny of the orthodox concept of the city-state as the one possible social environment for the complete self-realization of man through his essentially human faculty of reason. The excesses of the Athenian democracy induced, to be sure, a reaction of political thought toward advocacy of a conservative, aristocratically dominated government, expressed in the doctrine of the mixed constitution. When the expansion of the Greek world demanded larger political entities, these took the practical form of monarchies because no effective thought had been devoted even to the existing alternative of federation. Attempts were made to develop theoretical justifications of monarchy, either along the traditional approach of the Near East that the king is a divine ruler over servile subjects in an ecumenical empire, or according to the Stoic doctrine that the wise ruler is an expression of universal reason and that all men are equally citizens of one, universal commonwealth. Such attempts, however, made little headway against the dominance of the orthodox theory of the city-state.

The later Stoics abandoned their universal political ideal and returned to the traditional mixed constitution. In it they saw, with Plato, the expression of natural reason and justice. When the Greeks were faced with the phenomenon of Rome, they found a practical explanation for her success in the close approximation of her government, the result of historical development, to the theoretical ideal of the mixed constitution. But Greek political thinkers never achieved a satisfactory theoretical pattern which would relate the republican system of government to Rome's imperial mission. Thus during the last century of the Roman republic, disruptive stresses were created within the constitution by the problem of ruling the empire. Two main solutions emerged. The obvious one, to sub-

stitute for the existing constitution a monarchy on the Hellenistic
model, ran counter to the whole tradition of ancient political
thought as well as to the prejudices both of the senatorial nobles
and of the Romano-Italic citizen body. These prejudices were
strong enough to prevent Caesar and Antony from completely revo-
lutionizing the Roman government along monarchical lines. The
only alternative seemed to be to perpetuate the Roman city-state
in a position of mastery over the Mediterranean world. If so, pre-
cautions were necessary to avoid the evil end to which imperial
Athens had come. It had to be ensured that Rome's government
should embody wisdom and justice.

Cicero was conscious of this need not only within the Roman
state but in the relations between Rome and her allies or subjects.
He offered a solution which went beyond that of his Stoic, Academic, and Peripatetic predecessors. He recognized the importance
of written law not as a second-best substitute for the "animate law"
by which the ideal, all-wise ruler might give expression to universal
reason, but as in its own right an approximate expression in a particular society of the basic principles of all human society and
therefore, since man's participation in the divine attributes of reason
and speech made human society possible, of the universal, divine
reason. This solution provided a necessary link between the ideal
state of Greek political theory and the practical state achieved by
men. It would have been more fruitful, however, had Cicero related the source of law more closely to the exercise of popular
sovereignty. He, like the Greeks, held that sovereignty must rest
ultimately with the whole community and must be expressed in the
popular assemblies. But the Roman constitution, even more than the
conservative Greek city governments of the Hellenistic period,
limited this expression of popular sovereignty to the acceptance or
rejection of what the wisdom of the intelligent and well-to-do, the
senate and, in particular, the leading citizens, put before the assemblies. Not the voice of the people but the wisdom of the leaders
expressed the "voice of God." Moreover, even the limited popular

sovereignty allowed by Cicero had already been rendered unreal by the extension of Roman citizenship far beyond the limits possible for its effective exercise in the Aristotelian sense of being governed and governing in turn. This unreality was concealed because, though sovereignty rested with the people, actual government was vested by Cicero in the senate, supported by the equestrians and led by the far-sighted wisdom of leading citizens, the *principes*.

Augustus faced the practical problem of compromising between the necessity for an imperial government which, in terms of thinking with which he was familiar, could only be monarchical, and the traditions and prejudices of the Roman republic, whose strength had balked Caesar and enabled Augustus himself to defeat Antony. He achieved this compromise. He restored the Republic, with its apparatus of magistrates, senate, and assemblies and its favored position of Roman citizens vis à vis the subject peoples. But he developed Cicero's concept of a leading citizen, a *princeps*, into that of an extraordinary official, a person who received special powers from the Senate and Roman People to perform certain functions on their behalf, notably to unify the command of their armies under a proconsular *imperium* superior to those of other governors, covering many provinces, and held, with titular renewals, for life. The "prince" moreover actually kept a guiding hand on all the affairs of state by his prestige and influence, his *auctoritas*.

The fault in the Augustan compromise did not lie, as Tacitus and most modern critics have held, in the fact that it afforded an opportunity for monarchy to develop at the expense of the republic. It is a tribute to the political acumen of Augustus that the structure which he erected to meet one set of premises was able to adapt itself to the gradual change toward a totally different concept of government. The government of the Roman empire achieved its most effective balance during the second century of our era. By then, the emperor was frankly recognized as the head of the state. The senate no longer consisted of a narrow group of hereditary nobles but represented the best elements drawn from all the empire. And the privileges of citizenship were rapidly being extended to all persons capable of political self-realization in a local city-state under the general oversight of the central government. To condemn Augustus because his Roman principate became in fact an ecumenical monarchy under the Antonines would be as unfair as to condemn the creators of the United States because, a century and a half later, the constitution which they established to protect states' rights against an undue growth of the federal government has become the vehicle of just the sort of centralization which they distrusted.

The fundamental fault in the Augustan compromise is one which it shared with all political theory in antiquity — its inability to escape from the orthodox view of the city-state and from the belief in the direct exercise of citizenship. Augustus failed to bridge the gulf between government and governed in the Roman empire. Neither Caesar's monarchy nor Cicero's *de Republica* offered any guidance toward solving this problem. But in the end Cicero's *de Republica*, not Caesar's monarchy, set the theoretical pattern for the Augustan principate. In this sense, Augustus fulfilled Greek political theory and Roman political experience as wedded in the political theory of Cicero. It is perhaps not too extreme a claim to hold that the greatest contribution which Augustus made to the culture of Western Europe was not the actual government under which the Roman empire flourished but the perpetuation of the ideals of Cicero. The concept of government for the sake of the whole commonwealth and the concept that sovereignty proceeded from the will of the commonwealth, not from any divine favor or brute force, were transmitted by Cicero from Greek thought to the Roman empire and the Middle Ages. To these concepts Cicero added that of the paramount rule of law. His noble ideals were frequently overriden by force during the succeeding centuries. They were often compromised with theories of absolutism and the divine right of kings. But they have not yet lost their validity.

On the other hand, it is still possible to learn also from the

weakness of Greek political theory as expressed by Cicero and
applied by Augustus. That weakness is one which Augustus attempted to offset in practice when he supplemented the mixed
constitution by the *princeps*. But the dominance of the Aristotelian
concept of the direct exercise of citizenship under the mixed constitution was such that no theoretical solution was found for active
participation by ordinary citizens in the affairs of an imperial state.
The lesson for the world of today is not, however, that this adjustment must be made. Representative democracy has achieved government of the people, by the people, and for the people on a scale
not dreamt of in antiquity. The lesson which the ultimate failure
of classical civilization in its phase of a world state teaches is that
stagnation is inevitable when orthodox political theory fails to
progress in response to changed political conditions. Today national
sovereignty dominates political thought as firmly as did the orthodox theory of the city-state with its mixed constitution in the classical world. Only in so far as individuals throughout the world are
able to conceive of a citizenship and of political participation on a
scale larger than the nation will the "one world" from which this
discussion took its departure be realized in any fruitful sense. The
alternative is that presented by the Roman empire — a government
imposed from above and divorced from the governed. Such a government has historically meant, in Toynbee's terms, stagnation and
the decay of civilization.

Notes

Selective Bibliography

Index

NOTES

INTRODUCTION

1. Matthias Gelzer briefly propounded the thesis of this book in his chapter entitled "Gibt es eine klassische Form in der politischen Entwicklung?" in *Das Problem des Klassischen und die Antike*, ed. W. W. Jaeger (Leipzig and Berlin, Teubner, 1931) 99–108. He argued that Aristole, on the basis of previous Greek political thought and experience, established the city-state as the "classical" form of the state and denied that other forms, as tribal monarchies or composite empires, were fully "states." The dominance of the Aristotelian concept prevented later political thinkers from developing a theoretical framework for the world state, whether of the Persians, of Alexander, or of the Romans. The city-state remained canonical for Cicero, Augustus, and even St. Augustine. Konrad Glaser, "Die Bewertung der Staatsformen in der Antike," *Wiener Studien* LVII (1939) 38–57, surveys the evaluation of the various types of pure constitution and the development of the concept of the mixed constitution in Herodotus, Plato, Aristotle, Polybius (from Theophrastus and Dicaearchus), and Cicero. He concludes that in all of these authors the personality of outstanding leaders outweighed the particular forms of constitutions and that the consummation of this view in Cicero directly influenced Augustus. This emphasis on the "Führerpersönlichkeit" smacks of Nazi thought.

2. Mason Hammond, "Hellenistic Influences on the Structure of the Augustan Principate," *Memoirs of the American Academy in Rome* XVII (1940) 1–24.

3. Arnold J. Toynbee, *A Study of History*, abridged by D. C. Somervell (New York and London, Oxford University Press, 1947).

4. A recent attempt to show the weakness of Cicero as a statesman and as a man is Jérôme Carcopino, *Les Secrets de la Correspondance de Cicéron* (Paris, L'Artisan du Livre, 2 vols., 1947).

5. Ernest Barker, *The Cambridge Ancient History* VI 504, quoted by permission of the Cambridge University Press.

6. The intellectual and emotional gulf between "classical" and Christian thought is well presented by C. C. Cochrane, *Christianity and Classical Culture* (London, New York, and Toronto, Oxford University Press, rev. ed. 1944). For the continuity between classical and medieval (Christian) culture, see E. K. Rand, *Founders of the Middle Ages* (Cambridge, Mass., Har-

vard University Press, ed. 2, 1928) and *The Building of Eternal Rome* (Cambridge, Mass, Harvard University Press, 1943).

I

GREEK POLITICAL THOUGHT BEFORE PLATO: MONARCHY, ARISTOCRACY, AND DEMOCRACY

1. The view that Pericles was the true "inventor" of democracy is that of J. A. O. Larsen, "Cleisthenes and the Development of the Theory of Democracy at Athens," *Essays in Political Theory Presented to George H. Sabine* (Ithaca, N. Y., Cornell University Press, 1948) 1–16. Professor Larsen has an interesting discussion of the relation between the introduction of balloting and the rise of democracy in his article on "The Origin of the Counting of Votes," *Classical Philology* XLIV (1949) 164–181.

2. Thrasymachus in Plato, *Rep.* 338 A — 354 C, especially 338 C; see also Callicles in Gorgias 483 D. These passages are discussed by J. de Romilly, *Thucydide et l'Impérialisme Athénien* etc. (Paris, Les Belles Lettres, 1947) 251–253.

3. The "Old Oligarch" on the *Constitution of the Athenians* has recently been fully handled by Hartvig Frisch (Copenhagen, Gyldendalske Boghandel, 1942; a Danish version appeared in 1941). On p. 62 he abandons the traditional dating in the late 420's in favor of a date before 432. Ernest Hohl, "Zeit und Zweck der pseudoxenophontischen *Athenaion Politeia*," *Classical Philology* XLV (1950) 25–35, also argues for a date during the Thirty Years' Peace and regards the author as a well-

to-do merchant rather than a landed aristocrat. See also a recent translation of this work and of Aristotle by L. C. Stecchini, *Athenaion Politeia: The Constitution of the Athenians* etc. (Glencoe, Ill., The Free Press, 1950), who on p. 13 dates this work in the second half of 431 B.C.

4. The relation of Thucydides to the Sophists is the theme of J. H. Finley, Jr., *Thucydides* (Cambridge, Mass., Harvard University Press, 1942). For the contrast between the political philosophies of Plato and Thucydides, see David Grene, *Man in His Pride: a Study in the Political Philosophy of Thucydides and Plato* (Chicago, University of Chicago Press, 1950).

5. Herodotus discusses the three forms of government in III 80–84. See the *Commentary on Herodotus* by W. W. How and Joseph Wells (Oxford, Clarendon Press, 1912) I 277–279; also Wells' chapter on "Herodotus and the Intellectual Life of his Age" in his *Studies in Herodotus* (Oxford, Blackwell, 1923) 183–204 and W. Nestle, *Herodots Verhaltnis zur Philosophie und Sophistik* (Stuttgart, Stuttgarter Vereinsbuchdruckerei, 1908) 28–34. For Herodotus on tyranny, see How and Wells, *Commentary* II 338–347. For Herodotus' love of freedom, see Wells, *Studies* 153; T. R. Glover, *Herodotus*

(Berkeley, Calif., University of California Press, 1924) 187–221.

6. George Grote eloquently defended the Sophists against Plato in part II chapter LXVII of his *History of Greece*. See W. W. Jaeger, *Paideia* vol. I, bk. ii, ch. 3, for an appreciation of their importance in developing a "humanistic" education but their fundamental weakness in philosophy and ethics.

7. The *Clouds* of Aristophanes is alluded to by Socrates in Plato's *Apology* 18 B, 18 D, 19 C as a prime source of the prejudice against him.

II

PLATO AND ARISTOTLE: THE ORTHODOX THEORY

OF THE MIXED CONSTITUTION

1. The origin of legal philosophy among the Greeks and particularly in Plato's later works and in his Academy is the subject of W. W. Jaeger's "Praise of Law" in *Interpretations of Modern Legal Philosophies* etc., ed. P. L. Sayre (New York, Oxford University Press, 1947) 352–375. See also G. R. Morrow, "Plato and the Law of Nature," in *Essays in Political Theory Presented to George H. Sabine* (Ithaca, N. Y., Cornell University Press, 1948) 17–44; J. P. Maguire, "Plato's Theory of Natural Law," in *Yale Classical Studies* X (1947) 151–178. C. B. Welles alludes to Plato's contribution to jurisprudence on p. 112 (esp. n. 15) of his "Economic Background of Plato's Communism" in *The Tasks of Economic History*, supplement VIII (1948) to *The Journal of Economic History*.

2. The "Constitutions" collected by Aristotle are mentioned as the one hundred forty-third item in a list of his works given by Diogenes Laertius, V 27 (Loeb ed. I 474): "constitutions of 158 (literally '2 less than 160') cities, (public) and private, democratic, oligarchic, aristocratic, and tyrannical."

This list was copied by Hesychius in a life and list preserved in a single Vatican manuscript, see Valentin Rose, *Aristotelis qui ferebantur librorum fragmenta* (Leipzig, Teubner, 1886) 9–18; the item is on p. 16 line 135: "constitutions of cities which are private and democratic and oligarchic (and) aristocratic and tyrannical, 158." The fragments are given by Rose on pp. 258–367. The "Constitution of the Athenians" as recovered from a papyrus was first published by Sir Frederick Kenyon in 1891; for later editions, see Stecchini, above, ch. I, n. 3.

3. E. von Ivanka, *Die Aristotelische Politik und die Städtegründung Alexanders des Grossen (Ungar-hellenischen Untersuchungen* IV, Budapest, 1938), was not available but the title suggests a direct connection between Aristotle's theory of the city-state and Alexander's concept that Greek culture could best be spread by the founding of city-states throughout the Near East.

4. Aristotle, *Politics* III 13.12 (1283 b 42): "A citizen is he who shares in common ruling and being ruled in

turn;" see Newman's note, in his ed. III 240, also IV 209 n. on 1295 a 34 for Aristotle's "mean constitution," that in which the moderately well-to-do hold the balance of power. Aristotle had remarked earlier, Pol. I 2.9 (1253 a 2–3) that "man is by nature a political animal," *anthropos phusei politikon zoon,* which Seneca, *de Beneficiis* VII 1.8, rendered "a social animal and born for community," *sociale animal et in commune genitus.* Compare also similar Stoic phrases, quoted by Max Pohlenz, *Die Stoa* etc. (Göttingen, Vandenhoeck und Ruprecht) II (1949) p. 66, n. on p. 115 line 14, and p. 76, first n. on p. 138.

5. F. D. Wormuth, "Aristotle on Law," in *Essays in Political Theory Presented to George H. Sabine* (Ithaca, N. Y., Cornell University Press, 1948) 45–61, concludes on p. 61 that Aristotle's "attitude towards law was thoroughly pragmatic."

6. For a reiteration of the view that, at least in the Roman period, *Alexandria ad Aegyptum* was not equivalent to *Alexandria in Aegypto,* see H. I. Bell in the *Journal of Roman Studies* XXXVI (1946) 130–132.

7. The fragments of Dicaearchus have been most recently revised and discussed by Fritz Wehrli in his *Dikaiarchus* (Basel, Schwabe, 1944), the first volume in a series of texts and commentaries of *Die Schule des Aristoteles.* The relevant fragments appear on pp. 28–29 with commentary on pp. 64–66. Photius, *Bibl.* 37 (Wehrli, frag. 71), speaks of the "mixed constitution" in which the three pure forms are combines, as *Dikaiarchikon.* This word is generally regarded as a proper adjective derived from Dicaearchus rather than as a common adjective meaning "characterized by just rule," see Martini's article on *Dikaiarchus* in *RE* V (9) col. 551 lines 9–18. *Dikaiarchia,* meaning "just rule," is however attested by Hesychius, see Liddell and Scott's *Greek Lexicon* (new ed. by H. S. Jones; Oxford, Clarendon Press, 1925 ff.) I 428 *s.v.* The theory of the "mixed constitution" is assumed to have been expounded by Dicaearchus in his *Tripolitikos,* a title mentioned by Cicero, *ad Att.* XIII 32 and by Athenaeus, IV 141 A; see Wehrli frags. 70, 72. Diogenes Laertius, VII 131, refers to the great formulator of Stoic doctrine Chrysippus, head of the School during the second half of the third century, the statement that "the best constitution is the one mixed from democracy, monarchy, and aristocracy," Hans von Arnim, *Fragmenta Stoicorum Veterum* III (Leipzig, Teubner, 1913) 175; see below, ch. iv, n. 5, and, for Panaetius, ch. vi, n. 7.

III

HELLENISTIC LEAGUES AND MONARCHIES

1. J. A. O. Larsen published a discussion of "Representative Government in the Panhellenic Leagues" in two parts in *Classical Philology* XX (1925) 313–329, XXI (1926) 52–71. Larsen argues, pp. 69–71, that in the Hellenic

League of the fourth century B.C. a true representative federation was developed in which to some extent the conflict between the concept of "free and autonomous members" and an effective central authority was solved, compare p. 324. He feels that Alexander did not continue the League because it was Panhellenic and therefore incompatible with his ecumenical aim of uniting Greeks and barbarians, and because it was incapable of extension to his whole empire since the difficulty of communications would render a central authority impossible on a worldwide scale. Reference may also be made to Professor Larsen's articles on "The Constitution and Original Purpose of the Delian League," *Harvard Studies in Classical Philology* LI (1941) 175-213, "*Consilium* in Livy xlv. 18. 6-8 and the Macedonian *Synedria*," *Classical Philology* XLIV (1949) 73-90, and "Aristotle on the Electors of Mantinea and Representative Government," *Classical Philology* XLV (1950) 180-183.

2. André Aymard's study of *Les Assemblées de la Confédération Achaienne* (Paris thesis, also published as fasc. XXI of the *Bibliothèque des Universités du Midi*, Bordeaux, Feret, 1938) is concerned with the detailed history and operation of the league, rather than with the general problem of representation and federation. Aymard doubts Larsen's arguments for representation in Greek leagues in his article "L'Orginisation de la Macéduine en 167 et le régime représentatif dans le monde grec," *Classical Philology* XLV (1950) 96-107. For double citizenship in these leagues see Mason Hammond, "*Germana Patria*," *Harvard Studies in Classical Philology* LX (1951) 147-174.

3. W. S. Ferguson has some suggestive remarks on leagues as against monarchy in the *Cambridge Ancient History* VII 7-12; his whole chapter on the "Leading Ideas of the Period," pp. 1-40, should be consulted. For the failure of political Panhellenism and federalism, which left Greece open to unification by force under the Macedonian monarchy, see Victor Martin, *La Vie Internationale* etc. (cf. bibliography), especially the final chapter, pp. 577-594, called "L'Anarchie Panhellénique." Martin concludes that, politically, Panhellenic solidarity existed only in the minds of a limited elite, which lacked influence (p. 589; cf. p. 21 for the wider consciousness of cultural homogeneity). Professor W. Y. Elliott of Harvard University suggests that the Greek concept that political rights must be exercised directly and not through elected representatives might well be compared to the similar view of Rousseau.

4. Recent studies of the concepts of divine kingship in the Near East are the relevant chapters in a volume of essays edited by Henri and H. A. Frankfort on *The Intellectual Adventure of Ancient Man* (Chicago, University of Chicago Press, 1946) and Henri Frankfort's more detailed treatment in his *Kingship and the Gods* etc. (Chicago, University of Chicago Press, 1948). See also T. H. Gaster's review article on "Divine Kingship in the Ancient Near East" in *A Review of Religions* IX (1944-1945) 267-281. The Byzantine Research Institute at Dumbarton Oaks (Washington, D. C.) organized in 1950 a conference on oriental ideas and symbols of kingship, particularly in its ecumenical aspects, and

their later influence on Roman and medieval concepts. The papers will presumably be published. For Aristotle's definition of the citizen, see above, ch. ii, n. 4.

5. Authorities differ on the degree to which the army, representing the people, played a constitutional part in the Macedonian state and it is possible that Archelaos (414–399 B.C.) considerably "democratized" the army and gave the peasants more say as against the nobles; see Geyer's article *Makedonia* in *RE* XIV (27) 712, 769–770, followed by Tarn in the *Cambridge Ancient History* VII 201–202, 751. Julius Kaerst gives a more conservative view in his *Geschichte des Hellenismus* I (Leipzig and Berlin, Teubner, ed. 2, 1917) 181–189, which is adopted by Ferguson in *CAH* VII 9.

6. The Macedonians were considered as non-Greeks down to the time of Philip; Kaerst (see n. 5) I 154–162. Kaerst argues even that Philip was made a member of the Amphiktyonic Council personally, as of Greek descent from the Heraklidae, and not as a representative of the Macedonians, who were still regarded as non-Greek.

See also Julius Jüthner, *Hellenen und Barbaren* etc. (*Das Erbe der Alten*, Neue Folge, VIII, Leipzig, Dieterich'sche VBH, 1923) 30–33.

7. The relationship, both theoretical and administrative, between Hellenistic monarchs and the city-states under their rule is the subject of a detailed study by Alfred Heuss, *Stadt und Herrscher des Hellenismus in ihrem staats- und völkerrechtlichen Beziehungen* (*Klio*, Beiheft XXXIX, neue Folge XXVI, Leipzig, Dieterich'sche VBH, 1937). The difficulty of reconciling a monarchical overlord with the tradition of the independent and self-governing city-state seemed to W. S. Ferguson, *Greek Imperialism* (Boston and New York, Houghton Mifflin Co., 1913) 145–148, the reason why Alexander introduced the deification of the ruler, in order that his interference in the city-states might be looked on as that of a god. This is perhaps an extreme and one-sided view of the reasons for Alexander's self-deification but illustrates how the monarchical practices of the Hellenistic period came into conflict with the orthodox theory of the city-state.

IV

PHILOSOPHIC JUSTIFICATIONS FOR THE HELLENISTIC MONARCHIES

1. Hellenistic attempts to establish a political theory of monarchy, which seem to have originated in "Pythagorean" and Stoic circles, are discussed by E. R. Goodenough, "The Political Philosophy of Hellenistic Kingship," *Yale Classical Studies* I (1928) 55–102.

Louis Delatte, *Les Traités de la Royauté d'Ecphante, Diotogène, et Sthénidas,* (*Bibliothèque de la Faculté de Philosophie et Lettres de l'Université de Liège* XCVII [1942]), concludes, pp. 285–288, against Goodenough that both external evidence and language and thought place these three Neo-Pythagorean treatises on the divine monarch not in the early third century B.C. but in the third century A.D., sometime between Clement of Alexandria and the commentary of Porphyry on the *Iliad*; compare p. 163. In his survey of ancient theories of monarchy, pp. 123–163, he recognizes in the Hellenistic period, pp. 137–144, an adoption of oriental ideas of the divine ruler by the Ptolemies and Seleucids (but not by the Attalids and Antigonids, pp. 139–140) but he confines political speculation on royalty particularly to the Stoics, see p. 140. Goodenough, reviewing Delatte's book in *Classical Philology* XLIV (1949) 129–131, agrees that the actual treatises may be late but still regards the thought as Hellenistic Pythagoreanism. Reference may also be made to an interesting attempt to trace the general theory of balance in constitutions to the Pythagorean doctrine of numbers, by Armand Delatte, "La constitution des États-Unis et les Pythagoriciens," *Collection d'études anciennes* (Association Guillaume Budé, Paris, Les Belles Lettres, 1948), an extract from the *Bulletins de l'Académie Royale de Belgique*, classe des lettres, 5e série, XXXIV fasc. 6.

2. The statements that the Stoics and Epicureans traced back respectively through the Cynics and Antisthenes and the Cyrenaics and Aristippus to Socrates is traditional; see, for example, F. M. Cornford in *CAH* VI 310, based ultimately on Eduard Zeller, *Socrates and the Socratic Schools* (Eng. trans. by O. J. Reichel, ed. 2, London, Longmans, Green, 1877) 50, 390–391; see also R. D. Hicks, *Stoic and Epicurean* (New York, Scribners, 1910) 9–10. Farrand Sayre, in his "Antisthenes the

Socratic," *Classical Journal* XLIII (1948) 237–244, has given good reasons to support his contention that neither Antisthenes nor Diogenes were Cynics and that the Cynic School did not appear until the third century B.C. According to Sayre, Stoics of the imperial period, seeking a connection between Zeno and Socrates, invented the descent through Antisthenes and misrepresented him completely by so doing. Sayre repeats the view that the Cynics were not Socratics throughout his *The Greek Cynics* (Baltimore, Furst, 1948); see for instance pp. 24, 95–96 (conclusion). He derived it from the opening chapter of D. R. Dudley, *A History of Cynicism* etc. (London, Methuen, 1937) 1–15. His view is contradicted by Ragnar Höistad, *Cynic Hero and Cynic King* etc. (Uppsala, no publisher, 1948) 12–15. Höistad concerns himself with the Cynic concept that the king should be solitary, poor, and suffering but with high ethical qualifications, pp. 221–222. For the influence of the concept of the ethical ruler on the official titles of Hellenistic kings, Höistad refers to Wilhelm Schubart, "Das hellenistische Königsideal nach Inschriften und Papyri," *Archiv für Papyrusforschung* etc. XII (1936/1937) 1–26.

3. Plato describes the philosopher as a traveler taking refuge from a dust storm in *Rep.* VI 496 D. In a similar vein, the Roman poet of Epicureanism, Lucretius, in his *de Rerum Natura* II 1–13, beautifully described the ideal of withdrawal as that of looking on life from calm temples built by wisdom, like one who, himself in safety, watches from afar others tossed in a storm at sea, or the conflict of opposing armies. Lucretius here anticipates the idea of

the "ivory tower," a phrase whose origin is uncertain. Burton Stevenson, in the *Home Book of Quotations* (ed. 5, New York, Dodd, Mead, 1947) 2225 no. 16a, gives as its earliest occurence Sainte-Beuve's description (in 1837) of Alfred de Vigny "comme en sa tour d'ivoire."

4. For Cicero's attitude towards Epicureanism, see J. S. Reid's preface to his edition of the *Academica* (London, Macmillan, 1885), M. N. P. Packer, *Cicero's Presentation of Epicurean Ethics* etc. (New York, Columbia University Press, 1938), and H. M. Howe, "Three Groups of Roman Epicureans," an abstract in *Transactions and Proceedings of the American Philological Association* LXXIX (1948) 341–342.

5. For the Stoic "utopia" of a commonwealth of all men, a "Kosmopolis," governed by the dictates of reason rather than by a written constitution, and the compromise which they made between this ideal and the practical demands of life in specific city-states, see Max Pohlenz, *Die Stoa* etc. (Göttingen, Vandenhoeck und Ruprecht), I (1948) 137–141 and compare above, ch. ii, n. 7 at the end for Chrysippus, and below ch. vi, n. 7 for Panaetius. How far Alexander was influenced by the concept of the brotherhood of all men has been much disputed. Besides the works cited in the bibliography, especially Tarn, *Alexander* II 399–449, see, recently, H. M. de Mauriac, "Alexander the Great and the Politics of *Homonoia*," *Journal of the History of Ideas* X (1949) 104–114, and Philip Merlan, "Alexander the Great or Antiphon the Sophist," *Classical Philology* XLV (1950) 101–161. Merlan finds the concept already formed in the fifth century B.C. Roman Stoicism under the Early Empire laid particular emphasis on the concept of the true king, the embodiment of reason who rules with the consent of and in the interest of the people, as against the tyrant; but at the same time they continued to advocate political activity by the individual, Pohlenz, pp. 285 and 313 for Seneca, 337 for Epictetus; see also C. G. Starr, Jr., "Epictetus and the Tyrant," *Classical Philology* XLIV (1949) 20–29; Mason Hammond, "Pliny the Younger's Views on Government," *Harvard Studies in Classical Philology* XLIX (1938) 121–126.

6. For Antigonus Gonatas and Stoicism, see W. W. Tarn, *Antigonus Gonatas* (Oxford, Clarendon Press, 1913) 30–36 (early association with Zeno), 230–241 (philosophers at his court), and 249–256 (Stoic character of his rule); see also his brief statement in *The Cambridge Ancient History* VII 202–203. The anecdote from Aelian, *Var. Hist.* II 20 is quoted in *Antigonus* 256, n. 122.

7. Tarn, *Antigonus* 253, nn. 114–115, quotes Suidas' article on "kingship," *basileia*, for the statement that the rule of Philip and of the *Diadochi* was based not on nature or justice but on military backing and political intelligence. Later, on pp. 255, n. 120, and 256, n. 122, he cites the same article for the use of *philanthropia* in the collection of taxes as characteristic of kingship rather than tyranny. In his article on "king," *basileus*, Suidas distinguished kingship from tyranny on the ground that the former is hereditary and limited, the latter forceful and arbitrary. These articles are nos. 144–148

under B on pp. 457–458 of Part I of *Suidae Lexicon*, ed. Ada Adler (Leipzig, Teubner, 1928), which is vol. I of an edition of the *Lexicographi Graeci*.

8. For the connection between oriental and Hellenistic monarchies and the Roman empire, see Ernest Barker's chapter on "The Conception of Empire" in *The Legacy of Rome*, ed. Cyril Bailey (Oxford, Clarendon Press, 1923) 45–89. The last sentence in the text is based on his statement on p. 71. The *lex regia* is mentioned by Ulpian as cited in Justinian, *Digest* I 4.1 pr.; see also Justinian, *Institutes* I 2.6; Gaius, *Inst.* I 5, who uses *lex de imperio* without *regia*. Theodosius II and Valentinian said in an edict of 429, Justinian, *Codex* I 14.4, that "it is a saying worthy of a ruler's majesty that a prince should profess himself bound by the laws, for our authority depends on the authority of law." Compare the statement of Severus Alexander in an edict of 232, Justinian, *Codex* VI 23.3, that "even though the *lex* of his *imperium* releases the emperor from the obligations of law, yet nothing is so appropriate to the *imperium* as to live according to the laws." See the similar statements from Paul, *Sententiae* IV 5.3 (= Justinian, *Digest* V 2.8.2) and V 12.9a (= *Dig.* XXXII 23). E. A. Thompson, in *Attila and the Huns* (Oxford, Clarendon Press, 1948) 185–186, compares the sentiments of Theodosius' edict of 429 with a story told by the historian Priscus (p. 305, dated about A.D. 449). Priscus went on a mission to Attila and in his encampment interviewed a Greek merchant who had settled among the Huns and who compared his free and easy life among them with the oppression which he had suffered in the Empire. Priscus replied that life in organized society was better than in a disorganized one and that the Empire was organized and under the rule of law, to which even the emperor was subject. Thompson comments that these are "incredibly unreal and pedantic phrases from the philosophical schools" and cites Gibbon's phrase "a feeble and prolix declamation." But the story shows that the phrases of the lawyers did represent a generally held belief, however unfounded that belief was.

V

THE DEVELOPMENT OF THE ROMAN CONSTITUTION

1. For statements on early Roman history attributed by ancient authors to Aristotle, see Valentin Rose, *Aristotelis qui ferebantur librorum fragmenta* (Leipzig, Teubner, 1886) frags. 609–610, from Dionysius of Halicarnassus I 72; Plutarch, *Quaest. Rom.* 6; Festus *s.v. Roma* (p. 269 M); and Plutarch, *Camillus* 22. Rose includes these under the four (?) books of *Nomima*, which, he suggests, were a supplement to the *Politeiai*; see his earlier edition of the fragments, *Aristoteles Pseudepigraphus* (Leipzig, Teubner, 1863) 537–538.

2. Dionysius of Halicarnassus discusses early writers on Roman history

in I 6; see generally Schanz und Hosius, *Geschichte der römischen Literatur* I 168–209.

3. The extreme skeptical position toward early Roman history and the view that no records survived the sack of Rome by the Gauls in 390 B.C. is expressed by Ettore Pais in his various critical studies, particularly in his *Storia di Roma* (Vol. I in two parts, Turin, Clausen, 1898, 1899), especially in ch. I, pp. 1–128 on the sources, and in his *Ricberche sulla storia* etc. (4 vols., Rome, Loescher, later Maglione, 1915–1921). A more conservative approach is that of H. S. Jones in *The Cambridge Ancient History* VII 312–332, ch. x on "The Sources *etc.*" Even more conservative is the study of Roman history through the beginning of the Republic by Emanuele Ciaceri, *Le Origini di Roma* (Milan etc., Soc. An. Ed. Dante Alighieri, 1937), the first chapter of which, pp. 1–46, surveys briefly the history of the modern criticism of early Roman history, and the second, pp. 47–120, the question of credibility. That the Gallic sack did not destroy the city is the conclusion drawn from a study of the remains of early buildings by L. G. Roberts, "The Gallic Fire and Roman Archives," *Memoirs of the American Academy in Rome* II (1918) 55–65.

4. For the "prehistory" of Italy, see Joshua Whatmough, *The Foundations of Roman Italy* (London, Methuen, 1937). For the archaeological evidence of conditions in early Rome, see I. S. Ryberg, *An Archaeological Record of Rome from the Seventh to the Second Century B.C.* (Philadelphia, University of Pennsylvania Press, 1940).

5. That the Tarquins were "tyrants"

in the Greek sense was argued by P. N. Ure, *The Origin of Tyranny* (Cambridge, Eng., Cambridge University Press, 1922) 215–256, 295–296. Though his general conclusion seems extreme, he makes a good case against Pais's skepticism concerning Tarquin the Elder and Servius Tullius.

6. On the name "Tullius," see *RE2* VII (13) 800 *s.v.* and 805–807 under *Tullius* 18 (Servius T.). He was said to have come from the Latin town of Corniculum, which may have lain in the hills north of Tibur (Tivoli), *RE* IV (2) 1604 *s.v.* 1.

7. Tenney Frank argued that the history of the early Roman republic was much adapted to fit conditions in the late second and early first centuries B.C.; see his "Roman Historiography before Caesar," *American Historical Review* XXXII (1926/7) 232–240, substantially reprinted as ch. vi, "Republican Historiography and Livy," in his *Life and Literature in the Roman Republic* (Berkeley, Calif., University of California Press, 1930: *Sather Classical Lectures* VII) 169–196; see also M. L. W. Laistner, *The Greater Roman Historians* (Berkeley, Calif., University of California Press, 1947: *Sather Classical Lectures* XXI) 23–44.

8. For a recent edition of the fragments of the Laws of the Twelve Tables, see E. H. Warmington, *Remains of Old Latin* III (Loeb Classical Library, 1938) 424 ff. The skepticism concerning the traditional date and character of the Laws of the Twelve Tables which was expressed at the turn of the present century by such scholars as Lambert and Pais is now generally abandoned; see H. F. Jolowicz, *A Historical Introduction to the Study of*

Roman Law (Cambridge, University Press, 1932) 109–11; Vincenzo Arangio-Ruiz, *Storia del Diritto Romano* (Naples, Jovene, ed. 3, 1942) 53–62.

9. The genuineness, scope, and purpose of the Licinio-Sextian "Rogations" has been much disputed. A recent discussion by Kurt von Fritz, "The Reorganization of the Roman Government in 366 B.C. and the so-called Licinio-Sextian Laws," appeared in *Historia* I (1950) 3–44. Von Fritz takes a middle position between the traditional account and modern skeptics. He concludes that the changes in the consulship and the establishment of the praetorship were dictated by the administrative needs of a growing state but that the plebeians took advantage of the reorganization to secure recognition of their demands. The slowness with which they actually secured the benefits of this recognition is evidenced by Livy's account, VII 42, of the further guarantee of 342 B.C. and by the appearance of a wholly plebeian pair of consuls only in 172 B.C., Livy XLII 9; *Fasti Capitolini* for the year of Rome 582, *Corpus Inscriptionum Latinarum* I (ed. 2) part 1 p. 25 (= *Inscriptiones Italiae* XIII 1 p. 51). A pair of plebeian censors appear only in 131 B.C., Livy, *Epitome* LIX. Though approximately half the places in the enlarged colleges of pontiffs and augurs were reserved to plebeians by the *lex Ogulnia* of 300 B.C., the first plebeian *pontifex maximus* was Tiberius Coruncianus in 253 B.C., Livy, *Epitome* XVIII. For the scope and purpose of the *Lex Hortensia* of 287 B.C., see G. W. Botsford, *The Roman Assemblies* (New York, Macmillan, 1909) 313–316. For the view that the new plebeio-patrician senatorial aristocracy contained an even narrower

group of families who claimed a hereditary right to the consulship and were the *nobiles* of Cicero's day, see below ch. vii pp. 89–90 and n. 11.

10. The traditional arrangement of the fragments of Naevius, which placed the mythological material first, was questioned by H. T. Rowell in his article on "The Original Form of Naevius' *Bellum Punicum*" in the *American Journal of Philology* LXVIII (1947) 21–46. Professor Rowell argued that the epic opened with the beginning of the war and that the legendary material was introduced as a long digression inspired by the representations of the fall of Troy depicted on the temple of Zeus at Agrigentum, which was taken by the Romans in 262 B.C. The poem, originally a single whole, was later divided into seven books.

11. Warmington, *Remains of Old Latin* II (Loeb, 1936) 72–73 lines 59–62.

12. Cicero gives Ennius' estimate of Naevius in *Brutus* 75. A bibliography on Virgil's debt to his Latin predecessors, including Naevius, is given in Schanz und Hosius, *Geschichte der römischen Literatur* II 66.

13. Nepos, *Cato* 1.4, relates that Cato as quaestor in 204 B.C. had brought Ennius back from Sardinia to Rome. "Aurelius Victor," *de Viris Illustribus* 47, announces that Cato as praetor in Sardinia in 198 B.3. was taught Greek by Ennius. Schanz und Hosius, *Geschichte der römischen Literatur* I 50–51, conclude that Naevius left Rome in 204 B.C. and died at Utica in 201 B.C. They give no evidence for Naevius' birth other than that he fought in the First Punic War and began producing plays at Rome about 235 B.C. This suggests that his service may have been in

the later years of the war and that he was not necessarily contemporary with its earlier events.

14. The fragments cited from Ennius will be found in Warmington, *Remains of Old Latin* I (Loeb, 1935).

15. For *Moribus antiquis res stat Romana virisque*, see *Remains of Old Latin* I 174–175 line 467. The original location in the *Annales* is uncertain. The line was quoted, according to Augustine, *de Civ. Dei* II 21, by Cicero at the opening of *de Rep*. V.

VI

POLYBIUS: THE MIXED CONSTITUTION ADAPTED

TO ROME

1. Polybius VI, frag. 1, translated by W. R. Paton in the Loeb ed. III (1923) 269–271 and reprinted by permission of the Harvard University Press.

2. C. H. McIlwain, *The Growth of Political Thought in the West* etc. 100. Professor McIlwain refers to Hermann Rehm, *Geschichte der Staatsrechtswissenschaft* (Freiburg i. b., Mohr, 1896) 136–137, for this contrast between Aristotle and Polybius, but admits that at the end of *Pol*. VI 14, Aristotle does seem to conceive of a balance of power between organs, representing social classes, rather than of a fusion of principles; see his n. 2.

3. The arguments that Polybius' inconsistency as between a balance of constitutions and a cyclical succession shows different revisions is most recently reëxamined by F. W. Walbank, "Polybius on the Roman Constitution," *The Classical Quarterly* XXXVII (1943) 73–89. Polybius tells the story of Scipio quoting *Iliad* VI 448–449 over the ruins of Carthage in XXXVIII 22. 2–3 (XXXIX 4) as quoted by Appian, *Punica* 132.

4. Polybius comments unfavorably on the Macedonian support of Andriscus in XXXVI 17.12–15.

5. Wilhelm Capelle, in his article on "Griechische Ethik und römischer Imperialismus" in *Klio* XXV (1932) 88–113, argues that the debate in the third book of the *de Republica* about whether government depends on justice or injustice represents the conflicting opinions of the skeptic Carneades and the Stoic Panaetius; see also Karel Sprey in *de M. T. C. Politica Doctrina* 23–52, who refers to Hans von Arnim on "Karneades" in *RE* X (20) 1978. Sprey finds the same opposition expressed not only in *de Rep*. III but also in *de Leg*. I and *de Off*. III. Compare also Max Pohlenz in *Antikes Führertum* etc. (Leipzig and Berlin, Teubner, 1934) 33.

6. The embassy from Athens came to Rome to request the reduction of a fine imposed on the former city by the senate as a penalty for the devastation of Oropus. It comprised Carneades the Academician (Skeptic), Diogenes the Stoic, and Critolaus the Peripatetic (Aristotelian). They lectured during their stay in Rome; Gellius, *N. A.* VI (VII) 14.8; Plutarch, *Cato* 22; Pausa-

nias VII 11. During the twenty years from 170 to 150 B.C., a number of Greek philosophers and rhetoricians were expelled from Rome by the conservative, anti-Hellenistic party, probably led by Cato; see the references in Schanz und Hosius, *Geschichte der römischen Literatur* I (ed. 4, 1927) 179–181, T. J. Haarhoff, *The Stranger at the Gate* (London, New York, and Toronto, Longmans, Green, 1938; reëdited with same pagination, Oxford, Blackwell, 1948) 209–215.

7. B. N. Tatakis, *Panétius de Rhodes* etc. (Paris, Vrin, 1931) 211–216, Modestus van Straaten, *Panétius* etc. (Amsterdam, H. J. Paris, 1946) 203–211, and Max Pohlenz, *Die Stoa* etc. (Göttingen, Vandenhoeck und Ruprecht) I (1948) 204–205, agree that Panaetius, as a prac-

tical matter and because of his close association with the Roman state, abandoned the traditional Stoic universalism (for which, see above, ch. iv, n. 5) in favor of the orthodox theory of the city-state with a mixed constitution. For this he perhaps had the precedent of Chrysippus, above, ch. ii, n. 7 at the end. Pohlenz, II (1949) 102, third n. on p. 204 (but apparently not the other two), recognizes that the arguments in *de Rep.* III on behalf of justice derive from Panaetius. For Cicero's statements about Panaetius' political discussions, see Tatakis, p. 215, and van Straaten, p. 207. For the five fragments of Panaetius which deal with politics, four of which come from Cicero's *de Off.* and one from his *de Rep.*, see van Straaten, pp. 367–368, frags. 118–122.

VII

CICERO'S WORLD

1. L. R. Taylor has recently published an excellent study of *Party Politics in the Age of Caesar* (Berkeley, University of California Press, 1949). This supplements Ronald Syme's *Roman Revolution* (Oxford, Clarendon Press, 1939) and the fundamental studies by Matthias Gelzer, *Die Nobilität der römischen Republik* (Leipzig and Berlin, Teubner, 1912), and by Friederich Münzer, *Römische Adelsparteien und Adelsfamilien* (Stuttgart, Metzlersche VBH, 1920). Anton von Premerstein casts much light on politics of the Ciceronian period in his posthumous *Vom Werden und Wesen des Prinzipats* (*Abhandlungen der Bayerischen Akademie der Wissenschafter*, Phil.-

hist. Abt., neue folge XV, Munich, 1937).

2. That the Roman republic collapsed because the Roman aristocracy failed to live up to the motto "noblesse oblige" is the view of Tenney Frank in the concluding essay of *An Economic Survey of Ancient Rome* V: *Rome and Italy of the Empire* (Baltimore, The Johns Hopkins Press, 1940) 296–304; of Michael Rostovtzeff in *The Social and Economic History of the Roman Empire* (Oxford, Clarendon Press, 1926) 486–487; and of F. M. Heichelheim in his *Wirtschaftsgeschichte des Altertums* (Leiden, Sijthoff, 1938) I 859. See Mason Hammond, "Economic Stagnation in the Early Roman Empire" in

The Journal of Economic History, Suppl. VI, "Tasks" (1946, publ. 1947) 88–89. •

3. The apothegm "power tends to corrupt and absolute power corrupts absolutely" occurs in a letter from the distinguished British historian and founder of *The Cambridge Modern History*, Lord Acton (1834–1902), to Mandell (later Bishop) Creighton dated April 5, 1887. It may be found on p. 364 of Gertrude Himmelfarb's edition of Lord Acton's *Essays on Freedom and Power* (Boston, Beacon Press, 1948). It is cited in the most recent edition of Bartlett's *Familiar Quotations* (1948) on p. 1041 from *Time*, 22 July 1946, p. 28, where it is used in an article on Portugal under Salazar. The editors of Bartlett, perhaps confused by the fact that Lord Acton does not occur in the original volumes of the *Dictionary of National Biography* but only in the *Second Supplement, 1901–1911*, attribute the phrase to his grandfather, Sir John Francis Edward Acton (1736–1811), who became the unprincipled minister of the corrupt rulers of Naples, Ferdinand and Caroline, at the beginning of the nineteenth century. Lord Acton did not approve of his grandfather (introduction by Himmelfarb, p. xvi), which may have occasioned his dislike for power. The thought is not original, see Stevenson's *Home Book of Quotations* (ed. of 1947) under "Power" pp. 1573–1575, especially p. 1573 no. 16, from a speech of Burke in 1771: "the greater the power, the more dangerous the abuse," and p. 1574 no. 14 from Pitt on John Wilkes in 1770: "unlimited power is apt to corrupt the minds of those who possess it" (see also the *Oxford Dictionary of Quotations* pp. 59b, 297a, which gives

the text of Pitt as here quoted). Montesquieu remarked in *De l'Esprit des Lois* (publ. 1748) XI ch. iv, first par.: "mais c'est une expérience éternelle, que tout homme qui a du pouvoir est porté à en abuser; il va jusqu'à ce qu'il trouve des limites," or, as the English translation by Mr. Nugent, published at London in 1750, says: "every man invested with power is apt to abuse it; he pushes on until he comes to the utmost limit."

4. The aims and political alignment of the Gracchi have been the subject of much discussion. Appian, *Bella Civilia* I 1.9–11, states that Tiberius wanted to restore the small citizen farmers in order to increase the reservoir of citizens with enough property to be recruited for the legions. Plutarch, *Tiberius Gracchus* 8.4–7, suggests various motives and calls attention to the influence of Greek philosophical doctrines. Münzer, *Römische Adelsparteien* 257–281, thought that the Gracchi were spokesmen for a group of senatorial nobles allied by blood or marriage in opposition to Scipio Aemilianus; see also Syme, *Roman Revolution* 60. Hugh Last, in *The Cambridge Ancient History* IX (1932) 89–93, thought that Tiberius was concerned to get the idle urban population back on the land and that Gaius saw the imperative need of reorganizing the "Roman confederacy." Jérôme Carcopino, *Histoire Romaine* II (1935) 265, thought that the Gracchi might have saved the republic had the senate not defeated them.

5. Appian, *Bella Civilia* I pref. 1–2, remarked that Tiberius Gracchus was the first man to perish in civil strife at Rome since the attack of Coriolanus in 491 B.C., and adds that the attack by

Coriolanus was that of a deserter, not really internal strife; see also Velleius Paterculus II 3.3.

6. Passages from Cicero and other authors relevant to the period from the Gracchi through Sulla are collected by A. H. J. Greenidge and A. M. Clay, *Sources for Roman History* B.C. *133–70* (Oxford, Clarendon Press, 1903). In *de Rep.* I 31, Cicero remarks that the death of Tiberius Gracchus and, before that, the whole conduct of his tribunate, divided the people into two parties, see also III 29; *de Leg.* III 20–24. In *de Off.* I 76, he ranks the removal of Tiberius by Scipio Nasica as a service to the state equal to the victories of Scipio Aemilianus; compare also I 109, II 43, below, ch. x, n. 10.

7. W. W. Fowler, *Social Life at Rome in the Age of Cicero* (London & New York, Macmillan, 1909 and later reprints), gives a good picture of conditions in Rome at the end of the republic. The empire, despite material and administrative improvement, did not make the life of the lower classes much more attractive; see Jérôme Carcopino, *Daily Life in Ancient Rome* etc. (trans. from the French by ·E. O. Lorimer and ed. by H. T. Rowell, New Haven, Yale University Press, 1940).

8. Sallust, *Jugurtha* 35.10, says that Jugurtha, when ordered from Rome by the senate, exclaimed, "A city for sale and doomed to speedy destruction if it finds a purchaser."

9. Two families named Pompeius were prominent in the early first century B.C. That to which Pompey the Great belonged originated from Picenum, according to Syme, *Roman Revolution* 28, especially n. 1, following Münzer, *Römische Adelsparteien* 48.

Gelzer, *Die Nobilität* 77, cited by Münzer, says simply "die Pompejer sind picentische Grundbesitzer." The name seems Oscan, on the analogy of the city Pompeii; Drumann und Groebe, *Geschichte Roms* etc. IV (ed. 2, 1908) 312.

10. For Pompey as a "dynast" as much as Caesar, see most recently Taylor, *Party Politics* chs. vi and vii.

11. For the *optimates* and *populares* as political groupings in the senate rather than parties, *partes*, in the modern sense, see most recently Taylor, *Party Politics* 11–15, where Cicero's concept is well analyzed. Miss Taylor's book is mainly an elaboration of the conflict between these two groups, or political programs. Miss Taylor, p. 186, n. 6 on ch. i, like Syme, *Roman Revolution* 10–11, accepts Gelzer's definition, *Die Nobilität* 22, of *nobiles* as the descendents of men who had held the consulship, the military tribunate with consular powers, or the dictatorship, see above ch. V pp. 63–64 and n. 9. Adam Afzelius, in two articles, "Zur Definition der römische Nobilität in der Zeit Ciceros" and the same "vor der Zeit Ciceros," in *Classica et Mediaevalia* I (1938) 40–94 and VII (1945) 150–200, reëxamines the evidence and concludes that Gelzer's definition is warranted for the Ciceronian period but that in the third and early second centuries B.C. any curule office gave "nobility." These articles present the substance of his (unavailable) thesis for Copenhagen University, *Den romerske Nobilitets Omfang* (Copenhagen, Nyt nordisk Forlag, 1935). For *novus homo* see below, ch. viii, n. 10. The *nobiles* tended, of course, except for such unusual men as Catiline or Caesar, to belong to the optimate

group. Cicero differentiates between *optimates* and *populares* in idealistic terms in the *pro Sestio*, for which see Taylor, pp. 227–228, n. 1 on ch. viii. Cicero delivered this speech in 56 B.C., ostensibly in defense of Sestius against a charge of having used violence to force the passage of his tribunician bill. Sestius, as quaestor in 63 B.C., had assisted in the suppression of Catiline and, as tribune in 57 B.C., had been active for Cicero's recall from exile. Cicero was grateful to him and also hated the instigator of the prosecution, Clodius. Moreover, Pompey urged him to undertake the defense. Nevertheless, Cicero felt only a lukewarm interest in Sestius, in part because the latter had not urged the restitution of Cicero's property as well as his recall, and in part because the violence of which Sestius was accused had actually occurred in a street fight between his gang and that of Clodius. Cicero therefore devoted most of the speech to a glorification of his own career and in particular to a description of the iniquity of his exile and the unanimous support given by all the best elements in the state for his recall. In sec. 21, he indicates the respect enjoyed by the *nobiles:* "All good men, *omnes boni*, always favor nobility, *nobilitati*, because it is useful for the state for noble men to be worthy of their ancestors and because there prevails among us the memory of famous men who have deserved well of the state, even when they are dead and gone." He goes on to describe the *optimates*, particularly in secs. 96–99, as all those who place public interest above private and rally to the support of good causes. Such men are contrasted in sec. 105 with *populares* like the Gracchi

and Saturninus. These last win the support of the mob by catering to its desires; the *optimates* prevail in the senate and are often opposed by popular favor. Nevertheless, in a crisis, the people are guided by the *auctoritas* of the *optimates*. Pierre Boyancé, "Cum dignitate otium," *Revue des Études Anciennes* XLIII (1941) 172–191, analyzes Cicero's excursus on the *optimates* in the *pro Sestio* and concludes that it is directly relevant to the training of the statesman in the *de Rep.* and that its inspiration was Aristotle's *Nicomachean Ethics*, perhaps through Theophrastus and Panaetius. *Otium* is not idleness but freedom to pursue the political activity in which *dignitas* finds expression.

12. Torsten Petersson, *Cicero* etc. (Berkeley, University of California Press, 1920) 31–32, points out that Cicero had nothing in common with Marius and that his admiration was purely sentimental. For Cicero's poem on Marius, see W. W. Ewbank, *The Poems of Cicero* (London, University of London Press, 1933) 13–16. Since Hugo Merguet's *Handlexicon zu Cicero* does not contain proper names, recourse must be had to the *Onomasticon Tullianum* in the seventh volume of Orelli and Baiter's edition (Turin, Orelli and Fuesslini, 1838) 383–386. The passages there collected show that Cicero did not admire Marius' later acts and that he expressed his admiration most warmly in speeches to the people.

13. Senators were actually forbidden to own a vessel of more than three hundred amphora's burden by a *lex Claudia*, probably dating from 218 B.C., Livy, XXI 63.3–4. For this and similar restrictions on senators, see Theodor Mommsen, *Römische Staatsrecht* (Leip-

zig, Hirzel, 1887) III 898–901. This law
was tacitly disregarded by 70 B.C., Cicero, *Verr.* II, V 45, and may have been
renewed by a *lex Iulia repetundarum*
of 59 B.C. (?), Justinian, *Digest* L 5.3.
It seems to have been still in force under the Flavians, Suetonius, *Domitian*
9.3, with R. F. Gephart's note in his
edition of this life (University of Pennsylvania thesis, Philadelphia, 1922) 63.

14. For commerce in the period 150–
80 B.C., see Tenney Frank in *An Economic Survey of Ancient Rome* I:
Rome and Italy of the Republic (Baltimore, The Johns Hopkins Press, 1933)
274–282. The whole of this volume
gives a full treatment of the themes discussed in the present chapter. For Cicero's own views on occupations which
were *liberales* or *sordidi*, see *de Off.*
I 150–151.

15. Instances of provincial corruption in Cicero's day are to be found in
any history of the period; see, for instance, R. S. Conway, *Makers of Europe*
(Cambridge, Mass., Harvard University
Press, 1931) 37–43; R. O. Jolliffe, *Phases
of Corruption in Roman Administration* etc. (University of Chicago thesis,
Menasha, Wisc., Banta, 1919); E. M.
Sanford, "Roman Avarice in Asia,"
Journal of Near Eastern Studies IX
(1950) 28–36; compare below, ch.
viii, n. 8. The story of Cato's lost
accounts is related by Plutarch, *Cato
the Younger* 38–40, and by Dio Cas-

sius, XXXIX 22–23. Cicero remarks in
ad Att. VII I 6 (50 B.C.) on the disgust
of his staff when he left the surplus from
his budget to be paid back into the provincial treasury at Laodicea rather than
distributed among them, *RE2* VII (13)
987. It would be an irony of history if
these sums were eventually spent by
Cicero's dissolute ex-son-in-law, Dola-
bella, when he vainly held Laodicea
against Cassius in the summer of 43 B.C.,
RE IV (7) 1308 under *Cornelius* 141.
As Carcopino sarcastically points out in
Les Secrets etc. I 110–111 and 203, Cicero personally acquired during his governorship two million two hundred
thousand sesterces without violating the
laws, *salvis legibus*. This he deposited
at Ephesus and in 48 B.C. turned half
of it over to the Pompeians but had
the rest concealed in a safe place, *ad
Att.* XI 1.1 and 2.3, *ad Fam.* V 20.9.
Catullus criticizes his governor Memmius for miserliness in poems 10 and
28. The "purse full of cobwebs," *plenus
saccus aranearum*, occurs in his invitation to Fabullus for dinner, 13.8, and
may reflect his general condition of
poverty, rather than specifically his un-
rewarded service in Bithynia.

16. On the identity of interest between rich equestrians and senators during the later republic, see Arthur Stein,
*Der römische Ritterstand (Münchener
Beitrage zur Pap.-Forsch.* etc. X, Munich, Beck'sche VBH., 1927) 49-53.

VIII

CICERO'S POLITICAL CAREER AND PROGRAM
THROUGH HIS CONSULSHIP

1. For Cicero and Arpinum, see *RE* I (1) 1218 on Arpinum; *RE2* VII (13) 827–828 under *Tullius* 29 (M. T. Cicero). The name *Tullius* first appears for the sixth king of Rome, the Latin Servius T., above, ch. v, n. 6. The next occurrence is of a Volscian leader in the tale of Coriolanus, early fifth century B.C., *RE2* VII (13) 800–801 under *Tullius* 3. Cicero jokingly connects himself with the king in *Tusc.* I 38, *Brut.* 62, and Plutarch, *Cic.* 1.1, connects him with the Volscian leader, but there is naturally no assurance of the truth of either assertion. Thereafter until the time of Cicero, the name is rare and appears for people of varied origin, *RE2* VII (13) 800. Though Cicero's family had connections with leading senatorial families at Rome in the second century B.C., *RE2* VII (13) 827–828, it remained at Arpinum and was of equestrian status until Cicero himself achieved senatorial and consular rank. Tenney Frank, *An Economic Survey of Rome* I: *Rome and Italy of the Republic* (Baltimore, The Johns Hopkins Press, 1933) 295–296, feels that down to about 80 B.C. the bulk of equestrians still were landowners and that banking and tax contracting were not as important sources of wealth as they were in Cicero's heyday, for which see pp. 387–392. It is impossible to determine whether Cicero was of narrowly Roman, of Latin, or of Volscian stock and this was probably unimportant in his day. More important, as the next note will indicate, was the strength of localism in towns outside of Rome despite the Romanization which had been going on for many centuries in the area immediately around Latium.

2. For Samnite (Oscan) survivals in Pompeii, see R. C. Carrington, *Pompeii* (Oxford, Clarendon Press, 1936) 32–38. Catullus, 39.10–13, distinguishes between a dweller at Tivoli, a dweller at Lanuvium, a Sabine, an Umbrian, and a Transpadane. In 44.1–5, he distinguishes between Tivoli and the Sabine country. Horace is full of allusions to the local characteristics of different parts of Italy. Livy was accused of "Patavinity" by Asinius Pollio, Quintilian VIII 1.3; some sort of provincialism, perhaps in speech, therefore attached to Padua in the Po Valley. Cicero's own municipal pride was great; see Michael Grant, *From Imperium to Auctoritas* (Cambridge, University Press, 1946) 405, with references in n. 13. Martin van den Bruwaene begins his "Étude sur le patriotisme de Cicéron" in *Nova et Vetera* XXI (*Revue d'enseignement et de pédagogie*, Brussels, 1939) 177–186, with Cicero's affection for Arpinum in the *de Leg.* In the opening of bk. ii, Cicero contrasts the simple love of one's native town and patriotism for one's country. Van den Bruwaene therefore goes on to discuss Cicero's concept of patriotism and its sources both in Panaetius and in the Roman concept of *pietas*. Joseph Vogt's book, *Cicero's Glaube an Rom*

(*Würzburger Studien zur Altertum-swissenschaft* VI, Stuttgart, Kohlhammer, 1935), deals very generally with Cicero's concept of Rome's past and its meaning and his belief that under the protection of the gods Rome would be eternal.

3. Jérôme Carcopino, *Les Secrets* etc. (Paris, L'Artisan du Livre, 1947) II 218–305, rather unfairly portrays Atticus as an "accomodator," if not a "timeserver." Epicureanism preached withdrawal from public affairs, above, ch. iv, pp. 44–45.

4. Carcopino, *Les Secrets* etc. I 79–230, gives an unfavorable description of the "fortune et train de vie de Cicéron" and of his "cupidité et indélicatesses." Cicero's correspondence reveals to us his financial worries and transactions but it is not fair to him to assume that simply because more is known about him, his conduct was improper according to the standards of his day. He himself remarks in *de Off*. I 25 that "increase of one's property that harms no one else is not to be condemned but injustice is always to be shunned"; compare also II 64. He does not seem to have himself violated this principle.

5. Later in life, Cicero expressed directly in the *pro Caecina* 101 and the *pro Domo* 79 the criticism of Sulla which he ostensibly denied but implicitly suggested in the *pro Roscio Amerino*. In *de Off*. II 51, he states that he had defended Roscius against the power of Sulla himself. See Richard Heinze's article on "Cicero's politische Anfange" (1909) in his *Vom Geist des Romertums* (Leipzig and Berlin, Teubner, 1938) 84; and further references in *RE2* VII (13) 835–838.

6. Cicero gives poor health as the reason for his trip to the East in *Brutus* 313–314. Plutarch, *Cicero* 3.4–5 and 4.3, attributes his trip both to poor health and to fear of Sulla's anger at the attack in the *pro Roscio Amerino*. J. S. Reid, in his preface to Cicero's *Academica* (London, Macmillan, 1885) 3, discounts Plutarch and accepts Cicero's account as correct.

7. Verres' remark about the destination of the proceeds of three years of governing Sicily is quoted by Cicero in *Verr*. I 40. On the trial and Cicero's combination of altruistic and ambitious motives, see Taylor, *Party Politics* 101–118. In general, see F. H. Cowles, *Gaius Verres* (Cornell University thesis, Ithaca, N. Y., 1917).

8. Cicero, *de Off*. II 27, calls the Roman rule over others a *patrocinium orbis terrae verius quam imperium*. In *Div. in Caecilium* 18, he says of the law against extortion: *haec lex socialis est, hoc ius nationum exterarum est, hanc habent arcem minum aliquanto nunc quidem munitam quam antea, verum tamen, si qua reliqua spes est, quae sociorum animos consolari possit, ea tota in hac lege posita est*. L. R. Taylor, *Party Politics* etc. (Berkeley, University of California Press, 1949) 102, renders this sentence: "This is the foreigners' charter of rights. . . This is their strong tower, somewhat less strong now certainly than it once was, but still if our allies have any hope left to comfort their sad hearts, it must all rest on this law alone"; see p. 217, n. 7 on ch. v. In *de Rep*. III 41, Cicero makes Scipio express the fear that the violation by Tiberius Gracchus of the treaty rights of Rome's allies and the Latins marked the beginning of lawlessness which would change Rome's rule from

one of justice to one of force so that those who until then had obeyed her willingly would be held faithful by fear alone and this abandonment of the customs of the ancestors would lead to the downfall of the state. This is an obvious retrojection of Cicero's opinion of the conduct of Rome toward her allies and subjects in his own day. Joseph Vogt, *Cicero's Glaube an Rom* (above, n. 2) 89–92, elaborates on the concepts of *fides* and *iustitia* as the basis of Roman rule; see also his *Orbis Romanus: zur Terminologie des römischen Imperialismus (Philosophie und Geschichte usw.* XXII, Tübingen, Mohr [Siebeck], 1929) for the identification of the *orbis terrarum* with the *oikoumene* and the *imperium Romanum*. But this identification, which he traces on p. 11 from the pre-Ciceronian *Rhetorica ad Herennium* IV 9.13, became common only under the empire. Certainly Cicero never conceived of the Roman empire as a true world state, but as the rule, just to be sure, of one city-state over other peoples, see below, ch. x, n. 15; W. W. How, "Cicero's Ideal in his *De Republica*," *Journal of Roman Studies* XX (1930) 35; E. M. Sanford, "Romans and Provincials in the Late Republic," *Classical Weekly* XLII (1949) 195–201, who contrasts Cicero's ideal of a just protectorate with the picture which his speeches give of unjust government; compare above, ch. vii, n. 15.

9. In 70 B.C., the consuls Crassus and Pompey seem to have permitted, if they did not back, the tribunician legislation which deprived the senators of their monopoly of the juries and freed the tribunes themselves of the restrictions imposed upon them by Sulla. For this last measure, Cicero defends Pompey

against the criticism of Quintus, *de Leg.* III 22, 26; see F. B. Marsh, *The Founding of the Roman Empire* (Oxford, Oxford University Press, ed. 2, 1927) 62–67, especially p. 65. Though the consuls soon fell into disagreement, it is significant that, presumably further to weaken the senate and strengthen the assemblies and to recognize the gains to the Italians from the Social War, which Sulla had attempted to restrict, a census was completed in this and the following year for the first time since 85 B.C. In this, the number of citizens was doubled, Taylor, *Party Politics* 109, following Tenney Frank, *Economic Survey of Ancient Rome* I: *Rome and Italy of the Republic* 314–315. Frank's figures are based on his article "Roman Census Statistics from 225 to 28 B.C." in *Classical Philology* XIX (1924) 331 and 337. He gives the increase as from 463,-000 (Hieron., Ol. 173.4) in 85 to 900,000 (Livy, *Ep.* XCVIII; Phlegon, XCI 177. 3, gives 910,000) in 69. He fails to note that the mss. of Livy's *Epitomes (Periochae)* differ; the reading copied by Pithou from a lost ms. gives DCCCCL but the *ed. princ.* gives CCCCL *milia*; see Otto Rossbach, *T. Livi Periochae* etc. (Leipzig, Teubner, 1910) 98, n. on this passage.

10. Taylor, *Party Politics* 3 and 186, n. 8, follows Gelzer, *Die Nobilität* 27–28, 40–41, in regarding Cicero as the only "new man" to achieve the consulship between C. Coelius in 94 B.C. and 48 B.C.; see further her chapter v and Adam Afzelius, "Zur Definition der römische Nobilität vor der Zeit Ciceros," *Classica et Mediaevalia* VII (1945) 152–153. In *de Leg. Agr.* II 3–4, of 63 B.C., Cicero said to the tribal assembly: "After a very long interval, in

fact almost the first in our memory and times, you made me, a new man, consul and under my leadership you broke down that place which the nobility held protected by its defenses and fortified in every way, and you wished it hereafter to lie open to merit . . . With this honor you endowed me first from among the new men after many years, at my first canvass and at the earliest age . . ." See the other passages collected by Hugo Merguet, *Lexikon zu den Reden des Cicero* (Jena, Fischer, 1882) III 373–374 under *novus homo*, particularly *de Leg. Agr.* I 27; *pro Murena* 17. In the *de Off.* II 59, Cicero again boasts that he was elected to all offices *nostro quidem anno*, at the earliest legal age, and *cunctis suffragiis*, by unanimous vote; see also *de Rep.* I 10. It should, of course be remembered that though the *de Leg. Agr.* was presumably a *contio* to the tribal assembly, since it was in opposition to a law introduced by a tribune, the praetorian and consular elections took place in the centuriate assembly; see Taylor, ch. iii, for the different uses of these two assemblies in the political maneuvers of the period. See in general Strasburger's article *novus homo* in *RE* XVII (33) 1223–1228, and, for *nobiles*, above, ch. vii, n. 11.

11. Cicero said to Servius Sulpicius in *pro Murena* 22 (63 B.C.): "How can you doubt but that for gaining the consulship, the glory of military success contributes far more dignity than that of civil jurisprudence?" He goes on in sec. 24 to say that although the highest dignity is in those who excel in military praise, the art of public speaking is also weighty and full of dignity. The *de Oratore* is devoted to the thesis that skill

in public speaking, based on a broad education, is the proper training for a political leader, see particularly the preface to bk. I, in which Cicero elaborates in his own person to Quintus on the rarity and importance 'of outstanding orators. In the *pro Plancio* 64–67 (54 B.C.), Cicero told on himself the story of how he came back from his quaestorship in Sicily and found that his friends in Rome hardly knew that he had been away. He then and there resolved to live in the public eye and haunt the forum and thus attained his eminence. The *Commentariolum Petitionis* (*De Petitione Consulatus*), written by Q. Cicero for his brother in 64 B.C., may have "carried coals to Newcastle" as far as Cicero himself was concerned but still gives a vivid firsthand picture of electioneering in Rome and advice not out of date today.

12. Heinze, *Vom Geist des Romentums* (above, n. 5) 134, cited *Comment. Pet.* 5 for Quintus' advice to Marcus to stand in well with the *optimates*. But Quintus was apparently always more of a conservative and social climber than his brother. See, however, Carcopino's criticism of the doctrine of the *concordia ordinum* as simply a program in the interests of the propertied classes, *Les Secrets* etc. I 376–378.

13. The discussion of "Concord" is based on Hermann Strasburger, *Concordia Ordinum; Eine Untersuchung Zur Politik Ciceros* (Frankfurt Dissertation, Borna-Leipzig, Noske, 1931). W. W. Tarn, *Alexander the Great* (Cambridge, University Press, 1948) II 415–416, sees Augustus as the fulfiller both of the Roman idea of *concordia* between conflicting classes in the state and of the Greek idea of *homonoia* of all peoples

in a world state. For the temple of
Concord in the Forum, see S. B. Platner
and Thomas Ashby, *A Topographical
Dictionary of Ancient Rome* (Oxford,
Oxford University Press, 1929) 138–140.
The view in the text, that the *concordia ordinum* was to be supported by
the *consensus omnium bonorum*, was
that of the late E. K. Rand. Gelzer,
RE2 VII (13) 890 and 913, follows
Strasburger, *Concordia Ordinum* 68, in
thinking that the *concordia* of the Catilinarian speeches in 63 B.C. became the
consensus of the *pro Sestio* 106 after
the return from exile in 57 B.C. Both, as
is pointed out at the end of this chapter,
head up to the leadership of the *auctoritas senatus*. E. D. Eagle, "Catiline
and the *Concordia Ordinum*," *The
Phoenix* III (1949) 15–30, argues that
though the conspiracy of Catiline initially strengthened the *concordia ordinum* by uniting equestrians and *optimates*, it foreshadowed the breakdown
of the political power of the *nobiles*,
based on family alliances, in the face
of the new social and economic group-

ings represented by such opponents of
the *nobiles* as Crassus and Caesar.

14. The considerable recent literature
on *auctoritas*, particularly in its connection with the Augustan principate,
is referred to by Michael Grant, *From
Imperium to Auctoritas* (Cambridge,
University Press, 1946) 443, n. 4; see
particularly Fritz Fürst, *Die Bedeutung
der auctoritas im privaten und öffentlichen Leben der römischen Republik*
(Marburg dissertation, Marburg, Hamel,
1934) and André Magdelain, *Auctoritas
Principis* (Paris, Les Belles Lettres,
1947). For *senatus auctoritas*, see
Moore's article on *senatus*, *RE* Suppl. 6,
718. The importance of *auctoritas* in
Roman law is emphasized by Fritz
Schulz (trans. Marguerite Wolff),
Principles of Roman Law (Oxford,
Clarendon Press, 1936) 164–168. In pp.
180–183, he discusses the personal *auctoritas* of Augustus. Earlier, pp. 87–90,
he accepts the sincerity of the Augustan
restoration of the Republic at least in
the field of constitutional law. Compare
below, ch. xi, n. 9 for the name *Augustus*.

IX
THE DOWNFALL OF THE REPUBLIC

1. A survey of the significance of
parens or *pater patriae* is given by Anton von Premerstein, *Vom Werden und
Wesen des Principats* (Munich, 1937)
166–175; see other references in Grant,
From Imperium to Auctoritas 444, n.
6. Cicero said, *in Pisonem* 6, that Q.
Catulus, *princeps senatus*, hailed him in
a crowded senate as *parens patriae*.
Plutarch, *Cic.* 23.3, stated that the

salutation was the result of a laudatory
speech by Cato in a public meeting
(*contio*) after Cicero had laid down the
consulship. Theodor Mommsen, *Römisches Staatsrecht* (Leipzig, Hirzel, ed.
3, 1887) II 2.779, n. 1, called the salutation of Cicero "etwas ganz Anderes"
than the later formal bestowal of the
title by the senate on emperors. For
Caesar and Augustus as *pater patriae*,

see Jean Gagé's edition of the *Res Gestae* 147–148, note on ch. 35.

2. The appointment of the dictator is discussed by Liebenam in *RE* V (9) 375–376 under *dictator*. He points out that the "creation" of Q. Fabius Maximus as dictator in 217 B.C. by the people was due to the absence and inaccessibility of the consul; see Livy XXII 8.5. The last dictator in a general sense was M. Junius Pera in 216 B.C. and the last for a specific purpose (holding an election) was C. Servilius in 202 B.C.; see col. 388.

3. O'Brien Moore, *RE* Suppl. 6, 756–758 under *senatus*, follows Gerhard Plaumann, "Das sogenannte Senatus consultum ultimum," *Klio* XIII (1913) 359–361, in stating that the *s.c. ultimum* was also used to implement the assassination of Tiberius Gracchus and his followers; for the view in the text, see Mommsen, *Staatsrecht* III 2.1242–1244; A. H. J. Greenidge, *Roman Public Life* (London, Macmillan, 1901) 281.

4. For the account in the text of the trial of Rabirius, see Gelzer, *RE2* VII (13) 870–972, in his article on Cicero. Torsten Petersson, *Cicero* etc. (Berkeley, University of California Press, 1920) 237, connects Cicero's speech with the first trial under the procedure for *perduellio*.

5. For *abdicatio* and *eiuratio*, see Neumann's article, *RE* I (1) 25–26; Mommsen, *Staatsrecht* I 625. The tribunes who blocked Cicero's speech were Calpurnius Bestia and Metellus Nepos; their ground, ill-omened for Cicero, was that since he had condemned others without a fair hearing, he himself should not have a hearing; see Cicero, *ad Fam.* V 2.8; Gelzer, *RE2* VII (13) 892.

6. The practical experience of men like Pompey and Lucullus had much to do with the shaping of the Roman provincial system and the powers developed for commanders under the later republic foreshadowed those assumed by Augustus for the administration of the armies and provinces. But there is no reason to assume that Pompey or Lucullus had any "theory" about the Roman empire other than that Rome should govern, as justly as was consistent with her and her rulers' interests, and that the *nobiles* should govern Rome and monopolize the honors and profits of empire. For Pompey's influence on the Augustan principate, see Mason Hammond, *The Augustan Principate* (Cambridge, Mass., Harvard University Press, 1933) ch. ii, "The Development of Extraordinary Commands," following Eduard Meyer, *Caesars Monarchie und das Principat des Pompejus* (Stuttgart and Berlin, Cotta'sche BH., ed. 3, 1922).

7. References for Clodius' adoption and election as tribune will be found in Gelzer's article on Cicero, *RE2* VII (13) 907–908 and in Frölich's, *RE* IV (7) 83–84 under *Clodius* 48.

8. W. W. Ewbank, *The Poems of Cicero* (London, University of London Press, 1933), discusses in his introduction the dating of Cicero's poems. Of the major poems, he would shift the *Marius* to the mid fifties, leaving the *Aratea* to Cicero's youth. With this Büchner agrees in his discussion of the fragments of the poems in *RE2* VII (13) 1236–1267, see especially cols. 1254–1255.

9. The evidence for the composition of the *de Republica* is given by Philippson in *RE2* VII (13) 1109 as well as in

the editions listed below in the bibliography.

10. The immediate purpose of Pompey's law was to make it possible to send a successor for Caesar in Gaul during 49 B.C. Without this innovation, Caesar would by traditional custom have continued in his command beyond the precise end of his five years until a magistrate of 49 B.C. was available to replace him. For the whole problem of the term of Caesar's command and the various maneuvers to which Pompey resorted to get him out before he became consul so that he could be prosecuted as a private citizen, see G. R. Elton, "The Terminal Date of Caesar's Gallic Proconsulate," *The Journal of Roman Studies* XXXVI (1946) 18–42, who gives full references to previous discussions.

11. A direct consequence of Crassus' death at Carrhae for Cicero was his election to the college of augurs in Crassus' place, on the nomination of Pompey and Hortensius, his old conservative rival; see *RE2* VII (13) 967. Cicero valued highly this religious office.

12. It should be remembered in discussing precise dates before the Julian reform of the calendar that the civil year, owing to faulty intercalation, had ceased to correspond to the seasons; thus the date on which Clodius was killed would have been December 8 according to the Julian calendar. An intercalary month was inserted between February and March of 52 B.C., on the twenty-fourth of which Pompey was made sole consul, 58 days after Clodius' murder. The day on which Caesar crossed the Rubicon, January 10 on the older reckoning, would correspond

to the Julian November 23. Drumann and Groehe, *Geschichte Roms* etc. III (ed. 2, 1906) 779–827, give for the years 65–43 B.C. a comparative table of dates on the old and the Julian reckonings.

13. *Cedant arma togae, concedat laurea laudi* is quoted by Cicero, *de Off.* I 77, from his own poem on his consulship; see Ewbank, *The Poems of Cicero* 77. Ewbank, n. on this line on p. 123, prefers to *laudi*, given by the best manuscripts, the reading *linguae*, attested in the invective against Cicero attributed to Sallust, in Plutarch's life of Cicero, and in Quintilian. He admits that *laudi* gives an alliteration which would have been pleasing to the Romans and quotes the suggestion of Morel that Cicero himself may have revised his own text because of criticisms. On pp. 13 and 123–124, he collects Cicero's other references to this passage, criticized by his contemporaries and by later scholars, notably Quintilian, XI 1.24.

14. For criticism of Pompey and of his sons in Cicero, see Jérôme Carcopino, *Les Secrets* etc. (Paris, L'Artisan du Livre, 1947) II 90–104.

15. These Marcelli had been consuls successively in 51, 50, and 49 B.C. The *Transactions of the American Philological Association*, LXXVII (1946) 321, contain a summary of a paper by M. N. P. Packard on "The Question of Cicero's Sincerity in His Addresses to Caesar." Miss Packard reaffirms the consistency of these speeches with Cicero's later hostility to Caesar's dictatorship, after he had despaired of influencing Caesar toward constitutionalism. For Cicero's hope that Caesar might restore the republic, see *ad Fam.* IX 17.2–3, to Paetus in

August, 46 B.C., cited by Carcopino, *Les Secrets* etc. I 388, n. 1. Noteworthy in this connection is the tendency of modern scholars to accept the genuineness of the two letters to Caesar attributed to Sallust and to find in them also an expression by a Caesarian of the hope that Caesar would remain loyal to the traditions of senatorial government and of the orthodox theory of the city-state; see Otto Seel, *Römischer Denker und römischer Staat* (Leipzig and Berlin, Teubner, 1937) 12–17; L. R. Taylor, *Party Politics* etc. (Berkeley, University of California Press, 1949) 1 and 185, n. 2 on ch. i; Carcopino, *Les Secrets* etc. I 22. Carcopino, I 352–372, is particularly critical of Cicero's behavior in the period from 49–43 B.C.

16. Petersson, *Cicero* 518–525, treats sympathetically Cicero's divorce of Terentia, his marriage and divorce of Publilia, and his feelings on the death of Tullia. Contrast, however, Carcopino's chapter, *Les Secrets* etc. I 231–307, on "une vie de famille inconsistante." For details about Cicero's wives, his son and daughter, and other members of his family, see Drumann and Groebe, *Geschichte Roms* etc. VI (ed. 2, 1929) 604–675. Terentia is said to have married twice again and to have died at the age of 103. The dates of her birth and of her marriage to Cicero are not known exactly; Groebe places the marriage about 80 B.C.

17. Thornton Wilder has fancifully reconstructed the events and personalities which led up to *The Ides of March* (New York and London, Harper and Bros., 1948). He introduced Cicero only as an onlooker and phrase-maker. Gelzer, *RE2* VII (13) 1030–1031, accepts Cicero's ignorance of the plot. The conspirators distrusted his lack of physical courage and his old age, according to Plutarch, *Brutus* 12.2 and *Cicero* 42.1.

18. Hartvig Frisch has recently reviewed the historical background of the *Philippics* in his *Cicero's Fight for the Republic* (*Humanitas* I, Copenhagen, Gyldendalske Boghandel, 1946).

19. Velleius Paterculus, II 62. 6, states that Cicero made the famous remark which annoyed Octavian: *Caesarem esse laudandum, orandum, tollendum,* with the double meaning of *tollendum,* either "exalt" or "remove." Cicero denies that he said this in a letter to Decimus Brutus of 43 B.C., *ad Fam.* XI 20.1, 21.1, see Frisch (above, n. 18), p. 294. Carcopino, *Les Secrets* etc. II 182–183, thinks that Cicero's words are evasive and do not constitute a firm denial.

20. L. R. Taylor, *Party Politics* ch. viii, discusses the compromise reached by Augustus between "Catonism and Caesarianism." She follows Syme's *Roman Revolution* and von Premerstein's *Vom Werden und Wesen des Prinzipats.* Recent studies of Cato's historical significance are also Matthias Gelzer, "Cato Uticensis" in *Die Antike* X (1934) 59–91, and Adam Afzelius, "Die politische Bedeutung des jüngeren Cato" in *Classica et Mediaevalia* IV (1941) 100–203.

X

CICERO'S POLITICAL THEORY

1. On the sources and content of the *de Republica*, see, in addition to the books listed in the bibliography, W. W. How, "Cicero's Ideal in his *De Republica*," *Journal of Roman Studies* XX (1930) 24–42 and the articles cited below in n. 14. For his treatment of the changes to which the simple forms of state are subject and the consequent advantage of the mixed form, see Friedrich Solmsen, "Die Theorie der Staatsformen bei Cicero de Re Publica I: Kompositionelle Beobachtungen," *Philologus* LXXXVIII (1933) 326–341. An article by S. L. Utchenko, "Uchenie Tsitserona o smeshannoi forme gosudarstvennogo ustroistva i ego klassocaia suschnost'" ("Cicero's Doctrine of the Mixed Constitution and its Classical Nature"), *Vestnik Drevnei Istorii* III (1949), was not available.

2. It was pointed out above, ch. vi, n. 5, that the debate on justice in *de Rep.* III probably reflects views expressed by Carneades and Panaetius in the mid second century B.C.

3. For Ennius' line *moribus antiquis* etc., see above, ch. v, n. 15.

4. The traditional view is that the *de Legibus* was composed immediately after the *de Republica*, between 53 and 51 B.C., but perhaps not completed, and certainly not published, until after 46 and perhaps as late as 44 B.C. or even posthumously; see Philippson, *RE2* VII (13) 1118–1119; Petersson, *Cicero* 445. The *Transactions of the American Philological Association* LXXVII (1946) 321–322 contains the summary, based on an unpublished Harvard doctoral thesis, of a discussion by E. A. Robinson on "The Date of Cicero's *De Legibus*," in which the author argues that even the composition of the work must be placed in the last year of Cicero's life, after the murder of Caesar. The principal passages which indicate that the work was not completed by 45–44 B.C. are a statement by Cicero that he was studying constitutions and laws which occurs in a letter, *ad Fam.* IX 2.5 (May 45 B.C.), and the absence of the work from the list which he gives in *de Div.* II 1–4. This latter work was published soon after Caesar's death in 44 B.C. See also the abstract of Robinson's thesis in *Harvard Studies in Classical Philology* LX (1951) 299–301.

5. Cicero compared his program of supplementing the *de Republica* by a *de Legibus* to Plato's two works in *de Leg.* I 15 and III 1. In II 17, Quintus remarked that his brother's ideas were quite different from Plato's, though there was a resemblance in his language. See Philippson, *RE2* VII (13) 1120–1121, who emphasizes the combination of Roman and Greek elements.

6. The significance of Cicero's remark in *de Leg.* II 5 that Italians had a double citizenship, that of Rome and that of their local town, has been discussed by A. N. Sherwin-White, *The Roman Citizenship* (Oxford, Clarendon Press, 1939) 134–135. With this statement may be contrasted that in the *pro Balbo* 28 (56 B.C.) that "by civil law, no citizen of ours (= Roman) can belong to two city-states"; see Kornemann's article on *Civitas* in *RE* Suppl.

I 311. Law lagged behind sentiment. For the development of the concept of double citizenship in Greece and Rome, see Mason Hammond, "Germana Patria," *Harvard Studies in Classical Philology* LX (1951) 147–174, which starts from these two conflicting views in Cicero.

7. "Religion is the sigh of the oppressed creature, the feelings of a heartless world, just as it is the spirit of unspiritual creatures. It is the opium of the people" is the translation of a remark by Karl Marx given by Eden and Cedar Paul in their translation of Otto Rühle's *Karl Marx* (New York, Viking, 1929) 57 and cited in Stevenson's *Home Book of Quotations* (New York, Dodd Mead, 1947) 1689 no. 14a. The remark comes from Marx's "Zur Kritik der Hegelschen Rechtsphilosophie" in *Deutsch-Französische Jahrbücher* 1844 (1ste & 2te Lieferung, all published, Paris, ed. Arnold Ruge and Karl Marx) 71–85. The passage runs from the bottom of p. 71 to the top of p. 72 and concludes: "Sie ist das *Opium des Volks.*"

8. While this is not the place to discuss in detail Cicero's religious views, it may be pointed out that his acceptance of divination in *de Leg.* II 32 contradicts his skeptical position in the *de Divinatione*; see Martin van den Bruwaene, *La Théologie de Cicéron* (Louvain, Bureaux du Receuil, 1937) 183–184 and A. S. Pease, *de Divinatione* (Urbana, University of Illinois, Bk. I 1920, II 1923) 11 n. 16. In general, Cicero distinguished between religion and skepticism, Pease, pp. 10–13, and he accepted the Stoic acceptance of religion as against Academic doubt, *de Nat. Deorum* III 94–95; van den Bru-

waene, p. 246. Consistently, he could argue that divination and augury had been sincere in origin and not merely devised to fool the ignorant, *de Div.* I 105, but that in his own day the more educated person might prefer reason to them, *ad Fam.* VI 6 (Tyrell and Purser, IV, no. 488 on pp. 347–353, to Aulus Caecina in 46 B.C.); *de Nat. Deorum* III 14–15 (Academic criticism). Nevertheless, they still had political value as a means to direct the minds of the unskilled toward right decisions, *de Div.* II 70; *de Nat. Deorum* II 12, and hence are recognized in the *de Legibus* and in the speech *de Haruspicum Responso.* At any rate, Cicero specifically denied the Marxian view of religion in *de Nat. Deorum* I 118: *ii, qui dixerunt totam de dis immortalibus opinionem fictam esse ab hominibus sapientibus rei publicae causa, ut, quos ratio non posset, eos ad officium religio duceret, nonne omnium religionem funditus sustulerunt?*, see J. B. Mayor, *de Natura Deorum* I (London, Clay, 1891) 221 n. *ad loc.* and 157 n. on I 61; compare also *de Nat. Deorum* II 45: *de Div.* II 148; *de Har. Resp.* 18–19. While, therefore, as Pease remarks, Cicero's attack on superstition in the *de Divinatione* has been compared with that of Lucretius, his position is actually fundamentally opposed to the Epicurean, since Lucretius regards all religion as superstition which keeps the mind in bondage to fear, whereas Cicero accepts religion as fundamentally valid and even properly directed superstition as having validity as a simplification of religious truth for unskilled minds.

9. Cicero asserts his Academicism against his son's Arisotelianism in *de Off.* II 8. In I 2, he claims that his views

and those of the Stoics equally descend
from Socrates and Plato; see below, n.
13. T. B. DeGraff, "Plato in Cicero,"
Classical Philology XXXV (1940) 143–
153, concludes that in the field of ethics,
where Cicero reproduces the views of
Plato, he does so with understanding
and accuracy and that, therefore, he
may be assumed to have done the same
for authors whose works are lost. Cicero himself, in *de Off.* I 1, tells his
son Marcus that he had always sought
to combine Greek and Latin studies.

10. Caesar's ambition is condemned
in *de Off.* I 26, 75, II 64. He is blamed
for the collapse of the republic in I 85
and II 82–83. Cicero was forced by
these conditions out of public life, II
2–5, III 54. Caesar's rule was unjust to
citizens, I 43–44, II 83–84, and to allies,
I 35, III 87–88. Caesar is a "tyrant" in
I 23. The Gracchi are condemned in I
79, 109, II 43, 80; see above, ch. vii, n.
6. Sulla was condemned in I 43–44 and
II 27–29; see above, ch. viii, nn. 5 and 6.

11. That the choice of moral duty
should aim at the general good is Cicero's conclusion in *de Off.* I 160; see
also I 55, 158.

12. Walter Miller, in his preface to
the Loeb edition of the *de Off.*, p. xi,
speaks slightingly of the third book.

13. The discussion of Cicero's healing of the dichotomy in Stoic political
theory by introducing law to mediate
between God and nature is derived
from Karl Vossler's *Die Göttliche
Komödie* (ed. 2, Heidelberg, Winters,
1925) I 204–223, 294; see the English
translation by W. C. Lawton entitled
Mediaeval Culture etc. (New York,
Harcourt Brace, · 1929) I 189–205, 268.
C. H. McIlwain, *The Growth of Political Thought in the West* (New York,

Macmillan, 1932) 115–118, emphasizes
the fact that Cicero's concept of natural
law went beyond that of Plato. G. H.
Sabine, *A History of Political Theory*
(New York, Holt, 1937) 161–167,
recognizes the significance of Cicero's
view that government depends on law
and this in turn is an expression of
popular sovereignty and morally justified, though he belittles Cicero's advocacy of the mixed constitution. R. N.
Wilkins's article, "Cicero: Oracle of
Natural Law," in the *Classical Journal*
XLIV (1949) 453–456, is only a plea
for the recognition by the modern
world that there exist those basic principles of human nature which Cicero,
de Rep. III 33, defined as "right reason
in accordance with nature." For further
support of Cicero's original contribution
to political theory, see J. S. Reid's preface to his edition of the *Academica*
(London, Macmillan, 1885) 1–28; R.
S. Conway, *Makers of Europe* (Cambridge, Mass., Harvard University
Press, 1931) ch. ii, "The Originality of
Cicero." For "natural law" in Plato and
Aristotle, see above, ch. ii, nn. 1 and 5.

14. There has been much written
about the Ciceronian concept of the
princeps and its influence on Augustus,
for which compare below, ch. xi, nn.
13, 16. Albert Brion's thesis for the
licence of the University of Louvain,
*La controverse autour de l'idée du
Princeps chez Cicéron*, mentioned in
the *Revue Belge de Philologie et d'Histoire* XIX (1940) 278 has apparently
not been published. Pierre Grenade's
"Remarques sur la Théorie Cicéronienne dite du 'Principat'," in *Mélanges
d'Arch. et d'Hist. de l'École franç. de
Rome* LVII (1940) 32–63, gives references to the earlier literature. He is

doubtful of Cicero's influence on Augustus, as is W. W. How, "Cicero's Ideal in his *De Republica*," *Journal of Roman Studies* XX (1930) 37–42; see the discussion of this problem below in ch. xi, nn. 13, 16, 17. How argues that Cicero adapted the views of Plato and Aristotle on the ruler to Roman figures like Scipio Aemilianus or himself. The *princeps* would have no unusual powers or position but be only an *optimus civis* in an *optimus status civitatis*, which is *in potestate optimorum*, see p. 59, citing *de Leg.* III 37. Carcopino, *Les Secrets* etc. II 184 n. 2, thinks that Cicero was even vaguer in his concept than does Grenade. On the other hand, Martin van den Bruwaene, in one of his *Études sur Cicéron* (Brussels, L'Edition Universelle, no date but apparently published in 1946) entitled "La Notion du Prince chez Cicéron," pp. 59–77, argues that Cicero was exact in his concept of the Prince, which derived from Theopompus through Polybius' description of Scipio Aemilianus and that Augustus adopted this concept of the *princeps* who excels in statesmanship and exercises *auctoritas*. Viktor Pöschl, *Römischer Staat und griechisches Staatsdenken bei Cicero* (Berlin, Junker and Dunnhaupt, 1936) 162–170, discusses the influence of Plato on Cicero's concept. Richard Meister, "Der Staatsdenken in Ciceros *De re publica*," *Wiener Studien* LVII (1939) 57–112, resurveys the discussion and accepts the presence of a *rector rei publicae* in Cicero's theory but thinks that the fragmentary nature of the text of the *de Rep.* prevents an exact determination of how Cicero fitted him into the republican constitution. André Magdelain, *Auctoritas Principis* (Paris, Les Belles Lettres, 1947), devotes his first chapter to the republican precedents for the *auctoritas* of Augustus, particularly the Ciceronian theory of the *princeps*. He concludes, pp. 35–36, that Cicero advocated a *princeps auctoritate* and, contrary to previous interpretations, that Cicero thought of the *princeps* as having two functions. He might act to free the state from some deleterious condition, in which case his initiative was his own, *privato consilio*, or he might be a *rector rei publicae*, the leader of public opinion as expressed in the organs of state, *auctor publici consilii*. Finally, Magdelain concludes that this Ciceronian theory of the principate was not purely idealistic; it represented a systematization of previous or contemporary political experience. See Mason Hammond, *Augustan Principate* 172 and 268, nn. 15–17 and Wilhelm Weber, *Princeps* I (Stuttgart and Berlin, Kohlhammer, 1936) 172*–173* for earlier literature.

15. Sherwin-White (see above, n. 6), 270–271, discusses the word by which Cicero and Sallust designated the provinces: *gentes*. He disagrees with Ernst Kornemann that this indicated a recognition of provincial unity as distinct from Rome and maintains that the concept of Rome as *gentium moderator*, Sallust, *Oratio Lepidi* 11, or *imperator omnium gentium*, Cicero, *de Domo* 90, is not inconsistent with Livy's phrase *princeps terrarum* in his *Praefatio* 3 or with the Hellenistic idea of the *oikoumene*. The passages in which Cicero indicates that Rome's empire depended on the maintenance of good faith toward her allies and that she should not look upon the empire simply

as a source of revenue are *de Rep.* III
35 and 41 (from Nonius), IV 7 (from
Nonius), *de Leg.* III 9, 17, *de Off.* II
27 (cited above, ch. viii, n. 8); see the
discussion of these passages by Karel
Sprey in his *de M. T. C. Politica Doctrina* (Zutphen, Nauta, 1928) 50–54,
185–186. See also the passages cited by
Mason Hammond, "Ancient Imperialism *etc.*," *Harvard Studies in Classical
Philology* LVIII–LIX (1948) 151–153,
nn. 96–102.

16. Philippson's general estimate of
Cicero's philosophy, *RE2* VII (13)
1181–1183, is that he was a borrower
and codifier, often inconsistent in the
views which he advocated and unable
to exemplify his principles in practice.
He concludes that Cicero was one of
the purest of men in his morals but not
great in character. Petersson, *Cicero*
580–591, is kinder but still does not
allow much originality to Cicero. E.
K. Rand, in *The Building of Eternal
Rome* (Cambridge, Mass., Harvard University Press, 1943) 18–30, gives a
genial picture of Cicero with especial
emphasis on his originality and on his
Roman *humanitas*, and with particular
reference to the *de Republica*. Cicero's
significance in the development of the
concept of *humanitas* is also emphasized
by O. E. Nybakken, *"Humanitas
Romana,"* *Transactions and Proceedings of the American Philological Asso-*

ciation LXX (1939) 396–413 and,
apparently, by Francesco Arnaldi,
"Humanitas," *Romana* V (1941) 169–
188, though the latter was not available
except in a brief summary. Carcopino,
in *Les Secrets* etc. I 372, concludes his
chapter on "Erreurs d'une carrière
manquée" with the statement: "il n'a
possédé aucune des qualités qui font
l'homme d'État; il eut tous les défauts
qui l'annihilent." In the first section of
his following chapter, "Les défauts d'un
homme d'État," he discusses Cicero as
"un doctrinaire sans doctrine," and
characterizes the *de Republica* as simply
the result of his Greek studies, bearing
no relation to the realities of Roman
politics as exposed in the letters; see
especially pp. 374–376. For Cicero's
originality in political theory, see
above, n. 13.

17. Michael Grant, *From Imperium
to Auctoritas* (Cambridge, University
Press, 1946) 401–412, has most recently
discussed the relation of *libertas* to
civitas, with particular reference to
the "free" cities under Rome's rule. He
refers to Hans Kloesel's dissertation on
Libertas (Breslau, Nischkowsky, 1935),
in which, on p. 16, the Roman concept
of *libertas* is connected with that of
respublica. The same theme is further
developed for the republican period
on pp. 23–47.

XI

CICERO AND AUGUSTUS:

PRINCIPATE AND RESTORED REPUBLIC

1. Suetonius, *Augustus* 62–64, gives briefly the basic information about Octavian's marriages and family. Fuller references will be found in any of the more detailed lives of Augustus, for instance in Victor Garthausen, *Augustus und Seine Zeit* (Leipzig, Teubner, 1891–1904) I 1018–1147, II (notes) 631–757. Jérôme Carcopino discusses "Le marriage de Livie" in *Revue Historique* CLXI (1929) 225–236 on the basis of new chronological information from the *Fasti* of Verula.

2. Eutropius, who dedicated his *Breviarium Historiae Romanae* to the Emperor Valens (A.D. 364–378), remarks in VIII 5 that the memory of Trajan was so esteemed that even in the author's own day emperors were acclaimed in the senate as *felicior Augusto, melior Traiano.*

3. Octavia was Antony's fourth wife. They were married in 40 B.C. to cement the reconciliation between Octavian and Antony after the unsuccessful revolt and death of the latter's third wife, Fulvia. What Antony thought his legal relations with Octavia and Cleopatra were does not appear in the tradition; see Mason Hammond's article in *RE2* XVII (34) 1862 under *Octavius* 96 (Octavia minor) and bibliography in col. 1868; also Michael Grant, *From Imperium to Auctoritas* (Cambridge, University Press, 1946) 44, 368–374. Hammond's article should be corrected in col. 1861 line 22, where the statue mentioned by Seneca, *Suasoriae* I 6, was not of Octavia but of Antony. The bibliography should be supplemented also by A. E. Raubitschek, "Octavia's Deification at Athens," *Transactions of the American Philological Association* LXXVII (1946) 146–150 and by Mary W. Singer, "Octavia's Mediation at Tarentum," *Classical Journal* XLIII (1947) 173–177. Miss Singer refers to her unpublished doctor's dissertation on *Octavia Minor* etc. (Duke University, Durham, North Carolina, 1944).

4. Chapter 34 of the *Res Gestae* gives Augustus' version of his position after Actium and of the settlement in 27 B.C. and the grant of the title *Augustus*: "In my sixth and seventh consulships, after I had extinguished the civil wars and when I controlled all public affairs by universal consent, I transferred the sovereignty from my power to the Senate and Roman People. For this meritorious act of mine, by decree of the senate I was called Augustus and the doorposts of my house were decked with laurel publicly and a civic garland was placed above my doorway and a gold shield was placed in the Julian senate house. That the Senate and Roman People gave me this shield on account of my bravery, clemency, justice, and piety was declared by the inscription thereon. After that time, I excelled all in authority but I had no more power than others who were colleagues with me in each magistracy." See the Greek and Latin texts and notes in Jean Gagé's edition (Paris, Les Belles Lettres,

1935) 142–147. In the note on p. 144 will be found references for *Respublica restituta*.

5. *The History of the Title Imperator under the Roman Empire* is discussed by Donald McFayden (Chicago Dissertation, Chicago, 1920). His treatment may be supplemented by Anton von Premerstein, *Vom Werden und Wesen* etc. (Munich, 1937) 245–260, and by W. F. Jashemsky's thesis, *The Origins and History of the Proconsular and the Propraetorian Imperium to 27 B.C.* (Chicago, University of Chicago Press, 1950), an excellent analysis of the Republican instances. Grant's treatment of *Imperator* and *imperium* in *From Imperium to Auctoritas* 408–442 should be supplemented by Hugh Last, "*Imperium Maius*: A Note," in *The Journal of Roman Studies* XXXVII (1947) 157–164. These scholars reject, because of lack of evidence in coins and inscriptions, the statement by Dio Cassius, XLIII 44.2, that Caesar received the *praenomen Imperatoris* from the senate in 45 B.C. This statement may be a retrojection of the grant to Octavian in 29 B.C., see secs. 40.2, 41.2–3, perhaps deliberately inspired either by Octavian himself or by Agrippa, who first used the name on coins for Octavian when he himself refused a triumph in 38 B.C. for victories won under Octavian's *imperium*.

6. Dio Cassius, LVII 8.1, states that Tiberius said that he would be "to his slaves *dominus*, to the soldiers *imperator*, but to the people *princeps*," to render Dio's Greek terms into Latin. Thus, despite Tiberius' refusal of the *praenomen*, Dio LVII 2.1 and Suetonius *Tib*. 26.2, he felt that the title (saluta-

tions?) indicated command of troops in virtue of an *imperium*.

7. The gentile name *Iulius* was not entirely abandoned for the family of Augustus. Both *RE* X (19) and the *Prosopographia Imperii Romani* (ed. 1) vol. II classify its members under this name and the immediate successors of Augustus are traditionally known as the Julio-Claudians. Tiberius and Gaius were *Iulii*. Claudius and Nero were *Claudii*. But the *Prosopographia* attests *Iulius* rarely: once for Agrippa Postumus; occasionally for Drusus the Elder, for his son Germanicus, and for the latter's son Drusus; dubiously once for Lucius Caesar, one of Augustus' two grandsons; once for Nero Caesar, son of Germanicus; and occasionally for Tiberius. This rarity of use is confirmed by the instances given by Hermann Dessau in Index III in *Inscriptiones Latinae Selectae* III 1 pp. 257–265 to illustrate the names and titles of the Julian family. *Iulia*, however, remained a common name, in the traditional Roman fashion, for girls in the family. Moreover, laws passed on the initiative of Augustus were known as *leges Iuliae*. Praise of the Julian *gens* occurs in the Augustan poets, see Münzer, *RE* X (19) under *Iulius*, and an altar was erected to this *gens* on the Capitol, see *RE* III (6) 1537 line 37 under *Capitolium*, and S. B. Platner and Thomas Ashby, *A Topographical Dictionary of Ancient Rome* (Oxford University Press, 1929) 247. Hence there was no legal change of Caesar from a family to a gentile name, see Michael Grant, *Aspects of the Principate of Tiberius* etc. (The American Numismatic Society, *Numismatic Notes and Monographs* 116, New York, 1950) 92–98.

Iulius became a commonly attested gentile name under the early empire when descendants of Julian freedmen or of provincials who had received citizenship from a Julius rose sufficiently in the social scale to leave a record of themselves.

8. A convenient discussion of the antecedents and forms of deification which Augustus either encouraged or accepted during his lifetime or which were bestowed on him after death is L. R. Taylor, *The Divinity of the Roman Emperor* (American Philological Association, *Philological Monographs* I, Middletown, Conn., 1931). For "Hellenistic Influences in the Structure of the Augustan Principate," see Mason Hammond in *Memoirs of the American Academy in Rome* XVII (1940) 1–24. Grant emphasizes Augustus' position in the East as successor to the Hellenistic monarchs, *From Imperium to Auctoritas* 356–367, see also G. I. Luzzato, *Epigrafia Giuridica Greca e Romana* (*Publ. dell' Ist. di Diritto Rom.* etc., R. Università di Roma, XIX, Milan, Giuffrè, 1942) 217–221 and F. de Vissher, *Les Édits d'Auguste découverts a Cyrène* (*Receuil de travaux d'histoire et de philologie*, Université de Louvain, 3e sér., 1er fasc., Louvain, Bureau du Receuil, Bibliothèque de l'Université, 1940) 51–54.

9. *Augustus* is philologically connected with the verb *augere,* "to increase," from which also *auctoritas* is derived. Besides the references for *auctoritas* in Grant, *From Imperium to Auctoritas* 443 n. 4, referred to above, ch.. viii, n. 14, see von Premerstein, *Vom Werden usw.* 176–225, and, for *Augustus,* Hammond, *The Augustan Principate* 110–111, 266 nn. 6, 7; Gagé, *Res Gestae* 145.

10. Augustus took another step toward winning senatorial favor when he made regular the practice of replacing the consuls during the course of the year with "suffects." Although the first pair, who gave their names to the year, had the highest honor, nevertheless, in this way the consulship could be held by four or more senators during the year. Six-month terms were customary at first; by the second century, they were reduced to two, so that there were normally twelve consuls in each year. It is likely that any senator who lived long enough and did not either refuse to go through the full career or get blocked for some reason or other would attain the consulship. The other face of the coin was, of course, that the multiplication of the consuls was possible only because their function became less significant, and the multiplication in turn furthered the reduction of the significance.

11. *Res Gestae* 34, on Augustus' relation to the other magistrates, is quoted above, in n. 4.

12. Augustus uses *me principe* in *Res Gestae* 13, 30.1, 33.3.

13. The passages in which Cicero refers, or is said to have referred, to a *princeps civitatis* or the equivalent are: *ad Att.* VII 11.1 (*de Rep.* V 8) for *moderator rei publicae; de Rep.* II 51, V 5, 8, VI 1, 13 for *rector et gubernator civitatis; de Rep.* I 34, St. Augustine *de Civ. Dei* V 13 for *principe civitatis;* Peter of Poitiers (cited in Loeb ed. of *de Rep.* p. 252 as part of Bk. V 9, along with the quotation introduced by St. Augustine with the words cited in the text) for *principem civitatis; de Or.* I 209, *de Leg.* III 32, and frequently for *principes civitatis; de Domo* 66, *pro*

Sestio 84, *ad Fam.* I 9.11 for Pompey as *princeps civitatis.* A selection of Cicero's usages of *princeps* may be found in Hugo Merguet's *Handlexikon zu Cicero* (Leipzig, Dieterich'sche BVH, 1906) 556 *s.v.*; fuller detail for the speeches in his *Lexikon zu den Reden des C.* III (Jena, Fischer, 1882) 769–771 *s.v.*; and for the philosophic works in his *Lexikon zu den philosophishen Schriften* III (Jena, Fischer, 1894) 163–165. Only references, not citations, for the *Letters* are given by W. A. Oldfather, H. V. Canter, and K. M. Abbott, *Index Verborum Ciceronis Epistularum* (Urbana, University of Illinois Press, 1938) 417 *s.v.* A modern index for the rhetorical works is not available. In an interesting passage in the *pro Sestio* 97–98, Cicero described the *principes civitatis* as those who by will, opportunities, or means serve in governing the republic. If they create peace, they are outstanding men and saviors of the state. With this definition may be compared a remark attributed to Augustus by Macrobius, *Sat.* II 4.18. In reply to a criticism of Cato by Strabo, Augustus said, "Whoever will not wish to change the existing condition of the state is a good citizen and man," *quisquis praesentem statum civitatis commutari non volet, et civis et vir bonus est*; see Taylor, *Party Politics* 240, n. 74 on ch. viii. In a well-known passage in his last speech, *Phil.* XIV 17, Cicero appealed to those *principes* who after his consulship regarded him as a fellow leader: *utinam quidem illi principes viverent, qui me post meum consulatum, cum eis ipse cederem, principem non inviti videbant!* If, as it appears, he referred to his position under Crassus, Pompey, and Caesar in the

fifties, his memory slightly romanticized the facts. For a discussion of various views as to how precise Cicero was in respect to the concept of the *princeps*, see above, ch. x, n. 14 and below, n. 16.

14. Augustus speaks of the embassy of 19 B.C., comprising magistrates and *principibus viris*, in the *Res Gestae* 12.1; Suetonius, *Aug.* 29.4, says that Augustus frequently urged not only members of his family but also *ceteros principes viros* to build or repair public buildings; Velleius Paterculus, II 89.4, also speaks of *principes viri* whom Augustus exhorted to beautify the city. Suetonius later, 66.3, remarks that many *principes* of both orders, senatorial and equestrian, enjoyed influence and wealth to the end of their lives despite quarrels with Augustus. A. H. Howard and C. N. Jackson, *Index Verborum C. Suetoni Tranquilli* (Cambridge, Mass., Harvard University Press, 1922) 190–191, Arnold Gerber and Adolf Greef, *Lexicon Taciteum* (Leipzig, Teubner, 1877–1903) 1181–1186, and Carl Lessing, *Scriptorum historiae Augustae Lexicon* (Leipzig, Reisland, 1901–1906) 474–478, have collected the examples of *princeps* from these, the chief Latin historians for the early empire. Their collections show some use of the term for chief men other than the emperor or for chiefs of other peoples, but the overwhelming majority of citations refer to the emperors.

15. The *Res Gestae* lists the virtues of Augustus in ch. 34.2, translated above in n. 4; see Gagé's edition p. 144. Cicero wrote not only two books *de Gloria*, but also, apparently, one *de Virtutibus*. Both are lost; the *de Gloria*, mentioned in *de Off.* II 31 and various

letters, seems to have covered the same ground as *de Off.* II 31–85; the *de Virtutibus*, only twice alluded to by late authors, presumably enlarged on the treatment in *de Off.* I. See *RE2* VII (13) 1167–1168, 1173. The connection of the public virtues with the *principes* of the state is discussed by Wilhelm Weber, *Princeps* I (Stuttgart and Berlin, Kohlhammer, 1936) n. 611 on pages of notes 172–173. See also M. P. Charlesworth, "The Virtues of a Roman Emperor etc.," *The Raleigh Lecture*, separate reprint from the *Proceedings of the British Academy* XXIII (London, Milford, 1937); R. S. Rogers, *Studies in the Reign of Tiberius* (Baltimore, The Johns Hopkins Press, 1943) 1–88, "Some Imperial Virtues of Tiberius." H. T. Rowell, "The Forum and Funeral *Imagines* of Augustus," *Memoirs of the Am. Acad. in Rome* XVII (1940) 131–143, regards the presence of statues of famous Romans in his Forum and the use of masks not of his family but again of famous Romans in his funeral procession as a further attempt to make him an epitomizer and representative of Rome's past and of her virtues. The concept of the virtues of the ruler undoubtedly had Hellenistic precedents as well as Roman, see above, ch. iv, end of n. 2.

16. The discussion of the relation between Cicero's ideals and Augustus has been advanced chiefly by the following works: Eduard Meyer, *Caesars Monarchie und das Principät des Pompeius* (Stuttgart and Berlin, Gotta'sche BH, ed. 1, 1918; ed. 2, 1919; ed. 3, 1922), especially pp. 174–191, 547–548, with a reference to his earlier "Kaiser Augustus," first published in *Historischen Zeitschrift* XCI (neue Folge LV,

1903) 385–431 and reprinted in *Kleine Schriften* (Halle A. S., Niemeyer, 1910) 441–492; Richard Reitzenstein, "Die Idee des Principäts bei Cicero und Augustus" in *Nachrichten von der königlichen Gesellschaft der Wissenschaften zu Göttingen*, phil.-hist. Klasse, 1917, III, pp. 399–436, 481–489; and Richard Heinze, "Ciceros 'Staat' als politische Tendenzschrift" in *Hermes* LIX (1924) 73–94, reprinted in *Vom Geist des Römertum* (Leipzig and Berlin, Teubner, 1938) 142–170. Carcopino, *Les Secrets* etc. I 374–375, quotes with approval the criticism of the direct influence of Cicero on Augustus advanced by Pierre Grenade in his "Remarques etc." (above, ch. x, n. 14) 33–35, 61–63. Actually, Grenade's analysis of the philosophical background of the theory of the *"princeps"* in Cicero and his warning against attaching too great importance to the actual use of this word by Cicero or in quotations from him do not militate against the view that Augustus may have taken up and developed the views advanced by Cicero, whether he derived them directly from Cicero or whether Cicero simply expressed the final evolution of the theory of the mixed constitution as applied to the Roman government. Other recent discussions include W. W. How in *Journal of Roman Studies* XX (1930) 37–42 (above, ch. x, n. 14) and André Oltramare, "La réaction Cicéronienne et les débuts du Principat," *Revue des Études Latines* X (1932) 58–90, who concludes that though Cicero had only a limited influence on Augustus, his influence on a considerable section of Roman society forced Augustus to mask his policy behind a republican facade; J(ean?) Béranger, "Pour une définition du Principat: Auguste dans Aulu-Gelle, XV, 7, 3," *Revue des Études Latines* XXI-XXII (1943-1944) 144-154, who thinks that the Augustan concept combined the need for a monarch, result of the troubles of the end of the republic, and the philosophical ideal of a *coniunctio potestatis ac sapientiae* expressed by Cicero, see *ad Quintum fratrem* I 1.29; Ernst Knierim, *Die Bezeichnung "dux" in der politischen Terminologie von Cicero bis Juvenal* (Giessen Dissertation, Giessen, Meyer, 1939), who connects the concept of *dux* with *princeps, auctoritas*, and the Greek term *hegemōn*; André Magdelain, *Auctoritas Principis* (Paris, Les Belles Lettres, 1947), who traces the idea of the *princeps* definitely from republican precedents and from Cicero. Magdelain's thesis that *auctoritas* and *princeps* were intimately connected and that *auctoritas* was the source for the validity of imperial constitutions resembles the general interpretation advanced by Michael Grant in *From Imperium to Auctoritas*. But Grant would find the vehicle of *auctoritas* in a specific imperial power, the *tribunicia potestas*, rather than in the general recognition of Augustus as *princeps*.

17. Plutarch relates Cicero's support of the young Octavian and the latter's abandonment of him to Antony's vengeance in his *Cicero* 44-46; he de-

scribed Augustus' later reinstatement of Cicero's memory in sec. 49.3-4. Grenade, "Remarques *etc.*" 35-40, denies that the account of Plutarch should be taken seriously and argues that there was no real reconciliation of Augustus to the memory of his opponent; see also Carcopino, *Les Secrets* etc. I 30-37. For the republicanism of Asinius Pollio, see *RE* II (4) 1601 under *Asinius* 25, by Groebe. For Augustus' patience with Livy's praise of Pompey, see Tacitus, *Ann.* IV 34.

18. Tacitus' denial of the sincerity of Augustus in the restoration of the Republic appears clearly in the opening chapters of *Annals* I. Tacitus speaks in sec. 2 of "Caesar, the only leader left . . . who gradually gained power and drew to himself the functions of the senate, magistrates, and laws," and at the end of sec. 3, he says that "the young men were born after Actium, and even most of the old during the civil wars; how far was anyone left who had seen the Republic?" At the beginning of sec. 3, he calls Augustus' rule *dominationi* and at the opening of sec. 4, he remarks *verso civitatis statu . . . exuta aequalitate*. The favorable and unfavorable estimates of Augustus given in secs. 9-10 are so arranged as to leave the unfavorable impression in the reader's mind.

SELECTIVE BIBLIOGRAPHY

Not all the works cited in the notes are listed in this bibliography, but chiefly those recent ones which will help the interested reader to pursue the various major topics.

GENERAL

The Cambridge Ancient History, ed. J. B. Bury and others, Cambridge, Eng., Cambridge University Press, vols. IV (1926)–X (1934).

Histoire Grecque and *Histoire Romaine*, parts II and III of the *Histoire Générale* directed by G. Glotz, Paris, Les Presses Universitaires, 1925 ff.

RE and *RE2* = Pauly-Wissowa-Kroll-Mittelhaus, *Real-Encyclopädie der klassischen Altertumswissenschaft*, published in two halves, from "A" on and from "R" on. Whole volumes are indicated by Roman numerals, with an Arabic numeral in parentheses for the half volumes.

The Loeb Classical Library, texts and translations of Greek and Latin authors, London, Heinemann; in the United States: formerly New York, Putnam, and later Cambridge, Mass., Harvard University Press.

POLITICAL THEORY

W. A. Dunning, *A History of Political Theories*, London and New York, Macmillan, vol. I, 1902, reprint 1923: "Ancient and Mediaeval."

W. W. Fowler, *The City-State of the Greeks and Romans* etc., London, Macmillan, 1921.

Mason Hammond, "Ancient Imperialism: Contemporary Justifications," *Harvard Studies in Classical Philology* LXVIII–LXIX (1948) 105–161.

M. R. Konvitz and A. E. Murphy, *Essays in Political Theory presented to George N. Sabine*,

Ithaca, N. Y., Cornell University
Press, 1948.
C. H. McIlwain, *Constitutionalism
Ancient and Modern*, Ithaca,
N. Y., Cornell University Press,
ed. 2, 1947.

C. H. McIlwain, *The Growth of
Political Thought in the West* etc.,
New York, Macmillan, 1932.
G. H. Sabine, *A History of Political
Theory*, New York, Holt, 1937.

CHAPTER I

Hans von Arnim, *Gerechtigkeit und
Nutzen in der griechischen Auf-
klärungsphilosophie*, Frankfurter
Universitätsrede, 1916.
W. S. Ferguson, *Greek Imperialism*,
Boston and New York, Houghton
Mifflin, 1913.
David Grene, *Man in His Pride:
A Study in the Political Philos-
ophy of Thucydides and Plato*,
Chicago, University of Chicago
Press, 1950.

W. W. Jaeger, *Paideia*, New York,
Oxford University Press, 3 vols.,
1939–1944 (vol. I ed. 2, 1945).
A. C. Johnson and others, *The Greek
Political Experience* etc., Princeton, Princeton University Press,
1941.
Wilhelm Nestle, "Politik und Moral
in Altertum," *Neue Jahrbücher
fur klassicher Altertum* usw. XLI/
XLII (1918) 225–244.

CHAPTER II

Ernest Barker, *Greek Political The-
ory: Plato and his Predecessors*,
London, Methuen, ed. 3, 1947.
Ernest Barker, *The Political
Thought of Plato and Aristotle*,
London, Methuen; New York,
G. P. Putnam Sons, 1906.

Plato

James Adam, *The Republic of Plato*,
Cambridge, University Press, 2
vols., 1902 and later reprints.
A. E. Taylor, *Plato: The Man and*

his Work, London, Methuen;
New York, The Dial Press, ed. 3,
1929.

Aristotle

The Oxford Translation of *The
Works of Aristotle*, ed. W. D.
Ross, vol. X: *Politica* by Benjamin
Jowett, *Oeconomica* by E. S. Fors-
ter, *Atheniensium Respublica* by
Sir F. G. Kenyon; Oxford, Clar-
endon Press, 1921.
W. L. Newman, *The Politics of Aris-*

totle, Oxford, Clarendon Press, vols. I–II (1887), III–IV (1902).

W. D. Ross, *Aristotle*, London, Methuen, ed. 3, 1937.

CHAPTER III

Louis Delatte, *Les Traités de la Royauté d'Ecphante, Diotogène, et Sthénidas, Bibliothèque de la Faculté de Philosophie et Lettres de l'Université de Liége* XCVII, Liége, Faculté de philosophie et lettres; Paris, E. Droz, 1942.

E. A. Freeman, *A History of Federal Government in Greece and Italy*, London and New York, Macmillan, ed. 2 by J. B. Bury, 1893.

E. R. Goodenough, "The Political Philosophy of Hellenistic Kingship," *Yale Classical Studies* I (1928) 55–102.

Pierre Jouguet, *Macedonian Imperialism and the Hellenization of the East*, trans. from the French by M. R. Dobie, London, Kegan Paul Trench Trubner & Co. Ltd., New York, Knopf, 1928.

Victor Martin, *La Vie International dans la Grèce des cités (VIe–IVe s. av. J.-C.)*, *Publications de l'Institut Universitaire de Hautes Études Internationales*, no. 21, Geneva, Georg, Paris, Sirey, 1940.

C. W. McEwan, "The Oriental Origin of Hellenistic Kingship," *Studies in Ancient Oriental Civilization* XIII, Chicago, The Oriental Institute of Chicago, 1934.

C. A. Robinson, *Alexander the Great* etc., New York, Dutton, 1947.

W. W. Tarn, *Alexander the Great*, Cambridge, Eng., Cambridge University Press, 2 vols., 1948; especially vol. II, appendices 22 on "Alexander's Deification," 24 on "Alexander's Supposed Plans and the 'World-Kingdom'," and 25 on "Brotherhood and Unity."

W. W. Tarn, *Antigonos Gonatas*, Oxford, Clarendon Press, 1913.

W. W. Tarn, *Hellenistic Civilization*, London, Arnold, ed. 2, 1930 and later impressions.

CHAPTER IV

E. V. Arnold, *Roman Stoicism*, Cambridge, University Press, 1911.

Cyril Bailey, *Epicurus* etc., Oxford, Clarendon Press, 1926.

Cyril Bailey, *The Greek Atomists and Epicurus*, Oxford, Clarendon Press, 1929.

R. D. Hicks, *Stoic and Epicurean*, New York, Scribners, 1910.

Robert Philippson, "Die Rechtsphilosophie der Epikureer," *Archiv fur Geschichte der Philosophie* (= *Archiv für Philosophie*, I abt.) XXIII (= Neue Folge XVI, 1910) 289–337, 433–446.

Max Pohlenz, *Die Stoa: Geschichte einer geistigen Bewegung*, Göttingen, Vandenhoeck und Ruprecht, 2 vols., 1948/49.

Max Pohlenz, *Stoa und Stoiker* I: *Die Gründer, Panaitios, Poseido-* nios (to be continued with volumes on the later Stoics), Zürich, Artemis, 1950 (in *Die Bibliothek der Alten Welt*).

August Schmekel, *Die Philosophie der mittleren Stoa* usw., Berlin, Weidmannsche BH, 1892.

Eduard Zeller, *The Stoics, Epicureans, and Sceptics*, trans. from the German by O. J. Reichel, London, Longmans Green, rev. ed., 1892.

CHAPTER V AND GENERAL FOR ROME

A. E. R. Boak, *A History of Rome to 565 A.D.*, New York, Macmillan, ed. 3, 1946.

Max Cary, *A History of Rome down to the Reign of Constantine*, London, Macmillan, 1935 and later reprints.

Emanuele Ciaceri, *Le Origini di Roma*, Milan etc., Soc. An. Ed. Dante Alighieri, 1937.

Tenney Frank, *Roman Imperialism*, New York, Macmillan, 1914.

W. W. Fowler, *The Religious Experience of the Roman People*, London, Macmillan, 1911.

Matthias Gelzer, *Die Nobilität der römischen Republik*, Leipzig and Berlin, Teubner, 1912.

A. H. J. Greenidge, *Roman Public Life*, London, Macmillan, 1901.

Louis Homo, *Roman Political Institutions*, trans. from the French by M. R. Dobie, London, Kegan Paul Trench Trubner, New York, Knopf, 1929.

Theodor Mommsen, *Römisches Staatsrecht*, Leipzig, Hirzel, vols. I–II, ed. 3, 1887; III, 1888.

Friedrich Münzer, *Römische Adelsparteien und Adelsfamilien*, Stuttgart, Metzlersche VBH, 1920.

E. K. Rand, *The Building of Eternal Rome*, Cambridge, Mass., Harvard University Press, 1943.

Martin Schanz und Carl Hosius, *Geschichte der römischen Literatur*, Munich, Beck'sche VBH, vols. I, ed. 4, 1927: "Die römische Literatur in der Zeit der Republik" and II, ed. 4, 1935: "Die römische Literatur in der Zeit der Monarchie bis auf Hadrian."

Otto Seel, "Römische Denker und römischer Staat," *Neue Wege zur Antike*, I Reihe (Darstellungen)

XIII, Leipzig and Berlin, Teubner, 1937.

E. H. Warmington, *Remains of Old Latin*, Loeb Classical Library, London, Heinemann, Cambridge, Mass., Harvard University Press,

I, 1935: "Ennius and Caecilius"; II, 1936: "Livius Andronicus, Naevius, Pacuvius, and Accius"; III, 1938: "Lucilius, The Twelve Tables"; IV, 1940: "Archaic Inscriptions."

CHAPTER VI

Wilhelm Capelle, "Griechische Ethik und römische Imperialismus," *Klio* XXV (1932) 88–113.

Polybius

Richard Laqueur, *Polybius*, Leipzig and Berlin, Teubner, 1913.

Erwin Sarrazin, *Das Führerideal des Polybius*, Breslau, Nischkowsky, 1934.

Walter Siegfried, *Studien zur geschichtlichen Anschauung des Polybius*, Leipzig, Teubner, 1928.

Carl Wunderer, *Polybius: Lebens- und Weltanschauung aus dem zweiten vorchristlichen Jahrhundert*, *Das Erbe der Alten*, zweite Reihe XII, Leipzig, Dieterich'sche VBH, 1927.

The Scipios

Konrad Bilz, *Die Politik des P. Cornelius Scipio Aemilianus*, *Würzburger Studien zur Alt.-*

wiss., Stuttgart, Kohlhammer, 1936.

R. M. Hayward, *Studies on Scipio Africanus*, *The Johns Hopkins University Studies in Historical and Political Science*, series LI, no. I (also published as a thesis for the Ph.D.), Baltimore, The Johns Hopkins Press, 1933.

Julius Kaerst, "Scipio Aemilianus, die Stoa, und der Prinzipät," *Neue Jahrbücher* V (1929) 653–675.

Werner Schur, *Scipio Africanus und die Begründung der römischen Weltherrschaft*, *Das Erbe der Alten*, zweite Reihe XIII, Leipzig, Dieterich'sche VBH, 1927.

Panaetius

Modestus van Straaten, *Panétius, sa vie, ses écrits, et sa doctrine avec une édition des fragments*, Amsterdam, H. J. Paris, 1946.

B. N. Tatakis, *Panétius de Rhodes* etc., Paris, Vrin, 1931.

CHAPTER VII

W. W. Fowler, *Social Life at Rome in the Age of Cicero*, London and New York, Macmillan, 1909 and later reprints.

Richard Heinze, *Vom Geist des Römertums, Ausgewählte Aufsätze*, ed. Erich Burck, Leipzig and Berlin, Teubner, 1938.

Wilhelm Kroll, *Die Kultur der Ciceronischen Zeit, Das Erbe der Alten* XXII–XXIII, Leipzig, Dieterich'sche VBH, 1933; especially in vol. I (XXII), chs. I on "Die Staatsidee," II on "Die Macht der Tradition," and III on "Der einzelne in der Politik."

F. B. Marsh, *The Founding of the Roman Empire*, Oxford, Oxford University Press, ed. 2, 1927.

F. B. Marsh, *Modern Problems in the Ancient World*, Austin, University of Texas Press, 1943.

L. R. Taylor, *Party Politics in the Age of Caesar*, Sather Classical Lectures XXII, Berkeley and Los Angeles, University of California Press, 1949.

CHAPTERS VIII AND IX

RE2 VII (13) 827–1274 under *Tullius* no. 29, *M. Tullius Cicero*: "als Politiker" by Matthias Gelzer, "rhetorische Schriften" by Wilhelm Kroll, "philosophische Schriften" by Robert Philippson, "Briefe und Fragmente" by Karl Büchner.

Jérôme Carcopino, *Les Secrets de la Correspondence de Cicéron*, Paris, L'Artisan du Livre, 2 vols., 1947.

F. R. Cowell, *Cicero and the Roman Republic*, London, Putnam, New York, Chanticleer, 1948.

Paul Groebe, ed. 2 of Wilhelm Drumann, *Geschichte Roms . . . oder Pompeius, Caesar, Cicero* usw., Berlin and Leipzig, Borntraeger, 6 vols., 1899–1929; especially vols. V–VI on Cicero.

Eduard Meyer, *Caesars Monarchie und das Prinzipät Pompeius*, Stuttgart and Berlin, Cotta'sche BH., ed. 3, 1922.

Torsten Petersson, *Cicero, A Biography*, Berkeley, University of California Press, 1920.

Otto Plasberg, *Cicero in seinem Werken und Briefen*, ed. Wilhelm Ax, *Das Erbe der Alten*, zweite Reihe, XI, Leipzig, Dieterich'sche VBH., 1926.

Ronald Syme, *The Roman Revolution*, Oxford, Clarendon Press, 1939.

CHAPTER X

Friedrich Cauer, *Ciceros politisches Denken*, Berlin, Weidmannsche BH., 1903.

Giovanni Galbiati (Johannes Galbiatius), *de Fontibus M. Tullii Ciceronis librorum qui manserunt de Re Publica et de Legibus Quaestiones*, R. Accademia Scientifica-Letteraria, Milano, Facoltà universitaria di filosofia e lettere, pubbl. 2, Milan, Hoepli, 1916.

Viktor Pöschl, *Römischer Staat und griechisches Staatsdenken bei Cicero; Untersuchungen zu Ciceros Schrift De Re Publica, Neue Deutsche Forschungen*, Abt. klass. Philol. V, Berlin, Junker und Dunnhaupt, 1936.

Max Pohlenz, *Antikes Führertum; Cicero De Officiis und das Lebensideal des Panaitius, Neue Wege zur Antike*, zweite Reihe (Interpretationen) III, Leipzig and Berlin, Teubner, 1934.

J. S. Reid, preface to *M. Tulli Ciceronis Academica*, London, Macmillan, 1885.

G. H. Sabine and S. B. Smith, *Cicero on the Commonwealth*, introduction, translation, and commentary, Columbus, Ohio State University Press, 1929.

Karel Sprey, *de M. Tullii Ciceronis Politica Doctrina*, University of Amsterdam Thesis, Zutphen, Nauta, 1928.

Hermann Strasburger, *Concordia Ordinum: eine Untersuchung zu Politik Ciceros*, Borna-Leipzig, Noske, 1931.

CHAPTER XI

John Buchan, *Augustus*, London, Hodder and Stoughton; Boston, Houghton Mifflin, 1937 (note that the English edition has different pagination from the American).

Jean Gagé, *Res Gestae Divi Augusti* etc., Paris, Les Belles Lettres, 1935.

Michael Grant, *From Imperium to Auctoritas: A Historical Study of the Aes coinage in the Roman Empire, 49 B.C.–A.D. 14*, Cambridge, University Press, 1946.

Mason Hammond, *The Augustan Principate* etc., Cambridge, Mass., Harvard University Press, 1933.

T. Rice Holmes, *The Architect of the Roman Empire*, 2 vols., Oxford, Clarendon Press, 1928–1931.

André Magdelain, *Auctoritas Principis, Collection d'Études Latines* publiée par la Société des Études Latines, série scientifique XXII, Paris, Les Belles Lettres, 1947.

Anton von Premerstein, *Vom Werden und Wesen des Prinzipäts, Abhandlungen der bayerischen Akademie der Wissenschaften*, phil.-hist. Abt., neue Folge XV, Munich, 1937.

INDEX